Free Will
and Determinism
in American Literature

Other books by PERRY D. WESTBROOK

Author:
Happy Deathday
The Red Herring Murder
Infra Blood
Acres of Flint: Writers of Rural New England, 1870–1900
It Boils Down to Murder
The Sting of Death
Biography of an Island
The Greatness of Man: An Essay on Dostoyevsky and Whitman
Trail Horses and Trail Riding (with Anne Westbrook)
Mary Ellen Chase
Mary Wilkins Freeman
John Burroughs
William Bradford

Editor:
Pembroke
Seacoast and Upland: A New England Anthology

Free Will and Determinism in American Literature

Perry D. Westbrook

Rutherford · Madison · Teaneck
Fairleigh Dickinson University Press
London: Associated University Presses

© 1979 by Associated University Presses, Inc.

Associated University Presses, Inc.
Cranbury, New Jersey 08512

Associated University Presses
Magdalen House
136–148 Tooley Street
London SE1 2TT, England

Library of Congress Cataloging in Publication Data

Westbrook, Perry D
    Free will and determinism in American literature.

    Bibliography: p.
    Includes index.
    1. American literature—History and criticism.   2. Free will and determinism in literature.   3. Free will and determinism.   I. Title.
PS169.F68W4   810'.9'12   77-89785
ISBN 0-8386-2150-3

I wish to thank the following publishers for having given me permission to quote from published works:

Little, Brown and Company, for permission to quote from *The Complete Poems of Emily Dickinson*, edited by Thomas H. Johnson: Poem #306: Copyright 1914, 1942 by Martha Dickinson Bianchi; Poem #376: Copyright 1929 by Martha Dickinson Bianchi. Copyright (c) 1957 by Mary L. Hampson; poem #593: Copyright 1935 by Martha Dickinson Bianchi. Copyright (c) 1963 by Mary L. Hampson.
Charles Scribner's Sons, for permission to quote from "The Children of the Night" and "The Night Before" from *The Children of the Night* by E. A. Robinson, 1905. Reprinted by permission of Charles Scribner's Sons from "The Children of the Night" and "The Night Before" from THE CHILDREN OF THE NIGHT by Edwin Arlington Robinson.

PRINTED IN THE UNITED STATES OF AMERICA

Contents

Acknowledgments

I wish to thank the following publishers for having given me permission to quote from published works:

Harvard University Press, for permission to quote from *The Poems of Emily Dickinson,* edited by Thomas H. Johnson, as follows: "The Soul selects her own Society—" (#303), "He fumbles at your Soul" (#315), "Of Course—I prayed—" (#376), "God made a little Gentian—" (#442), "At least—to pray—is left—is left—" (#502), and "Mine—by the Right of the White Election!" (#528). Reprinted by permission of the publishers and the trustees of Amherst College from THE POEMS OF EMILY DICKINSON, edited by Thomas H. Johnson, Cambridge, Mass.: The Belknap Press of Harvard University Press, Copyright (c) 1951, 1955 by the President and Fellows of Harvard College.

William Heinemann Ltd. Publishers, for permission to quote from Fyodor Dostoevsky, *The Brothers Karamazov,* translated by Constance Garnett, 1912.

Macmillan Publishing Co., Inc., for permission to quote from Fyodor Dostoevsky, *The Brothers Karamazov,* translated from the Russian by Constance Garnett, 1929; for permission to quote from "The Man against the Sky" from *Collected Poems* of Edwin Arlington Robinson, copyright 1916 by Edwin Arlington Robinson, renewed 1944 by Ruth Nivison; and for permission to quote from Robinson's "Captain Craig," copyright 1902—public domain.

Yale University Press, for permission to quote from the *Poems of Edward Taylor,* edited by D. F. Stanford and L. L. Martz, 1960.

Definitions and Introduction

Determinism: the doctrine that all occurrences in the universe are governed by inexorable laws of cause and effect. Since human activities, whether of the body or the mind, are subject to these same laws as part of the universal order, *determinism* is more narrowly used to denote absence of freedom in our volitions and choices.

William James in an address at the Harvard Divinity School in 1884 defined determinism as professing "that those parts of the universe already laid down absolutely appoint and decree what the other parts shall be. The future has no ambiguous possibilities hidden in its womb: the part we call the present is compatible with only one totality. Any other future complement than the one fixed from eternity is impossible. The whole is in each and every part, and welds it with the rest into an absolute unity, an iron block, in which there can be no equivocation or shadow of turning."[1] To cap his definition, James quotes from that most deterministic—or fatalistic—of poems, the "Rubaiyat" of Omar Khayyam:

> With earth's first clay they did the last man knead,
> And there of the last harvest sowed the seed.
> And the first morning of creation wrote
> What the last dawn of reckoning shall read.

A deterministic outlook may find its intellectual basis in various religious and philosophical beliefs: the three Fates of the Greeks or the Germanic Wyrd; Predestination and the Eternal Decrees of God of the Augustinians and the Calvinists; or the scientists' Naturalism—the conviction that all phenomena, including man and his activities, are subject to one set of natural laws. A frequent synonym of *determinism* is *necessity,* from which comes the adjective *necessitarian,* denoting the unwavering causation of all physical and psychological events. *Mechanism* is another synonym.

Indeterminism: the belief that some events in the universe are not under an iron necessity or determinism; more narrowly, the supposition that the human will is not entirely subject to forces beyond an individual's control. According to William James, *indeterminism* means "that the parts [of the previously described "block" universe] have a certain amount of loose play on one another, so that the laying down of one of them does not necessarily determine what the others shall be. It admits that possibilities may be in excess of actualities, and that things not yet revealed to our knowledge may really in themselves be ambiguous. Of two alternative futures which we conceive, both may now be possible. . . . Indeterminism thus denies the world to be one unbending unit of fact."[2]

The *will:* may be defined as a faculty, a state of mind, an action of the mind, a process of the mind and the emotions and instincts combined, and as much else. *Webster's Third New International Dictionary* (unabridged) provides as useful a set of definitions as any for this difficult word. In the present essay the word *will* is employed to designate that *process* by which one chooses from two or more alternatives a course of mental or physical action and attempts to initiate such action. The only usable synonym of *will* is *volition.*

Free will (or *freedom of the will,* or simply *freedom*): that condition, supposed or real, in which the means of choosing and attempting to initiate one of several possible actions is not predetermined by natural or supernatural forces either within or outside the mind or body of the would-be agent. It is not permissible or meaningful to limit the discussion to *freedom of choice,* as Corliss Lamont does in his book *Freedom of Choice Affirmed.* To be sure, free choice is fundamental in the process. The chosen action need not be carried through, but it must at least be initiated if we are to speak of any significant freedom of the will. A chronic drunkard, for example, may one day *choose* to be sober and then immediately proceed to consume a fifth of whiskey. However free his instantly violated choice may have been, such freedom is not worth much. If, on the other hand, the drunkard initiated his choice of action by refraining completely from strong drink for the ensuing twenty-four hours and then slowly consumed a half a pint instead of a fifth, one could argue that an act of free will, however limited, had taken place. If the alcoholic continued his efforts by seeking a cure, one could continue to describe his will as acting freely, even if eventually he relapsed into his former condition. Of course, one could maintain that, in the case in which the decision for sobriety was immediately followed by the consumption of a fifth of whiskey, the real choice was for continued alcoholism. Calvin would so argue, asserting that the unregenerate will of this man would be incapable of choosing and carrying out a good action. A Freudian[3] might assert that unconsciously a stronger will, energized by neurosis, was at work; the inebriate's real choice was to punish himself or others as a result of some hidden guilt or hostility. But neither Calvin nor Freud would call such a choice *free,* though Calvin would admit a rather limited freedom in the man's being able to carry out his perverted choice.

Such choices, however, are classic examples of *determinism.* One could also argue that the drunkard's relapse after a partial or temporary remission of his destructive habit can be explained only deterministically. This is true if he still consciously continued to choose and will sobriety even as he underwent relapse. Yet for a time at least he succeeded in following and realizing his choice for a return to health, and thus his choice and will might not have been under a total determinism. Of course, all his vagaries of choice and action *may* have been under an inexorable determinism, but we must not ignore the possibility that he did actually enjoy moments of *freedom of will* (including freedom of choice). The door is at least ajar for the entrance of *indeterminism* into the case. It is not plausible ever to assume a total indeterminism (whereas total determinism can be made to seem somewhat plausible). Assuming the maximum freedom of the will, there are still large areas where the will is helpless to effect its inclinations. One may will not to die and succeed in this desire by surviving for a normal lifetime, but not forever, since death constitutes an insurmountable determinism. What is meant by *freedom of will* in this essay is a limited scope of free choice and action within an encompassing framework of deterministic circumstances both physical and psychological. As synonyms for *freedom of the will* I shall use *indeterminism* (in the narrower sense noted above) and *libertarianism*.

The purpose of this study is not, assuredly, to resolve the knotty problem of the will and its possible freedom. Rather, it is to examine theories and attitudes on the problem as expressed directly and indirectly in American literature. The focus is on such relatively popular literary forms as poetry, essay, and, above all, prose fiction. However, other areas of literature—taken in its broadest sense—have been scanned in order to trace the scientific, theological, and philosophical sources of the ideas that find their way into belles lettres. Furthermore, since American thought has always been to a considerable degree derived from that of other and older cultures, some attention is directed to influences from Europe and Asia. It is hoped that the results of these efforts will be a deepened understanding of some of the impulses that underlie national assumptions regarding the individual and his potential ability to direct his own life and occasional national presumptions in undertaking to direct the lives of others.

Free Will and Determinism
in American Literature

1

The Predestinated Will

Writers like Moses Coit Tyler, Oliver Wendell Holmes, and Harriet Beecher Stowe have pointed out that around New England dinner tables, from the seventeenth century until well into the nineteenth, theology was a major topic of conversation. Counting Sunday sermons and Thursday lectures, the average New Englander annually was exposed to over one hundred hours of instruction in religious doctrine. As the years passed, each churchgoer would acquire something resembling a university education in the teachings of his sect. Prominent among the subjects of sermons and lectures and the discussions that followed them in the parishioners' homes would be the will—its freedom or servitude, its relationship with election and predestination, and God's use of it in achieving His purposes.

Throughout the history of Christian thought the problem of the will has received the attention of the greatest thinkers—St. Augustine, Boethius, St. Thomas Aquinas, Bishop Bradwardine, Luther, and Calvin. The dangers of speculation on the subject were fully recognized. As Aquinas pointed out, any meaningful concept of moral responsibility must be based on the assumption that a choice between good and evil actions is possible; and such choice can exist only where the will is free. Therefore, an argument undermining the freedom of the will, or at least freedom of choice, would undermine any system of ethics—such as the Christian—that is based on the receiving of rewards or punishments for our actions in this life. Most medieval speculators on the problem accepted the will's freedom as a matter of faith. They believed that an all-knowing, all-powerful God has foreseen from the beginning of time precisely how each individual will act in each circumstance of his life; but, nevertheless, the individual acts freely. This paradox was given the name *conditional necessity* and left at that. Occasional amateurs in philosophy and theology—like Chaucer in "The Knight's Tale" and *Troilus and Criseyde*—toyed with the enigma and perhaps even questioned the official conclusions. But only with the Reformation did the status of the will receive a totally new examination, which resulted in a radically different estimate of its power and function in God's plan for the universe.

American theology, for the first 250 years at least, was constituted overwhelmingly of Reformation theology. Hence, American concepts of the will were those of the Reformers, especially John Calvin, whose doctrines are basic to the Puritan, the Presbyterian, the Dutch Reformed, and even the Anglican sects—in other words, the denominations adhered to by the vast majority of early colonists in British America. Now it is obvious that the first emigrants from Europe were endowed with considerable fortitude, willpower, and confidence in their mission; without such endowments people do not set out on such ventures. It is also obvious that the religious beliefs of these colonists must have been in harmony with their convictions concerning the rightness and the feasibility of their project. Vernon Parrington, among others, has pointed out that their religion—that is, Calvinism—was peculiarly appropriate and serviceable as a support and stimulus for a group bent on settling a wilderness. Thus, to understand these settlers and their descendants down to the present, it is necessary to understand their religious faiths and especially those elements which provided them with the sheer determination to persevere under extreme hardship and bitter discouragement. Exactly what teaching concerning the relation of man's will with God's spurred these emigrants to the exertions that made possible their survival?

St. Augustine

St. Augustine is the ultimate important source of the theology subscribed to by the Protestant colonists, since he was the chief source of Calvinism. Among the basic tenets of Augustine that bear on the nature of the human will are: the doctrines of man's utter inability, after the fall of Adam, to will *not* to sin; his complete dependence on God's grace to enable him to acquire the faith necessary for salvation; the irresistibility of God's grace when it is offered; and, finally, God's election of only a few persons upon whom to bestow His saving grace.

Adam had had free choice, according to Augustine, but by his misuse of it he had punged man into bondage to sin in which no truly "free choice"[1] or direction of the will can exist. The will redeemed by God's grace, however, is capable of righteous choice and actions even though God has foreseen and foreordained all of men's choices and actions whether good or evil.

A logical sequel to this concept is that God's foreknowledge of all events constitutes a fate or determinism that nullifies any true freedom of the will. But Augustine has an answer to this objection: God, he readily agrees, "allows nothing to remain unordered . . . and knows all things before they come to pass."[2] He realizes that a paradox is involved, but he is not "dismayed by the difficulty that what we choose to do freely is done by necessity, because He whose foreknowledge cannot be deceived foreknew that we would choose to do"[3] what we do. "From the fact that to God the order of all causes is certain, there is no logical deduction that there is no power in the choice of our will. The fact is that our choices fall within the order of the causes which is known for certain to God and is contained in His foreknowledge—for, human choices are the causes of human acts."[4]

But invariably, to Augustine, the unregenerate will is not really free, since it can will only evil. The regenerate will is free, despite God's foreknowledge of what it will do. But the will is unable to will its own regeneracy without the influx of God's grace, which no one controls except God.

John Calvin

The reader will encounter Augustine's concepts and arguments concerning the will many times in the pages that follow. Nowhere are they more pervasive than in the writing of John Calvin, the chief source in early America of ideas on the freedom of the will and on necessity. So important and so basic are Calvin's thoughts that they must be examined in some detail.

Fundamental to Calvin's ideas on the subject is his famous doctrine of eternal decrees by which God is deemed to have irrevocably and from the beginning of time "determined with himself what he willed to become of each man. For all are not created in equal condition; rather eternal life is ordained for some, eternal damnation for others."[5] Beginning, as did Augustine, with this premise, Calvin discusses at length the limitations that it places upon the free agency of man. To begin with, Calvin borrows from Origen a definition of free will: "a faculty of the reason to distinguish between good and evil, a faculty of the will to choose one or the other."[6] Calvin next quotes Augustine to the effect that the will and the reason have the faculty "to choose good with the assistance of grace; evil, when grace is absent."[7] As stated in 2 Corinthians 3:17, "where the spirit of the Lord is, there is freedom," that is, the freedom to do good *but* only good. In Eden, man by his disobedience alienated himself from the spirit of the Lord and enslaved himself to sin. Only by God's grace, given solely at God's pleasure and discretion, can man be freed from this enslavement. Yet even in a state of grace, when man chooses good actions, God must receive the credit. A man's good works are attributed to God alone.

An appropriate text is: "Cursed is the man who trusts in man and makes flesh his arm" (Jeremiah 17:5).[8] Though even unregenerate man has some understanding as to right and wrong in respect to earthly matters, only regenerate man enjoys spiritual discernment. Calvin writes: "Flesh is not capable of such lofty wisdom as to conceive God and what is God's, unless it be illumined by the Spirit of God."[9] Man after the fall is filled with evil. He is not deprived of will; he simply is incapable of willing anything but evil. He wills as he chooses, but his choice is determined by his sinful nature. Actually, Calvin admits, this condition in no way constitutes free will as most conceive of it—which would be will operating independently of grace and original sin. The most that can be said is that man sins willingly through his corrupt nature, not by exterior compulsion. The corrupt will, indeed, creates its own necessity. As Bernard wrote, "It is guilty because it is free [to follow its own inevitable bent], and enslaved because it is guilty, and as a consequence enslaved because it is free."[10]

From this highly limited freedom—the freedom to do the wrong that a corrupt and guilty nature must desire—man is delivered by conversion, which is the result of God's indwelling grace rather than of efforts on man's part. In conversion, which is the lot of the small number of God's elect, the chosen one experiences no less than the gift of a new spirit to replace his former corrupt one. Gratuitously, at God's inscrutable whim, the old inclination for evil is eradicated and is replaced by a new will that, just as inevitably, must desire that which is good and pleasing to the Deity. All of this, it should be emphasized again, is entirely God's doing—the result of predestination from the beginning of time. Some individuals have been booked for damnation; some, by God's inscrutable mercy, have been booked for salvation.

As Calvin puts it, "a second creation . . . in Christ"[11] is undergone by the regenerate. The unregenerate's volition has been turned away from good by his own nature. Grace precedes every good work, including the very act of becoming a believer; that is, the act of becoming one of the saved. After conversion, the believer does not *cooperate* with grace. He becomes *the instrument* of grace, as supine in its clutches as he was in the grip of original sin. A "prevenient grace"[12], in fact, causes the person predestined for salvation to choose and will the acceptance of converting grace itself. Thus, in conversion, as well as in the good works that should follow conversion, Calvin sees only a nominal freedom of will. The "perseverance"[13] of a saint—that is, the continued willing and doing of good by the convert—is in no way to the faithful's credit but to God's. The saint may be subjected to temptation—that is, the seeming choice of sinning or not—but God, who has made him His instrument, will ensure his making the right choice. To Calvin the "freedom" of the saved is preferable to that of Adam, which was "to be able not to sin; but ours [that of the regenerate] is much greater, not to be able to sin."[14]

Doctrines such as these are incredible or offensive to many modern minds. Yet the controversies raging about them in the past have filled libraries with folio tomes. The hair-splittings engaged in by the polemicists are illustrated in some of Calvin's own remarks. For example, he makes "a distinction between compulsion and necessity from which it appears that man, while he sins of necessity, yet sins no less voluntarily,"[15] for he follows his inclination, albeit a predestinated inclination. Still Calvin is frank enough not to argue that on the basis of this distinction the will is really free. "In discussing free will," he continues, "we are not asking whether a man is permitted to carry out and complete, despite external hindrances, whatever he has decided to do; but whether he has in any respect whatever both choice of judgment and inclination of will that are free."[16] Since no such choices exist, according to Calvin, man can hardly be said to enjoy a freedom of the will. The most that can be conceded is that "something not subject to free choice [may be] nevertheless voluntarily done."[17]

This "voluntariness" in man's sinning was sufficient, in Calvin's eyes, to justify the punishment of unregenerate man for his evil nature and deeds. But Calvin is at least consistent: the good deeds that the regenerate "voluntarily" do and for which they achieve salvation reflect no credit on the doers.

Nor does Calvin fail to deal with Aristotle's and Aquinas's argument that "unless virtues and vices both proceed from the free choice of will, it is not consistent that man be either punished or rewarded." Calvin's rejoinder is indeed blunt: We deserve punishment. It makes no difference "whether we sin out of free or servile judgment." [18]

Such, then, are Calvin's views, often repeated and much elaborated in the *Institutes*. One caution, however, is necessary. Calvin's doctrine that the will is completely subservient to God's in no way constitutes a reason, in Calvin's view, for man's not using his will and not struggling to be righteous. The outcome of the struggle is, of course, in the hands of God and has been decreed through all eternity. Yet to Calvin, as to Augustine, the will is God's instrument for achieving His purposes. The elect may not cease their struggle to lead godly lives, even though they are sure that they are on the roll of the saved. Any such cessation, in fact, would be cogent evidence that one is not of the elect. Nor may those who are rather sure they are among the damned cease to strive to be converted; for conversion, even though eternally decreed, is accompanied by effort of will. That is God's way of accomplishing conversion.

Similarly, ministers must constantly exhort the unregenerate to seek to attain conversion, even though logic might indicate that mere human exhortation could have no effect on an issue written on God's scrolls since before the Creation. Exhortation is another of God's ways of bringing about that which He has decreed: a specific sinner's desire "to seek after and to attain . . . renewal." [19] Thus, there is no foundation for the often expressed wonderment that a thoroughgoing Calvinist predestinarian like Jonathan Edwards should deny the primary efficacy of the human will in determining one's salvation and at the same time deliver revivalistic sermons according to which the whole issue would seem to depend on the individual's efforts. True, the matter is entirely in God's hands, but if God has decided that such and such a person is to become regenerate, the regeneration will take place through the minister's spiritual wrestling with the sinner and the sinner's wrestling with himself.

A paradoxical tendency of Calvinism is thus to exalt rather than diminish the role of the human will and to lend it a dignity that it would not possess if conceived of as working entirely on its own. For the will of a converted man, at least, reflects God's will. And even the evil volitions of the unregenerate serve to fulfill God's mysterious purpose. The human will, though entirely circumscribed, is pivotal in the divine order of things. Hence the dogged determination, the downright stubbornness, so often associated with Puritans. The Puritan elect are persons who know they are right because they are doing what God wills them to do; they are no less than the tools of God in working out His plans for His creation.

The Thirty-Nine Articles and the Westminster Confession

The doctrines of John Calvin are basic to two great English statements of belief—the Thirty-nine Articles of the Anglican Church and the Westminster Confession of Faith of the Puritans. Of these the Thirty-nine Articles, drafted by the archbishops and other clergy at a convocation held in London in 1562, is older by almost a hundred years. Still to be found in small type at the end of the *Book of Common Prayer* currently in use in churches of the Anglican Communion, the Articles proclaim the tenets of Calvinism in greatly abridged but unmistakable terms. Though some of the doctrines stated therein have fallen into disuse, they were very much alive in the sixteenth and seventeenth centuries, providing the subject matter for many a sermon and many a discussion. Though the Puritans gradually broke with the liturgical practices and polity of the Anglican Church, they could, and did, adhere to much of the theology of the Articles.

Teachings in the Thirty-Nine Articles

Certainly the teachings in the Articles touching upon the will and its place in God's plan for the universe are unexceptionable to any orthodox Calvinist. Article 10 ("Of Free Will") reads: "The condition of Man after the fall of Adam is such, that he cannot turn and prepare himself, by his own natural strength and good works, to faith, and calling upon God: Wherefore we have no power to do good works, pleasant and acceptable to God, without the grace of God by Christ preventing us, that we may have a good will, and working with us, when we have that good will."[20] Article 11 ("Of the Justification of Man") states that good works are no substitute for faith which makes them "righteous before God" and we have seen in Article 10 that faith comes only by the grace of God. Good works before justification, or the onset of faith, are in no way pleasing to God; but, we are told in Article 12 ("Of Good Works"), after justification, though they "cannot put away our sins, and endure the severity of God's judgment . . . yet are they pleasing and acceptable to God in Christ, and do spring out *necessarily* [italics added] of a true and lively Faith; insomuch that by them a lively Faith may be as evidently known as a tree discerned by the fruit."

Ultimately, of course, everything is dependent on those ultra-Calvinistic doctrines of predestination and election, which are summarized in Article 17:

Predestination to Life is the everlasting purpose of God, whereby (before the foundations of the world were laid) he hath constantly decreed by his counsel secret to us, to deliver from curse and damnation those whom he hath chosen in Christ out of mankind, and to bring them by Christ to everlasting salvation, as vessels made to honour. Wherefore, they which be endued with so excellent a benefit of God, be called according to God's purpose by his Spirit working in due season: they through Grace obey the calling: they be justified freely: they be made sons of God by adoption: they be made like the image of his only begotten Son Jesus Christ: they walk religiously in good works, and at length, by God's mercy, they attain to everlasting felicity.

Teachings in the Westminster Confession

Eighty years later, in the years 1643–46, an assembly of divines from the Scottish and English Puritan churches drew up the famous Westminster Confession of Faith that has supplied the doctrinal standard for most branches of the Presbyterian Communion to the present day and, to within the last hundred years, for the Congregational Church. In matters concerning the priesthood, the government of churches, and the uses of the sacraments, the Westminster Assembly deviated radically from the Thirty-nine Articles. But theologically, there are many close parallels, most of which arise from the solid Calvinist core of each document. Though there is no need to quote extensively from the Westminster Confession, there are in it, especially as regards the will, several modifications of the precepts of Calvin's *Institutes* and of the Thirty-nine Articles.

The Anglican Article 10, as shown above, is exceedingly negative about the efficacy of the human will, or even its usefulness. It is in complete agreement with Calvin in stating that, without the grace of God working through and in it, the human will is totally incapable of initiating righteous acts. The will has its place, its function, but only as a tool of Deity.

The Westminster Confession does not deny this, but its statement is so worded that it lends slightly more dignity to man's efforts—values them perhaps more highly, even though they are as mere cogs in the divine machine. "God from all eternity," reads chapter 3 ("Of God's Eternal Decrees"),

> did by the most wise and holy counsel of his own will, freely and unchangeably ordain whatsoever comes to pass; yet so as thereby neither is God the author of sin; nor is violence offered to the will of the creatures, nor is the liberty or contingency of second causes taken away, but rather established.
>
> Although God knows whatsoever may or can come to pass, upon all supposed conditions; yet hath he not decreed anything because he foresaw it as future, or as that which would come to pass, upon such conditions.
>
> By the decree of God, for the manifestation of his glory, some men and angels are predestined unto everlasting life, and others are foreordained to everlasting death.[21]

In its further discussion of predestination, the Confession is adamant: the individual has nothing to do with his own destiny, whether of salvation or damnation. The choice is utterly and totally God's: God directs the human soul into repentance and conversion as he has seen fit from the beginning of time. Nothing that the individual does or tries to do will have the slightest effect. Yet the terms of this famous "double decree" (of election and damnation) are such that no violence is offered to the will of the creatures. More purely Augustinian than Calvinistic, this paradox, to most, must have remained one of the mysteries of faith. But mystery or not, it was a part of the faith, and on the basis of it Presbyterian and Congregationalist ministers for the next 200 or more years could insist that man's choice of salvation or damnation was free and that he could only achieve regeneration by energetic exertions of will.

Chapter 11 ("Of Free Will") hardly resolves the matter, though it attempts an explanation and at least provides further material for controversy: "God hath endued the will of man with that natural liberty, that is neither forced, nor by any absolute necessity of nature determined to good or evil." Apparently by its intrinsic nature the will is potentially capable of exercising free choice between good and evil acts. It labors under no fundamental incapacity that might direct it inevitably into evil. And indeed Chapter 11 says that in its prelapsarian state the will "had freedom and power . . . to do that which is good and well-pleasing to God; but yet mutably, so that he might fall from" innocency. But by Adam's wrong choice in Eden, this basically effective and godlike faculty has been crippled so that it "hath wholly lost all ability of will to any spiritual good accompanying salvation; so as a natural man, being altogether averse from that good, and dead in sin, is not able, by his own strength, to convert himself, or to prepare himself thereunto." After conversion, man once again is enabled "freely to will and to do that which is spiritually good," yet he is still capable of willing and doing evil. "The will of man is made perfectly and immutably free to good alone, in the state of glory only," a view contrary to Calvin's contention that the regenerate will could desire only good.

Thus far the situation, according to the Westminster Confession, would seem to be this: Since man's will was damaged by the fall, he now needs God's help in rehabilitating it. The act of rehabilitation is entirely God's doing—and He does it for His elect only. This does not mean that a sinful or fallen man cannot desire and struggle for his conversion; indeed, such desire and struggle are necessary and are part of the predestinated process. But one's efforts and wishes alone are of no avail in effecting regeneration of one's soul. According to the doctrine of Effectual Calling (chapter 12 of the Westminster Confession), God renews the wills of the elect and draws them to Christ, yet He does not compel or bludgeon the sinner into conversion. The function of man's renewed will for salvation is vital; yet it is totally dependent on God's aid or grace.

The process after calling, or conversion with accompanying

repentance, is essentially that outlined in chapter 17 of the Thirty-nine Articles, though the Westminster Confession goes into greater detail. Automatically following on conversion occurs justification, whereby man is made righteous (the root meaning of the Latin *justificare*) and becomes an eligible recipient of the redemptive powers of Christ. Once justified, the redeemed are "partakers of the grace of adoption: by which they are taken into the number, and enjoy the liberties and privileges of the children of God" (chapter 14). The regenerate now are "sanctified": that is, they lead godly lives, exhibiting in their character and actions their newfound holiness, though they are never entirely free from "some remnants of corruption . . . , whence ariseth a continual and irreconcilable war, the flesh lusting against the Spirit, and the Spirit against the flesh" (chapter 15). With the aid of the Spirit of Christ, the elect will now be able to perform good works, which are pleasing to God but in no way constitute in themselves assurance of salvation.

Most comforting, perhaps, to these favored ones of God is the doctrine of the Perseverance of Saints (chapter 19), which states that "they whom God hath accepted in his Beloved, effectually called and sanctified by his Spirit, can neither totally nor finally fall away from the state of grace: but shall certainly persevere therein to the end, and be eternally saved." This happy security again depends not upon the saints' free will but upon the immutability of the decree of election. Yet the saints do at times backslide and incur God's wrath and "bring temporal judgments upon themselves." Thus, though the final outcome does not depend upon free will, the saint must ever pit his will against temptation. The life of the elect is far from a bed of roses, for grace and salvation may not be taken for granted even by the true believer, who may be deceived as to his own state and thus must ever strive "to make his calling and election sure" (chapter 20)—that is, become assured of them in his own mind. He can achieve this assurance only by succeeding in leading a righteous

life and keeping his own faith alive. Most likely he will go
through periods of doubt and fear; yet if he is truly of the elect,
he will manage to keep himself "from utter despair."

Two Calvinist Poets: Michael Wigglesworth and Edward Taylor

The Teachings of Michael Wigglesworth

The most popular Puritan poet in New England in the
seventeenth century was Michael Wigglesworth, whose
lengthy doggerel summary of Calvinist theology, "The Day
of Doom," was "must" reading among the saints on either
side of the Atlantic. Didactic and devoid of aesthetic attrac-
tions, the poem nevertheless appealed to the emotions—
mainly that of fear—in the manner of a hellfire-and-brimstone
sermon. Remarkably, however, if one reads "The Day of
Doom" with care, one discovers that it addresses itself throughout to the knotty problem of the will. Are the saints and sinners
that are arraigned before Christ at the Last Judgment personally responsible for the condition in which they find themselves, and hence for the punishment or reward meted out to
them?

According to Wigglesworth's account, the saints are quickly
disposed of, being sent off to paradise with smug expressions
on their faces and obvious elation at the plight of their enemies, the damned. Wigglesworth deals much more lengthily
with the sinners, for it is their plight that raises, and has always
raised, the most embarrassing question which can be asked a
Calvinist: "If these wretches have been chosen by divine fiat
from the beginning of time for eternal damnation, how can
they be considered morally responsible for the misdeeds for
which they are punished?" Wigglesworth does not evade the
issue. Every type of sinner is paraded before the judge, but
despite their excuses they are all accused and sentenced on
the basis of *their choice* of evil rather than of grace *freely* offered.

The intellectual and emotional climax for Wigglesworth's readers must have come at that point when a group of unfortunates squarely put the question to Christ:

> How could we cease thus to transgress?
>   how could we Hell avoid,
> Whom Gods Decree shut out from thee,
>   and sign'd to be destroy'd?
>
> Whom God ordains to endless pains,
>   by Law unalterable,
> Repentance true, Obedience new,
>   to save such are unable. . . .[22]

The candor with which Wigglesworth states this and other arguments against the Calvinist eschatology is one of the few merits of the poem. Christ's answer, though to many today it will seem illogical, is presented with equal bluntness. "Here is the doctrine; take it or leave it," is what Wigglesworth is saying:

> Christ readily makes this Reply,
>   I damn you not because
> You are rejected, or not elected,
>   but you have broke my Laws:
> It is but vain your wits to strain,
>   the end and means to sever:
> Men fondly seek to part or break
>   what God hath link'd together.
>
> Whom God will save, such he will have,
>   the means of life to use:
> Whom he'll pass by, shall chuse to dy,
>   and ways of life refuse.
> He that fore-sees and foredecrees,
>   in wisdom order'd has,
> That man's free-will electing ill,
>   shall bring his will to pass.
>
> High God's Decree, as it is free,

> so doth it none compel
> Against their will to good or ill,
>   it forceth none to Hell.
> They have their wish whose Souls perish
>   with Torments in Hell-fire,
> Who rather chose their Souls to lose,
>   than leave a loose desire.
>
> ·
>
> You sinful Crew, no other knew
>   but you might be elect;
> Why did you then your selves condemn?
>   why did you me reject?
> Where was your strife to gain that life
>   which lasteth evermore?
> You never knock'd, yet say God lock'd
>   against you heav'ns door.
>
> ·
>
> You argue then: But abject men,
>   whom God resolves to spill,
> Cannot repent, nor their hearts rent:
>   ne can they change their will.
> Not for his *Can* is any man
>   adjudged unto Hell:
> But for his *Will* to do what's ill,
>   and nilling to do well. [23]

Wigglesworth's stanzas, in fact, present one of the clearest statements of the New England Calvinist insistence on the freedom of the will. The argument is identical with that of Jonathan Edwards, as the reader will soon see: man is free to follow his will, and what he wills determines his damnation or his salvation. That he is not free to choose the direction, or inclination, of his will in no way, so the argument goes, circumscribes the freedom of the will itself. A distinction is made here between choice, which is beyond individual control, and will, which "freely" translates the choice into action. Whether this can be validly called true freedom of the will is, as has already been pointed out, extremely questionable. Calvin himself questioned the worth of such freedom.

The Teachings of Edward Taylor

Wigglesworth's style was crude and his dialectic blunt to the point of cruelty. Another Massachusetts Puritan, Edward Taylor, approached the matter much more poetically and subtly. Taylor subscribed wholeheartedly to the Westminster Confession of Faith and in no significant way deviated from its tenets regarding eternal decrees, election, justification, preseverance of saints, santification, and freedom of will. There is no use in rehearsing his views on these doctrines, for he was in every way orthodox. Most of the rather extensive body of his poetry, which was undiscovered and unpublished until the 1930s, falls into one of two groups: the numerous "Preparatory Meditations," which he composed as spiritual exercises before administering the Lord's Supper; and the much less extensive "God's Determinations Concerning His Elect," which contains a somewhat systemized account of Christ's relations with those whom God has chosen for eternal life.

Outside these two categories is a small group of miscellaneous occasional poems and lyrics. The most pleasing introduction to Taylor is through one of these latter—the justly famous "Huswifery,"[24] which can rank with the best of Herbert or Donne in "metaphysical" ingenuity. Anticipating Melville's chapter on the matmakers in *Moby-Dick*, Taylor elaborates a complex metaphor based on the homely process of cloth-making—in which the poet becomes God's tool for working out His will in the fulfillment of His decree of the poet's election. Truly one of the finest poems in American literature, "Huswifery" epitomizes American Calvinist views on the relation of man's will to God's. In theological terms, the poem is an allegory of the saving processes of justification and sanctification, through "natural" endowments, such as "Understanding, Affections, Judgement,"[25] which God sets in motion in the elect and which the elect would be helpless to exercise by their own unaided efforts. Similarly, in the "Meditations," Taylor compares man to a musical instrument played upon by God:

> If thou wilt blow this Oaten Straw of mine,
> The sweetest piped praises shall be thine.[26]

Yet it would be wrong to say that Taylor considered man to be will-less. He has a will, but he is dependent on God for its direction and even its activation. The elect derive their will from God; the reprobates are capable of willing only that which results in damnation.

> Such as are Gracious, Graces have therefore [sic]
> They evermore desire to have more.
> But such as never knew this dainty fare
> Do never wish them 'cause they dainties are.[27]

For the elect, life will indeed be a constant struggle to maintain their state of grace, though they can be assured of successful perseverance to the end. One of their responsibilities—in fact, one of the "evidences" that one is chosen—is that one will be the object of assaults by Satan. If one were not of the elect, Satan

> . . . never would bestow
> Such darts upon [you] Grace to overthrow.
> The Bullets shot are blinde, the fowlers eye
> Aims at the marke before he lets them fly.[28]

To be God's chosen vessel is not to remain at rest; it entails, rather, a ceaseless exertion of the God-given will to fulfill His behests.

A humorous illustration of a "saint's" struggle against Satan's temptations occurs in Henry Ward Beecher's novel *Norwood: or, Village Life in New England.* Deacon Marble has an unseemly habit of breaking into laughter in church, despite desperate efforts to stifle his mirth. Being a deacon he is, of course, supposedly one of the elect; but as such he would be expected to possess a will capable of controlling his sacrilegious

impulses. His wife is alarmed and puts the question to him
squarely:

> ꞇou are as full of levity as flies are. Would you laugh if you
> was dying? I really believe you would! . . . A deacon at your
> time of life, chirpin' as if you was a cricket—and goin' round,
> as if you was nothin' better'n a bird, singing and hoppin',
> instead of being a deacon, with an immortal soul in him!
> Sometimes I am afeerd you are in the gall of bitterness yet
> [that is, unregenerate]. You ought to examine your evi-
> dences, deacon. Laughing is not one of the signs of grace, I'm
> sure. It's awful to be deceived; and you've a good many
> reasons to fear that you are deceivin' yourself.[29]

The deacon's dilemma is the classical Calvinist one, however amusing it may be. Had his conversion been genuine,
his will would have been sufficiently fortified by grace to
subdue his levity. Without grace, the will is helpless to do the
right thing. The deacon's wife, who is deadly serious, may
well be alarmed.

Later American Calvinism

American Calvinism in the Colonial and early Federal
periods did not deviate so widely from the doctrines of the
Institutes and of the Westminster Confession as some commen-
tators have assumed. This was particularly true as regards
teachings concerning the will. The difference, indeed, was
less in the eighteenth century than in the seventeenth. To
present the theology of American Calvinist thinkers after
1700 is to repeat much of what has already been stated; yet
a minimum of such repetition is unavoidable and is necessary
for purposes of comparison and as evidence of Calvinism's
continuing deeply ingrained influence on many phases of our
culture.

Most prominent among American Calvinist theologians of
any period is Jonathan Edwards, whose famous treatise *Freedom of the Will* emphasizes the place of struggle—or endeavor,

as he calls it—in the divine scheme of things. It has been said that Edwards's argument "results in the view that we are free to do as we please but we are not free to please as we please.[30] In other words, the bent of our wills—whether they direct us toward salvation or damnation—is decreed by God at the beginning of time. The damned choose to will evil to themselves and others; the elect choose what is beneficial to themselves and others. This is the decree of God. The will can always will as it chooses, but in attaining what it wishes to attain, it will not be exempt from "endeavor."

> Endeavors which we use, are things that exist; and therefore they belong to the general chain of events; all parts of which chain are supposed to be connected: and so endeavors are supposed to be connected with some effects, or some consequent things, or other. And certainly this don't hinder but that the events they are connected with, may be those which we aim at, and which we choose, because we judge 'em most likely to have a connection with those events, from the established order and course of things which we observe, or from something in divine revelation.[31]

The point emphasized by Calvin himself, as seen above, and by all his followers, is that man is given his will to use, and he must use it. The fact that God, omniscient and omnipotent, has long ago decreed exactly how the will is to be used by each individual—whether for good or for evil—and has decided how successful it is to be in its efforts, in no way excuses one from the utmost exertion within one's power in the direction that God, through the Scriptures, has pointed out to man. Thus Thomas Hooker writes in a sermon on sin: "The will of man [is] the chiefest of all [God's] workmanship, all for his body, the body of the soul, the mind to attend upon the will, the will to attend upon God and to make choice of Him and His will, that is next to Him and He only above that."[32]

"Simple Necessity" and "Conditional Necessity"

The Doctrine of "Simple Necessity"

Edwards explicitly rejects any mechanistic concept of the will, and in this he is in accord with all American Calvinists:

> As to that objection against the doctrine [of necessity] which I have endeavored to prove, that it makes men no more than machines; I would say, that notwithstanding this doctrine, man is entirely, perfectly and unspeakably different from a mere machine, in that he has reason and understanding, and has a faculty of will, and so is capable of volition and choice. . . .[33]

Yet, in one respect Edwards retreated to an even stricter Calvinism than that of the Westminster Confession, which states in chapter 3 ("Of God's Eternal Decrees") that God has "not decreed anything because he foresaw it as future, or as that which would come to pass. . . . " In the Middle Ages the free-will controversy frequently revolved around the question of God's foreknowledge. The question is simply stated but is probably unanswerable: Is man bound to act as an omniscient and omnipotent God foresees that he will act? In the Middle Ages there were two major doctrines on this matter, that of "simple necessity" and that of "conditional necessity." According to the theory of simple necessity, God's foreknowledge constitutes a binding determinism on all acts of man. What God foreknows will happen; man's will is nullified. The concept of simple necessity was present in America at least through the eighteenth century, for it is stated and upheld by Edwards:

> 'Tis . . . evident, that if there be a full, certain and infallible foreknowledge of the future existence of the volitions of moral agents, then there is a certain infallible and indissoluble connection between those events and that fore-

knowledge; and that therefore . . . those events [the volitions] are necessary events. . . .[34]

Against simple necessity there is an obvious and simple argument, and the best thinkers on the will from Augustine through Edwards have attempted to cope with it. The objection that had to be answered is this: If all man's volitions, let alone his actions, are inevitably bound to come to pass as God has foreseen them, why act at all? Edwards argues that man must will that which God decrees him to will. His volitions will be precisely as God has foreseen and foreordained them; the will of man is one of God's instruments in accomplishing His inscrutable purposes in this world.

In these concepts Edwards is in complete agreement with Calvin, with one exception. Calvin—apparently a bit touchy on the matter of the determining power of foreknowledge—contended that divine foreknowledge of man's sins in no way imposes the necessity of those sins on man, for the fact that God *decreed* these events is the reason He foresees them, and the decrees, not the foreseeing, are what necessitate the human actions and volitions. Thus one deterministic force is removed, and man becomes that much closer to qualifying as a moral agent.

But Edwards, too, despite his more rigid stance, insists that man is a moral agent, for he is free to do as he pleases even though he is not free to please as he pleases. God's binding foreknowledge of exactly what one's pleasure will be in every choice and action does not, according to Edwards, alter man's freedom to follow his choice. To most readers Edwards's inclusion of the problem of foreknowledge in his argument will weaken whatever cause he can make for man as a moral agent.

The Doctrine of "Conditional Necessity"

Earlier thinkers, including Augustine himself, stated the

case differently—through the postulation of "conditional necessity." Simple necessity, they realized, is untenable unless man be permitted to sink into despair induced by a sense of his own helplessness. Thus they contended that, though God foresees our actions, these actions are still the result of our own free choice and free volition. This, they stated, is one of the mysteries of faith and must be accepted. Edwards made the error of trying to rationalize the mystery.

The medieval mind was very much aware of these knotty questions, as is evident from their extensive treatment in Chaucer's *Canterbury Tales* and *Troilus and Criseyde*. In the Renaissance also they were in the foreground, appearing in such works as *Macbeth* and *Paradise Lost,* not to mention their all-pervasiveness in Puritan theology.

A classic statement of conditional necessity is found in *Paradise Lost.* This work is perhaps as much a humanist as a Puritan poem, but at any rate it was an influence—and mainly a liberalizing one—in both English and American Puritanism.

On the subject of free will Milton is forthright, going well beyond the concessions of strict Calvinsim. In book 3 of the epic, God says of man:

> I made him just and right,
> Sufficient to have stood, though free to fall. [35]

God did not wish to create a puppet, a helpless victim of necessity. Man must obey or disobey God by his own free choice—which is exactly the argument of Dostoevski in "The Grand Inquisitor" chapter in *The Brothers Karamazov.*

God, Milton continues, has given man two instruments whereby he can effect his choices: reason and will.

> But God left free the will, for what obeys
> Reason is free, and reason he made right;
> But bid her well beware, and still erect,
> Lest, by some fair appearing good surpriz'd,
> She dictate false, and misinform the will

> To do what God expressly hath forbid.
>
> (*Paradise Lost* 9. 351–56)

Such did God create not only man but all "the etherial powers." God, of course, knows that Satan will revolt and that man will fall but

> . . . they themselves decreed
> Their own revolt, not I: if I foreknew,
> Foreknowledge had no influence on their fault. . . .
>
> (3. 116–8)

These passages refer primarily to the prelapsarian dispensation, but they have a more general application as well. Though most Calvinists agree that Adam before the fall enjoyed greater liberties of choice and volition than he did after the fall, God foreknew—in fact decreed—the calamities that were to overwhelm him. But if Milton not only refuses to equate foreknowledge and necessity before the fall, he cannot—and does not—equate them in the postlapsarian world. In thus espousing "conditional necessity," he goes beyond the grudging concessions of orthodox Calvinism to the freedom of the will.

Proceeding to the doctrine of election, Milton strays again from strict orthodoxy:

> Man shall not quite be lost, but sav'd who will,
> Yet not of will in him, but grace in me
> Free vouchsaf'd. . . .
> Some have I chosen of peculiar grace
> Elect above the rest; so is my will:
> The rest shall hear me call, and oft be warn'd
> Their sinful state, and to appease betimes
> Th' incensed Deity, while offer'd grace
> Invites; for I will clear their senses dark,
> What may suffice, and soften stony hearts
> To pray, repent, and bring obedience due.
> To prayer, repentance, and obedience due,
> Though but endeavour'd with sincere intent,
> Mine ear shall not be slow, mine eye not shut.
>
> (3. 173–75; 183–93)

The will alone cannot save even the elect; only grace may do that. However, like Edwards, Milton states that the desire—the will—for salvation must be present as well as grace, for the will is the channel through which grace flows. But the radical departure from orthodoxy in Milton is his very clear assertion that those who are not elect—not slated from the beginning of time for salvation—may, through sincere effort, gain a hearing with God and achieve salvation. God foreknew that he would grant amnesty to these unchosen ones, but even so the solid wall of election has been breached. Neither Calvin nor Edwards would go so far as Milton has.

Practical Accommodations by the Puritans

Edwards's defense of Calvinism was prompted by a tendency among Protestants of his day to question the teachings on predestination and the will. Indeed, whether or not to believe in free will is, in fact, a perennial instance of what William James calls a genuine option—that is, one which is "forced, living, and momentous."[36] One's entire way of life is involved in one's estimate as to the extent to which one is in control of one's own destiny. Should one resign oneself to living passively like a vegetable? Or should one make some attempt to control one's environment, one's thoughts, the direction of one's own life?

The pragmatist's response is, of course, the latter, and consideration of the consequences of each approach leaves little hesitancy in most minds. Total fatalists do exist—at least in literature—as typified by Chaucer's Troilus, whose first response to any difficulty is to lie on his couch and meditate on the irrevocability of the decrees of Fortune. Yet such persons are rarities, both in literature and in real life.

Augustine was faced with the choice of admitting the futility of all moral effort or of accepting the paradox of conditional necessity: man is free but God knows how man will act. To maintain man's status as a moral agent, Augustine chose the latter. And Aquinas went so far as to warn against concentrated speculation on the matter, for in that direction lay despair and atheism.

Seemingly committed to a doctrine of determinism, the Puritans nevertheless developed personal wills of a stubbornness and purposefulness that still excite wonder. The elect, indeed, could not do otherwise; for they considered their exertions to be expressions of God's will, and thus they should strain themselves to the utmost. Yet the opposite view—that since God is on their side no strenuous effort is necessary—would be equally logical. This view was indeed held by some not of the elect, much to the distress of their rulers. But in general the Puritans became noted for their firmness of character and unbending determination in accomplishing their ends against every obstacle. Their wills appeared to be developed out of all proportion—even to the extent, as Hawthorne has pointed out, of becoming inhuman and destructive.

Thus, either as they were presented in fiction or as they were in actuality, the Puritans in their daily living did not behave like very thoroughgoing determinists. Each individual was taught that he had a will and was able to use it. In fact, he was encouraged to use it. Edwards himself went to great pains to refute the slander of the Arminians, who stated that Calvinism reduced man to a condition of will-lessness. Edwards argued that exactly the opposite is true:

> [Man's] will is guided by the dictates or views of his understanding; and . . . his external actions and behavior, and in many respects, also his thoughts, and the exercises of his mind, are subject to his will; so that he has liberty to act according to his choice, and do what he pleases; and by means of these things, is capable of moral habits and moral acts, such inclinations and actions as according to the common sense of mankind, are worthy of praise, esteem, love and reward; or on the contrary, of disesteem, detestation, indignation and punishment.[37]

By not regarding man as a machine—and no greater heresy could be imagined than to regard him as such—the Puritans, despite certain embarrassing deterministic implications of their dogma, insisted that man had originally been created in the image of God and thus could not be devoid of will of some sort—especially after the image, defaced by Adam, had been restored by grace. Though man might be infinitely vile and lowly in comparison to God, he was comparable to the fallen angels in that he had retained several divine qualities. The law for man and the law for things, to the Puritan mind, were not the same—as they were to be a few generations later to the scientific naturalists. For God had entered into a special covenant with man. The elect and God were almost on bargaining terms, as is virtually stated by the doctrine of the perseverance of saints.

2

The Predestinated Will in American Fiction of the Nineteenth Century

No notable instances of imaginative literature in Colonial America focused, on the question of will, outside of Edward Taylor's poems and Wigglesworth's doggerel (and I exclude the latter from the category of imaginative literature). Sermons, philosophical and theological tracts, and other didactic writing, of course, constantly attacked the problem. A number of such works have already been cited; others will be cited in later portions of this study.

But to understand the impact of Calvinist conceptions of the will on the artistically creative mind in America and thus on the profoundest levels of the American psyche, one must turn to the authors of the nineteenth century. The concept of the predestinated will is pervasively present as a formative and thematic literary force. I shall begin by exploring the treatment of the concept in the work of three writers of fiction— Nathaniel Hawthorne, Herman Melville, and Mary Wilkins Freeman—and one poet—Emily Dickinson. The approach of these four was in harmony with the Calvinist approach, though none of the four was orthodox in the old sense and only one, Mrs. Freeman, even belonged to a church. The doctrine of predestination lingered almost as an unconscious memory in these authors' and in their fictional characters' minds. It provided a determinism that was inherent in their

outlook on life and in that of many of their fellow countrymen in all social strata. Down to the present day, indeed,
few American writers of anything approaching tragic stature—
as these four did—have been entirely free of at least a vestige
of the old theology. It might be argued that this residue of
Puritanism is what has made American literature at its best
a great and profound literature. And in few cases have nations
achieved greatness in their literature without some such
communal intuition of a directing force behind their national
destiny.

Nathaniel Hawthorne

Nathaniel Hawthorne—as virtually all critics recognize—
was a Puritan in everything but dogma. His interest in the
psychology of guilt and its origins and nature; his certainty
about the existence of evil in the world, especially in the
heart of man; his acceptance of a rigid moral code, with its
emphasis on retribution for violations of it; and, not the least,
his use of a Puritan-shadowed New England milieu in most
of his best fiction—all combine to make him an unchurched
Calvinist. His ruminations upon fate, predestination, and
the will, which are all that concern me here, are especially
of a Puritan cast.

The Scarlet Letter

True to the Calvinist spirit, Hawthorne's greatest novel, *The
Scarlet Letter*, is characterized by a sense of doom arising out of
the unchangeable bent of certain characters.

Peace, Hester, peace!" replied [Chillingworth] with gloomy
sternness. "It is not granted me to pardon. I have no such
power as thou tellest me of. My old faith [Calvinism, ob-
viously], long forgotten, comes back to me, and explains
all that we do, and all that we suffer. By thy first step awry

thou didst plant the germ of evil; but since that moment, it has been a dark necessity. Ye that have wronged me are not sinful, save in a kind of typical illusion; neither am I fiend-like, who have snatched a fiend's office from his hands. It is our fate. Let the black flower blossom as it may![1]

In only one respect is Chillingworth's statement disingenuous. From long before Hester's transgression, the inclination of his will was toward evil. By his own admission he, an old man, was morally at fault in marrying a passionate young woman, and it is hinted that he had a part in the notorious Overbury murder. But at any rate, as he appears in *The Scarlet Letter*, Chillingworth is in the clutch of a motive that he could not shake off if he would (and he has no desire to)—the motive of revenge. This motive engrosses his will as thoroughly as the same motive engrosses the will of Captain Ahab in Melville's *Moby-Dick*. Each character is following his monomaniacal will to the exclusion of all else. Each realizes at times that he is, in fact, obsessed, but neither chooses to attempt to rid himself of the obsession. For it is over our choices that the Calvinists say we have no control.

A sense of doom oppresses not only Chillingworth in *The Scarlet Letter*. Dimmesdale describes himself as "irrevocably doomed,"[2] and the reader is told that upon Hester "there was a sense of inevitable doom."[3] The psychology of Dimmesdale, indeed, as it is traced through the novel, conforms exactly with the Calvinist concepts of the will. Despite his being a minister, he is clearly not yet among the saved—though he doubtless had some experience that he supposed to signify regeneracy. But he must have been deluded, for his sin of adultery and his inability to confess it and do public penance for it show him to be not yet under the influence of grace. Though he privately suffers remorse and inflicts punishment upon himself, even to the extent of placing himself under the care of the diabolical physician Chillingworth, he has not met the requirements for conversion. Public confession and expression of penitence for one's sins and acceptance of punishment for them are, according to Calvin, among the chief evidences of a genuine conversion.[4] Dimmesdale, to be sure, struggles to bring himself to confession before his congregation. All that is lacking, apparently, is the grace of God, without which the unregenerate soul is powerless to effect its own conversion. Lacking divine aid, the sinner is naturally in terror lest he not be one of the elect; for to the elect, confession and repentance are eventually possible. All Dimmesdale can do is to struggle and hope that, in time, will come the inflow of spirit that will prove him to be among the saved.

But everything points to Dimmesdale's being one of the damned. His interview with Hester in the forest culminates in their decision to flee from Boston—an act betokening a state of mind totally unfavorable to an inflow of grace. Whatever hopes he had for salvation are blotted out by the stronger hope of temporary escape in this world without the difficulty of confession and penance. As Dimmesdale reenters the town from the forest, the familiar scene seems entirely changed to him. But the change is within. His "own will, and Hester's will, and the fate that grew between them, had wrought this transformation."[5] The unregenerate will, writes Calvin, can desire only evil. Now the minister's will, previously undecided, surges headlong in the direction of evil.

> Before Mr. Dimmesdale reached home, his inner man gave him other evidences of a revolution in the sphere of thought and feeling. In truth, nothing short of a total change of dynasty and moral code, in that interior kingdom, was adequate to account for the impulses now communicated to the unfortunate and startled minister. At every step he was incited to do some strange, wild, wicked thing or other, with a sense that it would be at once involuntary and intentional; in spite of himself, yet growing out of a profounder self than that which opposed the impulse.[6]

The good minister thus is barely able to restrain himself from shocking, with the utterance of a blasphemy, one of his deacons whom he meets on the street; from stating arguments against the immortality of the soul to an elderly and pious woman of his congregation; and from encouraging to a life of sin one of the most innocent of the young girls in his church. Modern psychiatry would find Dimmesdale to be suffering from a compulsion neurosis. An orthodox Calvinist would conclude that here was a case of an unregenerate will's inevitable tendency toward evil.

Yet, as all readers of the novel know, Dimmesdale does finally, though belatedly, make his public confession, and thus he shows himself quite possibly to be among the elect. As he himself states, nothing less than an about-face of his volition is responsible for his dramatic act of penitence, and this shift he ascribes solely to God, "who gives me grace, at this last moment, to do what—for my own heavy sin and miserable agony—I withheld myself from doing seven years ago."[7] He enjoins Hester "to be guided by the will which God hath granted"[8] him, and he repeats, "Let me now do the will which [God] hath made plain before my sight."[9] Meanwhile Chillingworth, whom Hawthorne unmistakably presents as a stand-in for the devil, attempts to prevent his victim's confession, which would entail a release from present and future hell. The situation brings to mind the morality plays of the Middle Ages. God and the devil are struggling for the soul of the minister, who passively awaits the outcome.

If God has predestined Dimmesdale's soul for salvation, then of course the devil must inevitably relinquish it. But the Puritan could never be certain just what God's intentions were in such cases. The whole episode may have been staged by the devil alone to mislead and further torture his victim. Thus even now, the minister cannot be sure of his inclusion among the redeemed. Such doubts are normal to a regenerate mind, although they must never be permitted to banish hope. And Dimmesdale, as he approaches death, has hope as well as fear, as is evidenced by his last words:

[God] hath proved his mercy, most of all, in my afflictions. By giving me this burning torture to bear upon my breast! By sending yonder dark and terrible old man, to keep the torture always at red-heat! By bringing me hither, to die this death of triumphant ignominy before the people! Had either of these agonies been wanting, I had been lost forever! Praised be his name! His will be done! Farewell![10]

The major characters in most tragedies—and *The Scarlet Letter* is assuredly a tragedy—are usually ground beneath cosmic forces beyond their control. But in few tragedies is a major character so devoid of a will of his own as is Dimmesdale, whose control over his destiny is so slight as to be negligible. Hawthorne, of course, was not a thoroughgoing necessitarian or predestinarian. Many of his characters exert considerable direction over their own lives. Hester, for example, despite her own sense of inescapable doom and certainly by dint of will, masters the social forces ranged against her in Boston. And out of what promises to be a prolonged wretchedness, she cultivates a life ultimately rich in satisfaction, if not in pleasure.

The Blithedale Romance and The Marble Faun

Yet, will-less as well as obsessed characters can be found in Hawthorne's novels. In *The Blithedale Romance*, the meek and passive Priscilla is described as "only a leaf floating on the dark current of events, without influencing them by her own choice or plan."[11] And she herself says, "I am blown about like a leaf. . . .I never have any free will."[12] When Priscilla first appears, she is literally being carried into the house at Blithedale by the strong-willed Hollingsworth, and later she prostrates herself before the equally strong-willed Zenobia. Hollingsworth, on the other hand, is an obsessed spirit—totally at the mercy of his fanatical, chimerical plans for the reform of criminals. His volition in this direction is so strong that it precludes his willing anything else. Again the Calvinist formula applies: Hollingsworth wills as he chooses, but he has no control over his choice. Oddly, when his plans collapse, he is left in a state of abulia and places himself under the care and control of Priscilla, who gains in willpower as Hollingsworth declines.

In *The Marble Faun* Hilda is relatively passive, and Miriam is burdened with an overdeveloped volition. But in this novel there is the special case of Donatello, whose actions are directed by amoral impulse. His is a will unbridled by the knowledge of right and wrong that supposedly followed the fall of Adam and Eve in the Garden of Eden. In a sense, Donatello's is a perfectly free will, untrammeled by the inhibitions of the moral code. In another sense, it is a highly circumscribed will, inasmuch as the element of choice under which it operates is badly blurred. Instinct and impulse dictate its action; Donatello lacks any real set of ethical rules by which to gauge the consequences of his conduct.

It has often been said that without free will there is no moral responsibility. The converse is almost true: where there is no sense of moral responsibility for one's actions, the will may be anarchic but not free insofar as freedom entails some obligations to oneself, one's God, and one's fellows. To push a man off a cliff at a mere glance from one's sweetheart, as does Donatello, is acting with a completely unrestrained will, but not a free will. Can the person who is unable to control his impulses be said to enjoy freedom of will or to be a victim of whim? Each of us has his own answer. To Hawthorne, it is sufficient to pose the question.

But if Donatello's anarchic will can hardly be said to be free, neither, according to Hawthorne, is Miriam's controlled will. " 'As these busts in the block of marble,' thought Miriam, 'so does our individual fate exist in the limestone of time. We fancy that we carve it out; but its ultimate shape is prior to all our action.' " [13] Always, in assessing Hawthorne's determinism, one must bear in mind the latent Calvinism in his outlook. One must remember that the Calvinists never relieved humanity of responsibility for its actions, however great the sway of predestination and original sin.

It has just been seen how vehement Edwards was against any doctrine that would reduce man to a machine. Hawthorne, despite his recognition of the narrow limitations placed on the will, is no less vehement against any mechanistic tendency in contemporary thought or science. In *The Blithedale Romance* Coverdale launches into a diatribe against mesmerism because of its potential nullification of the individual's accountability for his actions:

> It is unutterable, the horror and disgust with which I listened, and saw that, if these things were to be believed, the individual soul was virtually annihilated, and all that is sweet and pure in our present life debased, and that the idea of man's eternal responsibility was made ridiculous and immortality rendered at once impossible, and not worth acceptance. But I would have perished on the spot sooner than believe it. [14]

Hawthorne thus shares in his thought the central paradox of Calvinism—the paradox of a drastically proscribed liberty of will existing with full responsibility for one's actions.

The House of the Seven Gables

The same paradox is to be found in Hawthorne's *The House of the Seven Gables*, in which free will is more extensively discussed than in his other novels. It, too, contains some weak-willed characters—Hepzibah, Phoebe, and above all the pitiable Clifford—and at least one—judge Pyncheon—who is endowed with an overpowering ruthlessness of will. But a further aspect of the problem of the will is treated here—that of transmitted guilt. In a way, *The House of the Seven Gables* is reminiscent of Oliver Wendell Holmes's *Elsie Venner*, which I shall discuss later. Both novels are romances and allegories. Indeed, the fact that the allegorical novel as written by Hawthorne, Holmes, Melville, and others found such a popular acceptance in America is symptomatic of our culture during the nineteenth century. It is one of the many indications of how close we were to the strictly religious—especially Calvinistic—interpretations of life. Allegory thrives in a religiously oriented society, and the most popular work, until recently, among English-speaking Protestants—the allegorical *Pilgrim's Progress*—was a favorite of Hawthorne's and admittedly an inspiration to him in his own writing.

The House of the Seven Gables, then, conveys through its romantic fantasy certain spiritual verities as Hawthorne sees them. The basic truth—the theme—of the novel is "that the wrong-doing of one generation lives into the successive ones, and, divesting itself of every temporary advantage, becomes a pure and uncontrollable mischief. . . ."[15] The word uncontrollable certainly implies determinism, as does the idea of the continuing influence of a misdeed through a number of generations. This is essentially the same situation with which Holmes deal in "Mechanism in Thought and Morals," as well as in *Elsie Venner*. But Holmes is mainly concerned with the transmissibility of responsibility for a hereditary taint traceable to a remote ancestor. And here Hawthorne and Holmes differ. Hawthorne says that there *is* responsibility *so long as the sin is repeated*; Holmes says that inherited tendency absolves us of responsibility for resulting sins.

Judge Pyncheon inherits all the characteristics of the original evil Pyncheons; he suffers from the same greed, the same animality of the passions, and the same tendency to apoplexy. Genetic heredity could in no way be better illustrated. And he inherits the same temptations—opportunities for riches and power—that caused the downfall of his progenitors. The man is morally tainted in a world where to do evil is all too easy, and he succumbs to evil. Holmes would treat such a man with leniency: circumstances and family blood are against him. But Hawthorne is moved by no clemency for Judge Pyncheon. A more detestable character would be hard to find in the world's fiction. He is exactly like the original Pyncheon, and he is exactly as guilty—not for what the original one did but for doing the same things himself.

Holmes was repeatedly testing the doctrine of original sin and finding it wanting. Hawthorne would agree with Holmes that we are not guilty of the sins of Adam, just as Judge Pyncheon is not guilty of the sins of his forebears. But so long as we repeat the sin of Adam—disobeying God's commandments—Hawthorne says that we are guilty, and the fact that we inherit Adam's weakness does not excuse us. Hawthorne is careful to draw the parallel between the history of the Pyncheon family and that of humanity since the fall. The Pyncheon garden—with its polluted well, its "rank weeds (symbolic of the transmitted vices of society),"[16] and the degenerate breed of chickens that inhabit it—is "the Eden of a thunder-smitten Adam, who had fled for refuge thither out of the same dreary and perilous wilderness into which the original Adam was expelled."[17] The Pyncheons are either an attenuated breed, like Hepzibah and Clifford, or strong-minded villains, like the judges both of the present and of witchcraft days. But this in no way relieves them from responsibility for their action or lack of action. The criminal mentality of the judge is the heritage of many generations, but each generation is responsible for its own misdeeds— even if they represent an "uncontrollable mischief," as Hawthorne calls it in his preface. Uncontrollability and responsibility do indeed constitute a paradox—the Calvinist one.

Herman Melville

Though no more a church member than Hawthorne, Melville was to an even greater extent conditioned by his Calvinist (in his case Dutch Reformed) background. In novel after novel, and in character after character, he grappled with the problem of the will, and his answers, or dilemmas, were the perennial ones of Augustinian and Calvinistic Christianity.

To begin with, Melville states categorically, in his famous essay "Hawthorne and His Mosses," that no thinking man can eliminate from his concept of the constitution of things something resembling original sin. The "power of black-ness,"[18] as he calls it, is inescapably present; it is perhaps the great adversary; and it certainly must be reckoned with. Not only this, but "all mature men, who are Magians, sooner or later know, and more or less assuredly—that not always in our actions, are we our own factors."[19] Deep among the foundation stones on which God's order rests is a principle of evil; and man, as he picks his way among the evils and goodnesses of this world, is not in control of his own destiny.

Billy Budd and *Moby-Dick*

We are not "our own factors"; this is the idea that haunts Melville's greatest works and is the essence of his psychology. The unregenerate are capable of willing only evil, said Calvin. The regenerate can will only good. The individual wills as he chooses, but the choice is determined by the God-decreed bent of the will. Thus Claggart in *Billy Budd* can, and does, will only evil. His is "a depravity according to nature,"[20] Melville says, but it corresponds to the evil of the unredeemed. On the other hand, Billy can will only good; and he is de-stroyed by his own goodness and innocence as much as by Claggert's malignancy. After he suffers a Christlike death, Billy's goodness lives in the hearts of his fellows. Total good-ness seems to be predestined to martyrdom in this world. Of course, Melville's conviction that the innocents (those who can will and think only good things) are at a disadvantage deviates from strict Calvinism—as do many other facets of his thought. But the spectacle he presents of rigidly channeled wills—either toward evil or toward goodness—is Calvinistic. The same spectacle is seen again in *Benito Cereno*, in which Babo is the Claggart, and Captain Delano, whose good nature blinds him to the perception of evil under his very nose, is only slightly less an innocent than Billy Budd.

The contrast is more notable in *Moby-Dick*, where the sensitive, kindly Starbuck, a Quaker, is paired off with Ahab, whose will has become slanted unalterably toward death and destruction. Ahab, in fact, has sold himself to "the power of blackness," impersonated by Fedallah and his crew of Parsees, and he revises the formula of baptism to contain the devil's name. Needless to say, Starbuck is no match for him, and the unequal contest requires no attention here beyond the remark that had Starbuck been less good-hearted he might have dealt with Ahab more effectively.

To repeat, Ahab is the mortal receptacle of a will devoted to its own destruction and to the destruction of his associates. He has not always been the monomaniac he is during the action of the novel, but there is no indication that he ever made a free and deliberate choice between Starbuck's way (that of reason and humaneness) and the devil's. He has become totally possessed by one motive—revenge upon an unreasoning brute that assaulted him in self-protection. He himself avows that he is in the clutches of a driving, destructive fate, and like that other fatalist, Macbeth, he consults oracles and soothsayers. In his inability and lack of desire to direct his will toward goodness, Ahab may be compared to Claggart and Babo—but there the comparison stops. Even in unredeemed man, Calvin wrote, there are glimmerings of prelapsarian Adamic grandeur. The outlines of the noble structure of God's own image are discernible amid the ruins. So it is with Ahab. At times he struggles against the overwhelming will to destruction, as Claggart and Babo never struggle. There is a king-like quality in Ahab, a greatness that Starbuck readily recognizes. But this quality is powerless against his destiny.

Everywhere the reader is met with ambiguities. So it is when the plight of Captain Vere in *Billy Budd* is examined. The captain, whose name signifies truth, has to sentence Billy to death in order to maintain discipline—itself a good—

on his ship. Groping his way between total evil and perfect goodness, he seems to have found something more than a blind alley. The goodness of Billy is not and cannot be completely annihilated, and there seems a fair chance of keeping the evil of Claggart somewhat in check. But Captain Vere has not made a free decision. It has been forced upon him by circumstances, against his better feelings, which are all with Billy. In no sense is the captain a free agent, though the determinism that dictates his actions may be a social rather than a divine or psychological one.

Pierre, or, The Ambiguities

Captain Vere is a man who can never be sure whether he is right or wrong—a predicament, says Calvin, which involves all humanity, the regenerate as well as the unregenerate, neither of whom can ever be sure of their status in God's election. The will that seems to its possessor to be motivated by justice and benevolence may actually be headed for perdition. This is the case with Pierre Glendinning in the novel *Pierre, or, The Ambiguities*. Pierre is a young man endowed with every advantage—good family, wealth, health, and the prospects of marriage with a beautiful and propertied young girl. But after learning that he has a half sister—born to his father's mistress—and meeting the girl, who is fascinatingly beautiful, he gives way to his "better feelings." He will forgo his marriage with the fair Lucy and instead undertake the support of his half sister, Isabel of the dark tresses. The impulse is good on the surface, and he conceives it as such. Certainly it would seem to be the generous thing to do—the Christian thing— though the family clergyman does not think so. Furthermore, it would involve great effort and sacrifice, for Pierre's strong-minded mother would have no truck with a project that could, and eventually does, disrupt her relations with her son. In other words, great willpower and steadfastness of purpose are required of Pierre in carrying out his brotherly plan. Would not one say that a man so selflessly motivated was acting under a benign volition—a volition that could be taken as an earnest of divine grace, or regeneracy? But the Calvinists warn us that we may be deceived by our own actions and motives. Absolute certainty of the presence of grace is never attainable. The most favorable indications may turn out to be the machinations of Satan insinuating himself into the unregenerate will.

Such may be the case with Pierre. One thing is certain: his project does not prosper. But this alone is not proof of evil motivation; the saints have often suffered for their good deeds. Yet Melville insists that what at first glance seems to be a beneficent will—for example, the will to protect one's sister—may on further examination reveal itself to be evil in the extreme. "Deep, deep, and still deep and deeper must we go, if we would find out the heart of a man; descending into which is as descending a spiral stair in a shaft, without any end, and where that endlessness is only concealed by the spiralness of the stair, and the blackness of the shaft."[21]

Pierre's conscious motives may be impeccable. But his unconscious motives are something else again. There is much that anticipates Freud in this novel. To begin with, Pierre and his mother playfully pretend to be brother and sister—playmates. When he decides to go away with his real half sister, he does so in the guise of a husband. As Melville points out, there is a predisposition in Pierre's unconscious mind to convert the real relationships of life—mother and son, sister and brother—to other more intimate and perhaps more satisfying relationships: "Pierre felt that never, never would he be able to embrace Isabel with the mere brotherly embrace; while the thought of any other caress. . .was entirely vacant from his uncontaminated soul, for it had never *consciously* intruded there."[22] (Italics added.)

Consciously, no; but unconsciously, yes—to the extent that it was his major motive. Only a little over halfway through the novel the reader is told: "Over the face of Pierre there shot a terrible self-revelation; he imprinted repeated burning kisses upon [Isabel;] pressed hard her hand; would not let go her sweet and awful passiveness."[23] Pierre's will, without his knowing it, has been directed toward incest. To plead unconsciousness is irrelevant. Incest is what he has willed and what he has achieved at least symbolically. By any standards the motive has been an evil and a selfish one. Incest in our society can bring nothing but destruction, as it does in this case: the death of Pierre's mother; the loss of his fiancée Lucy and of his property; and, finally, his own death and the deaths of Isabel, Lucy, and his cousin. Perhaps only Pierre and Isabel were aware of the incestuous element in their relationship, but that does not alter the situation. Underlying the violence of Pierre's actions was the lust for Isabel; this lust generated the forces that destroyed the others. One cannot say that Pierre freely chose to bring about these calamities or the relationship with his sister; yet he willed a series of actions that led to them, albeit unconsciously. We will as we choose, but we do not choose as we choose. The depths of Pierre's nature determined his choice of action. The bent of our will is beyond our control. The case of Pierre is a perfect example of the Calvinistic concept of the will's inability to determine its own direction.

To be sure, Melville does not use Calvinistic terminology. *Fate*, rather than *predestination* or *foreordination* or *necessity*, is the word he most frequently employs in describing his protagonist's plight. "If this night, which now wraps my soul," cries Pierre, "be genuine as that which now wraps this half of the world; then Fate, I have a choice quarrel with thee. Thou are a palterer and a cheat; thou hast lured me through gay gardens to a gulf."[24] And Isabel exclaims elsewhere: "But Fate will be Fate, and it was fated"[25] that she meet her brother. And constantly in his commentary, Melville makes reference to the "Three Weird Ones."[26] "Pierre was not arguing Fixed Fate and Free Will, now; Fixed Fate and Free Will were arguing with him, and Fixed Fate got the better in the debate."[27] And in another place in the book Melville writes, "how then shall you escape the fateful conclusion, that you are helplessly held in the six hands of the Sisters?"[28] In still another place he writes, "then, first in all his life, Pierre felt the irresistible admonitions and intuitions of Fate."[29] Enmeshed in this web, man seeks in vain to extricate himself by his own efforts. Melville gives his unequivocal stamp of approval to "that most true Christian doctrine of the utter nothingness of good works."[30]

But it is not a mere arbitrary, mechanical fatalism—like that suggested by Mark Twain in *What is Man?*—that oppresses humanity. Melville is aware of the tragic profundities of man's nature and he elucidates them by citing copiously from Shakespeare and Dante. "Appalling is the soul of a man! Better might one be pushed off into the material spaces beyond the uttermost orbit of our sun, than once feel himself fairly afloat in himself!"[31] Such words could not have been written by the naturalists, or Holmes, or Twain—all of whom, in mechanizing man's will, simplified man and hence diminished his stature. More in accord with Melville's writing is Dostoevski's famous passage:

> Yes, man is broad, too broad, indeed. I'd have him narrower. The devil only knows what to make of it! What to the mind is shameful is beauty and nothing else to the heart. Is there beauty in Sodom? Believe me, that for the immense mass of mankind beauty is found in Sodom. Did you know that secret? The awful thing is that beauty is mysterious as well as terrible. God and the devil are fighting there and the battlefield is the heart of man.[32]

To the Calvinists, to the great tragic world-writers, and perhaps to certain of the depth psychologists, a fate is undoubtedly at work in a man's destiny, but this fate operates at so deep a level and in such harmony with the basic, hidden desires of the human heart that at times it seems scarcely distinguishable from the will itself. Melville employs several striking symbols in *Pierre* to represent man's destiny—the vast boulder precariously teetering on a ledge deep in the forest and threatening to crush whoever comes beneath its shadow; and the almost-buried rocks beneath the mountain cliffs that remind one of the fate of the buried Enceladus who dared revolt against the gods. These symbols, of course, do not imply forces extraneous to man but rather some self-annihilating, crushing power deep within his nature. This is a vision of humanity far closer to the Calvinist's concept of a God-like nature in ruins than to the mechanist's notion of a human being as a peripatetic biochemical laboratory ticking off inevitable reactions with clocklike precision. Above all else, Melville was impressed by man's potential for evil—a potential that man by his very nature cannot avoid fulfilling. As Melville states in *Clarel* this potential for evil gives "in the conscious soul's recess / Credence to Calvin,"[33] a corroboration of "Calvin's creed."[34]

Mary Wilkins Freeman

Writers whose concept of the will has been conditioned by Calvinism are likely to contrast dehumanization caused by an overdeveloped and uncontrollably misdirected will with what Hawthorne called the "great and warm heart"[35] of normal humanity. Some examples of this are: Judge Pyncheon as contrasted with Phoebe and Holgrave; Ahab as contrasted with Starbuck; Hollingsworth's reforming fanaticism and Zenobia's self-devouring intensity as contrasted with Priscilla's gentle compassion. The same pattern may be found in the works of other writers of the latter part of the nineteenth century. Some of these works were of a popular though not subliterary sort, and thus they are significant because they reflected widespread views. Harriet Beecher Stowe's *Poganuc People*, for instance, contains in the character of Zeph Higgins an amazing example of stubborn willfulness, one-tracked and unyielding. Though perhaps not unrealistically drawn, Zeph's character is so lopsided that he gives the impression of a caricature and, as the author intended, he elicits laughter. He is not analytically presented, as are Hawthorne's and Melville's characters. Yet he provides a significant specimen of a warped will. He is a bumpkin Ahab and a country cousin of Judge Pyncheon, formidable enough in his home territory, though not awe-inspiring.

Another Connecticut writer, Rose Terry Cooke, is scarcely more analytical of the "wrong-headed" farmers who people her short stories. Yet in a few pieces—"Grit," "Squire Paine's Conversion," "Mrs. Flint's Married Experience," and especially "Freedom Wheeler's Controversy with Providence"—her effects transcend the humorous and strike some faint chords of tragedy. Like Zeph Higgins, her characters are intended to be products of Calvinism gone to seed; the strength and wholesomeness have long since been bred out of them; they are mere grotesques with little or no theological significance.

By all odds the most skillful anatomist of what Fred Pattee called "the terminal moraine of New England Puritanism"[36] is Mary Wilkins Freeman, who in several prefaces to her books announced herself as a specialist in the New England will, especially in its diseased and warped aspects. A close follower of Hawthorne, she is fascinated by the dehumanizing effects of a fanatically directed volition and, still like Hawthorne, she sees love as the only cure for the resulting ravages. Mrs. Freeman was brought up and lived most of her life in New England villages, and she claimed that her characters and their ills were drawn from real life. She has recorded her observations in two or three volumes of expertly written short stories and several novels of medium merit—not to mention a shelfful of distinctly second-rate output.

She also had a firsthand knowledge of the religious stresses of a lingering Puritanism. She was a converted member of a somewhat liberal church in Randolph, Massachusetts, the town of her birth. But she tasted a stronger Calvinism during a year as a student at Mt. Holyoke Female Seminary, where discipline was rigid and theology orthodox to a degree that would win the approval of the sternest Puritan of Colonial days. Soul-searching, public confession of one's sins followed by abject penitence, nerve-shattering seasons of religious revivalism, and Sabbaths devoted in their entirety to church-going and edifying lectures were the standard regimen originally imposed by the first headmistress, Mary Lyon, who won fame as a pioneer in education for women.

Pembroke

A glance at the major characters in Mary Wilkins Freeman's best novel, *Pembroke* (an unjustifiably neglected book), should be sufficient to establish her view point. Barnabas Thayer, the chief male character, is affianced to a neighboring farmer's daughter, Charlotte Barnard. One night the young man has a political quarrel with Charlotte's father, who orders him from the house never to return. Barney stalks out, ignoring his fiancée, who anxiously follows him. He vows to himself not to go back to that house again, even if the old man relents. "It never occurred to him that he could enter Cephas Barnard's house again, ask his pardon, and marry Charlotte. It seemed to him settled and inevitable; he could not grasp any choice in the matter."[37] His will has been jolted from one rut into another, and no thought of ever deviating enters his mind. Deprived of even the recognition of an alternative course, he can thus hardly be said to enjoy any choice in the matter. Yet he does do what he wills. In Barney's makeup, a volition once made is inviolable, inevitable, predestinated; it must be followed to its ultimate and most bitter conclusion.

Accordingly, for years Barney lives in the half-finished house he had been building for his bride. He knows no pleasure, no companionship; his days and years are consumed with incessant labor. An acquaintance notices that his back is becoming bent.

> 'Have you hurt your back?' Thomas asked in a subdued
> tone.
> 'I've hurt my soul,' said Barney. 'It happened that Sunday
> night years ago. I—can't get over it. I'm bent like this back.'[38]

But he does get over it. Charlotte, who with an inflexible
stubbornness of her own has stayed away from him, finally,
with equal stubbornness, goes to his house to nurse him after
he collapses with rheumatic fever. This is Puritan country,
and even in the mid-nineteenth century the times are still
Puritan in the villages. The minister and a deacon call upon
Charlotte at Barney's house. Their expostulations ricochet
off the surface of Charlotte's will. But after they leave, Barney
orders her to go home, and to *his* will she finally submits.

Barney's volition has now veered from the path on which
it had been traveling so long and starts wheeling off in another direction. He readies himself to go to Charlotte's house
and ask for her hand properly. This more reasonable course
is not of his choosing; he is directed into it willy-nilly; yet
this new purpose is as irresistible as his earlier one. After
Charlotte left him,

> he waited fifteen minutes, with his eyes upon the clock.
> Then he got up out of his chair. He moved his body as if
> it were some piece of machinery outside himself, as if his
> will were full of dominant muscles. He got his hat off the
> peg, where it had hung for weeks; he went out of the house
> and out of the yard.[39]

Barney is like an automaton under the direction of volitions
over which he has no control—his is the Calvinist will path-
ologically developed.

But both Barney and Charlotte appear as weaklings compared to Barney's mother, Deborah Thayer. She disapproves
of Barney's breaking with Charlotte, orders him forever

from her house, and devotes herself to trampling upon her doormat of a husband and whipping the Westminster catechism into her son Ephraim's dense skull. To Deborah, the Assembly's catechism is the word of God, and the only word of God outside Scripture. Further, she considers that God has appointed her to beat the catechism's truths into her son. Unfortunately, the son is not only a poor scholar but also suffers from a weak heart, and the doctor has cautioned against severely punishing him. But God's will must be done, and Deborah knows that she has been put on earth to do it.

One day when Ephraim is both stupider and sicker than usual, she whips him severely. It is God's intention that she do so, she thinks; nor does she "realize the part her own human will had in it."[40] She informs Ephraim that it is God's will and hers—the two were synonymous—that he learn the catechism, and she brings down the stick. She raises the stick again, and Ephraim falls dead to the floor.

> Then Deborah stood over him, and began to pray aloud. It was a strange prayer, full of remorse, of awful agony, of self-defense of her own act, and her own position as the vicar of God upon earth for her child. 'I couldn't let him go astray too!' she shrieked out. 'I couldn't, I couldn't! O Lord, thou knowest that I couldn't! I would—have lain him upon—the altar as Abraham laid Isaac! Oh, Ephraim, my son, my son, my son![41]

Emily Dickinson and the Hope of Conversion

Like Mary Wilkins Freeman, Emily Dickinson was a product of a New England village and attended Mt. Holyoke Female Seminary, which, if it accomplished nothing else, succeeded in impressing on its pupils an indelible Calvinist cast of mind and mood. But unlike Mrs. Freeman, Emily Dickinson came from a highly educated home in a college town and was never a communicant even in a liberal church.

In addition, of course, she was a much greater writer.

Many recent critics of Dickinson, such as Charles Anderson, William R. Sherwood, and Theodora Ward, have focused attention on the influence on her work of the spiritual climate in which she lived. Unquestionably she was profoundly affected in her intellectual, emotional, and artistic life by the religious beliefs and practices of her time and place. The greatest difficulty—and one that seems almost insurmountable—is to determine whether in her poetry and even in her letters she employs religious terminology metaphorically or literally. A valid assumption is that she does not do one or the other exclusively—that her intention varies with her mood and situation. Thus her ideas on conversion, election, and the will, whether she states them as convictions or as indications of a state of mind, are analogous to those accepted as dogma by the orthodox churchgoers of her community, and are expressed in the conventional language, or jargon, used by them. With her, as in the teachings of the denomination under whose influence she lived, the question of the will was but one facet of the larger question of election and conversion and, more specifically, the hope of conversion, which must precede the spiritual "turning" itself.

Hope, in a religious sense, had a single important meaning—hope that one was among the chosen for salvation and that one was about to experience the act of repentance and the influx of faith that would assure one of salvation. In many of her poems Dickinson uses the word "hope" in its theological sense, and in many other, and usually better, poems, she assesses the state of her own hope (or her persona's) without actually using the word. Since hope is that aspect of the conversion process most outside the control of the conscious will, it is pivotal in an examination of Dickinson's attitudes concerning the will and its part in directing her life. But before any conclusions can be reached regarding her thoughts on the will, it will be necessary to examine the somewhat modified form of Calvinism to which she was exposed. Such an examination will also reveal much about nineteenth-century Calvinism, not only in New England but in the country as a whole.

Western Massachusetts (where Dickinson was born and lived her life) and most of Connecticut were bastions of a conservative theology that also held sway in large parts of the Eastern hinterland and much of the Midwest, as opposed to the liberalism and Unitarianism of Boston and other eastern metropolitan areas. Indeed, Amherst College was "founded to revive and preserve the faith of the Puritans."[42] In the early years Edwards's *Freedom of the Will* was required reading for all students there, and the presidents of the college were regularly orthodox ministers. The spirit of Edwards still haunted the whole of western New England, either directly or through the teachings of his most influential disciples, the Reverend Samuel Hopkins of Connecticut and the Reverend Nathanael Emmons. These ardent Edwardsians emphasized revivalism as the pathway to conversion and played down other "means"—without discarding them—such as adherence to the forms of religion, study of religious books other than the Bible, and good works or exemplary living. The overwhelming personal experience of conversion was the only reliable sign of, and entrance into, saving grace, and all of an individual's and his pastor's efforts were to be directed toward producing that one all-important experience. But grace was solely the gift of God; He alone could grant it. As a president of Amherst College said: "It is the most solemn truth to which you can listen. . .that unless God saves you, you are lost."[43] This did not mean that one could sit idly waiting for the overwhelming moment. Grace came slowly, after great struggle on the part of the pastor and his charge. Its onset was heralded by "hope," which was a manifestation of God's intentions and hence was beyond the individual's power to generate for himself.

As for the stand of the Hopkinsians on the doctrine of the irresistibility of grace, church historians differ. One reports that these "New Divinity" parsons, as they were called, supported irresistibility: If man so *wills*, he can submit to divine will. But he *cannot make himself so will*. Man's only hope is in "an interposition not only of divine, but of irresistible grace."[44] Another holds that in the Hopkinsian scheme man is seemingly endowed with "complete moral autonomy,"[45] including the privilege of refusing or choosing grace when offered. This rather startling degree of libertarianism would mark a concession to the archenemy of Calvinism—Arminianism, which was opposed to the doctrine of irresistible grace. In general, one may assume, the idea of free choice in the acceptance or resistance of grace once it was offered was gaining ground in American Calvinistic religion, though the offer was still considered to remain under the decree of God alone. The question seems relatively unimportant since any believer finding himself suddenly flooded with grace would doubtless welcome his new condition and not exercise his option of refusal.

One thing is certain. From childhood Dickinson was continuously aware of the critical importance of conversion. Revivals were almost annual occurrences at Amherst College and among the townspeople. In some years the revivals were more intense than in others and the "harvest of souls" would be greater, but always they were occasions of excitement and generators of gossip as to who had or had not appeared among the saved. A book titled *Revival Sketches and Manual* (1859) written by the Reverend Heman Humphrey, who was president of Amherst College from 1823 to 1845, is doubtless typical of the teachings on religion to which Dickinson was accustomed. Humphrey refers to conversion as a "pearl of great price"[46] and threatens with hellfire any who do not find it. He insists that those whom God chooses have not earned their good fortune by any merit in themselves. But he equally insists that the convert accepts the freely offered "bread of life"[47] by his own choice, emphasizing in almost the same words that Jonathan Edwards used that man is not a machine. Moreover, the would-be Christian must strive for his own conversion; everything cannot be left to God. Though Humphrey shies away from a discussion of the doctrine of the irresistibility of grace, he never specifically rejects it, and he affirms the "sovereignty and efficiency of God"[48] in all matters.

When she went away to school at Mt. Holyoke Female Seminary, Dickinson experienced no relief from the urgency for salvation that characterized religious life at Amherst. Mary Lyon, the founder of the seminary, was an admirer of the theology of Jonathan Edwards. The major purpose of her school was to advance the spiritual lives of its students. At the beginning of every year each girl classified herself as to her spiritual condition: a professing Christian (converted), "hopefully pious," or "without hope."[49] Most of the girls belonged in the first two categories, but Dickinson was one of those "indulging no hope," and as such she was assigned to a small group that received special and intensive exhortation and instruction from Miss Lyon herself. The time of her admission was one of spiritual exaltation at Mt. Holyoke, since in the previous year fifty students had been converted and Miss Lyon was able to say that "the Holy Spirit had never before exercised his converting influence in the family for so long a time."[50] Entering such an environment, a girl "with no hope" would feel self-conscious and perhaps unworthy. That Dickinson was ill at ease is amply testified by her letters of the period, especially those to her friend Abiah Root.

Dickinson remained in this tense atmosphere for only one year, after which, as with Mary Wilkins Freeman, her weakened health caused her to withdraw. One needed strong nerves and a strong body to flourish at Mt. Holyoke. But back in Amherst the religious pressures persisted, though perhaps less oppressively. For a time Dickinson may have felt some optimism concerning herself, since neither her brother, her sister, nor her father had yet been converted.

But in a great "harvest" in 1850, all three experienced saving grace, and she was the only one in her family who was unconverted. Much has been made of her supposed revolt from orthodoxy; and doubtless some such revolt took place; but it did not occur suddenly, and it is not easy to gauge how throughgoing it was. Her attendance at church, which finally ceased altogether, did not begin to fall off till after 1855, when she was twenty-five years old. About 1854, in a letter to Susan Gilbert Dickinson, she still seemed not to have totally despaired of conversion though she feared that "Jesus Christ. . . [may] remark he does not know" her, in which case "there is a darker spirit will not disown it's [*sic*] child."[51]

Throughout her life she consulted ministers, both orthodox and Unitarian, at times of personal crisis or puzzlement. George Whicher has pointed out that "Mr. and Mrs. Clergyman, whoever they happened to be," at the family church, "were always numbered among her friends."[52] One of them, the Reverend Jonathan L. Jenkins, interviewed Dickinson in 1873 on the subject of her soul and reported to her father that she was "sound."[53] This discovery by an orthodox minister clashes with the usually held theory that she broke entirely with the Amherst brand of theology. Whether Mr. Jenkins discovered that she had undergone conversion or was merely "hopeful" is not certain. The Hopkinsian deemphasizing of "means" would perhaps cause him to regard with leniency her failure to attend his, or any other, church.

Another indication—usually overlooked by biographers—that Dickinson was not a complete skeptic in regard to Calvinism is the influence in her life of the Reverend Charles Wadsworth of Philadelphia, one of the most popular Presbyterian preachers of his day. Whether or not she was in love with Wadsworth, she did confer with him several times. The first time was in 1855, which appears to have been a time of soul-searching for her, and she exchanged many letters with him. No one knows on what matter she first sought his advice; but either then or later he must have known that she was unconverted, and it is inconceivable that he did not advise her, at least indirectly, on her plight. All are agreed that Wadsworth was theologically conservative. A sample of his doctrine on the will and conversion may be found in his sermon "Grace and Works," published in 1869. Wadsworth saw "*a union of Divine and human agencies in the work of salvation* [italics his]. . . .God is sovereign. God does foreordain whatsoever comes to pass. There is a decree of election. The names of the elect are from eternity in the Lamb's book of life. But, meanwhile, man is a free agent—as verily free to choose salvation—as honestly invited to find justification in Christ, and final glory in heaven—as if there were no decree of election and God were not sovereign on salvation."[54] Man must accept these two conflicting truths; he must not try to understand or reconcile them. Obviously, for Wadsworth, the doctrine of conditional necessity was a living truth.

But immediately Wadsworth backs away from what appears to be almost a libertarian stand. Man, he hastens to assure us, does not enjoy "a self-determining power in the will." The will or willingness to be saved must be wrought in the soul by God. "God makes us willing and that very willingness is man's free choice. . . .*A man's ability to comply with the condition of election is absolutely and entirely a divine gift* [italics are Wadsworth's]."[55] Finally, Wadsworth warns, one must always strive for one's conversion; like Humphrey, he cautions against leaving everything to God. Above all, the unconverted must not succumb to despair, no matter how discouraging the struggle. Any message Dickinson got from Wadsworth on the subject of conversion must have struck her as a repetition of what she had always heard. Could she admire a man as sincerely as she did and still reject the very foundations of the faith by which he lived?

Many of Dickinson's poems on conversion deal either literally or figuratively with her (or her persona's) chances for salvation through redeeming grace. The language and the figures she uses reflect Calvinism as it existed in the nineteenth century, and thus she deserves consideration among those writers who, without being strongly dogmatic, yet retained as truth much that underlay the orthodox doctrine. She employs most of the Calvinist vocabulary of redemption: hope, justification, salvation, grace, sanctification, and election. Frequently, of course, the use of such terms is obviously metaphorical, as in this stanza on how she was affected by reading Elizabeth Barrett Browning:

> I could not have defined the change—
> Conversion of the Mind
> Like Sanctifying in the Soul—
> Is witnessed—not explained—[56]

Even to the suggestion that uncontrollable forces are at work in determining her literary appreciation, this poem sustains the Calvinist parallel. Indeed, Dickinson defines greatness in poetry as that quality which overwhelms us willy-nilly.

Many poems containing theological terms and concepts may be taken either figuratively or literally, as is the case with the following famous one, which could spring from an assurance of salvation or from the experience of falling in love.

> Mine—by the Right of the White Election!
> Mine—by the Royal Seal!
> Mine—by the Sign in the Scarlet prison—
> Bars—cannot conceal!
>
> Mine—here—in Vision—and in Veto!
> Mine—by the Grave's Repeal—
> Titled—Confirmed—
> Delirious Charter!
> Mine—long as Ages steal![57]

It is unthinkable that in writing the word "election" the poet did not have in mind its religious meaning. And the rest of the poem fits: "the Royal Seal" is God's decree of her election; "the Sign in the Scarlet prison" is the "evidences" and feeling of conversion in the heart imprisoned in the body, yet visible to her and others; "here—in Vision—and in Veto" explains that whether visible or denied to vision, the conversion is sure and cannot be taken from her; "the Grave's Repeal" is the promise of immortality "confirmed" by conversion. Along with the theological terms and concepts are a series of legal ones—"Right," "Seal," "Veto," "Repeal," "Titled," "Confirmed," and "Charter,"—which themselves build up a metaphor of the finality and permanence of whatever the poem celebrates. This choice of words echoes not only the speech of Emily's lawyer father but also the old Puritan legalistic view of the Covenant of Grace whereby God enters into a contract with His elect. There is, of course, in the poem an implication that a power—a king, God— stronger than the human will is involved. Yet the question still remains whether the poem is about literal religious conversion or an undying love for a mortal—though the former seems more probable.

Hope, or hopelessness, is a frequent subject of Dickinson's poetry. The following lines may refer to hope of conversion or hope of something else that is highly desired. In any event, the presence or absence of hope is independent of her will or choice to control or assist (it never "asked a crumb—of me").

> "Hope" is the thing with feathers—
> That perches in the soul—
> And sings the tune without the words—
> And never stops—at all—
>
> And sweetest—in the Gale—is heard—
> And sore must be the storm—
> That could abash the little Bird
> That kept so many warm—

> I've heard it in the chillest land—
> And on the strangest Sea—
> Yet, never, in Extremity,
> It asked a crumb—of Me.[58]

A human being's helplessness to bring about his or her conversion, or some other desired end, by his or her own efforts, if not backed by God's wishes, is the subject of two stunning poems on prayer:

> Of course—I prayed—
> And did God Care?
> He cared as much as on the Air
> A Bird—had stamped her foot—
> And cried "Give Me"—
> My Reason—Life—
> I had not had—but for Yourself—
> 'Twere better Charity
> To leave me in the Atom's Tomb—
> Merry, and Naught, and Gay, and numb—
> Than this smart Misery.[59]

The futility of prayer—unless it fits in with God's plans—in the above poem and the one that follows stems from the helplessness of the human will in achieving its goals.

> At least—to pray—is left—is left—
> Oh Jesus—in the Air—
> I know not which thy chamber is—
> I'm knocking—everywhere—
>
> Thou settest Earthquake in the South—
> And Maelstrom, in the Sea—
> Say, Jesus Christ of Nazareth—
> Hast thou no Arm for Me?[60]

One gets the feeling in such poems—and there are many others equally despairing—that Emily Dickinson is attempting what her mentors from Mary Lyon to the Reverend Charles Wadsworth had exhorted her to do: to pray to a tyrannical God for something—whether conversion or not—that He could give us but only if we exert ourselves sufficiently. Eventually Dickinson seems to have tired of this sort of activity, and her poems of skepticism are the result.

Some of her poems deal unmistakably with conversion or the sequels of it, leaving no other interpretation reasonably possible. The following poem describes moments of ecstasy ("Superior instants") known only to the elect ("favorites") and scarcely controllable by the will (like "Apparition — subject to Autocratic Air"):

> The Soul's superior instants
> Occur to Her—alone—
> When friend—and Earth's occasion
> Have infinite withdrawn—
>
> Or She—Herself—ascended
> To too remote a Hight [*sic*]
> For lower Recognition
> Than Her Omnipotent—
>
> This Mortal Abolition
> Is seldom—but as fair
> As Apparition—subject
> To Autocratic Air—
>
> Eternity's disclosure
> To favorites—a few—
> Of the Collossal substance
> Of Immortality[61]

If the previous poem describes moments that may follow conversion, the next describes the preliminaries of conversion as well as the full experience itself:

He fumbles at your Soul
As Players at the Keys
Before they drop full music on—
He stuns you by degrees—
Prepares your brittle Nature
For the Etherial Blow
By fainter Hammers—further heard—
Then nearer—Then so slow
Your breath has time to straighten—
Your Brain—to bubble Cool—
Deals—One—imperial—Thunderbolt—
That scalps your naked Soul—

When Winds take Forests in their Paws—
The Universe—is still—[62]

And finally, with a lighter touch, the poet speculates as to whether she is a late bloomer so far as conversion goes. Purple, the color of repentance and of royalty, has a twofold appropriateness to the theme:

God made a little Gentian—
It tried—to be a Rose—
And failed—and all the Summer laughed—
But just before the Snows

There rose a Purple Creature—
That ravished all the Hill—
And Summer hid her Forehead—
And Mockery—was still—

The Frosts were her condition—
The Tyrian would not come
Until the North—invoke it—
Creator—Shall I—bloom?[63]

Any careful reader will find many more of Dickinson's poems to fit each of these three categories. Indeed, fully half of the total number employ religious language or ideas. Not surprisingly, those which are ambiguous are usually her most impressive. For example, the poem that follows would be weaker if the reader knew whether the "one" chosen was Christ or some lover or friend, or whether "Majority" refers to a spiritual coming of age through conversion or through an earthly love.

> The Soul selects her own Society—
> Then—shuts the Door—
> To her divine Majority—
> Present no more—
>
> Unmoved—she notes the Chariots—pausing—
> At her low Gate—
> Unmoved—an Emperor be kneeling
> Upon her Mat—
>
> I've known her—from an ample nation—
> Choose One—
> Then—close the Valves of her attention—
> Like Stone—

It is an interesting poem in that it states both the soul's freedom to select its destiny (as Calvinists insisted it must do) and the finality of its act ("Like Stone—"), which carries a connotation of momentousness and irrevocability suggestive of the doctrine of the perseverance of saints. Whatever the intention of the poem, it has muted overtones of predestination. Like the other three authors considered in this chapter, Dickinson thought and expressed herself in Calvinist terms, no matter how completely she may have rejected the forms and dogma of her ancestral church.

3

Nineteenth-Century Authors
Actively Hostile to
Calvinistic Predestination

The four authors considered in the previous chapter are outstanding among a group who analyzed the will from a point of view deeply tinged with Calvinism, though not theologically orthodox. They were at times appalled by what a Calvinist sense of predestination could do in warping or hardening a person's will. Yet they did not reject outright the idea of predestinated action of the will as an expression either of philosophical truth or of innate bent of character. They might not accept literally the doctrine of "eternal decrees," but they were not prepared to grant a high degree of freedom of choice or action to humanity. They might admit that the wills of Ahab, Chillingworth, and Deborah Thayer were diseased, certainly lopsided; but they invested these people with a dignity befitting those in the clutch of a destiny beyond human control. They created tragic characters within the philosophical and psychological but not the theological framework of Calvinism. Like Milton, they recognized that the Protestant system imparted a certain grandeur to mankind that a merely mechanistic system would not. The death of a theology, like that of Calvinism, does not always immediately entail the death of the modes of thought it has engendered.

A group of authors of approximately the same period as

those discussed in the previous chapter adopted a much more hostile view toward Calvinist dogma, especially as it dealt with human will. Prominent among these were Charles Brockden Brown, Harriet Beecher Stowe, Oliver Wendell Holmes, and Mark Twain. Their antagonism seems largely to have stemmed from feelings of personal revulsion against orthodoxy, although they were doubtless influenced by contemporary intellectual currents, which will be examined later. Yet these authors had by no means rid themselves of all vestiges of the rejected or despised theology. Three of them, at least, subscribed to a determinism more rigid than anything preached by the churches.

Charles Brockden Brown

Charles Brockden Brown's *Wieland* presents a will enslaved not by religion but by disease in the form of religious mania. Brown was himself no Calvinist; he was a Quaker by upbringing and an eighteenth-century rationalist by conviction. Religious fanaticism such as that of Wieland, and Wieland's father before him, could be nothing but abhorrent to Brown. The younger Wieland has totally surrendered his will to what he believes is the will of God. But paradoxically, this surrender of the will fortifies the will. Once Wieland believes that he is being directed by God, whose voice he hears clearly instructing him to kill his wife and children, his will to perform the deed becomes irresistible. The madman's logic, in this case, parallels the Calvinist logic. God achieves His ends through our will. Not only do we dare not, but we cannot, disobey. By the grace of God we become superhuman; we become instruments of Deity. Clara Wieland, the madman's sister, speculates:

> His wife and children were destroyed; they had expired in agony and fear; yet was it indisputably certain that

their murderer was a criminal? . . .None but a command from heaven could have swayed his will; and nothing but unerring proof of divine approbation could sustain his mind in its present elevation.[1]

To his sister, whom he had also attempted to murder, the imprisoned brother says: "Thinkest thou that thy death was sought to gratify malevolence? No. I am pure from all stain. I believed that my God was my mover!"[2] Wieland consistently protests his innocence and reiterates that he has simply done God's will. His religion was that of the Camisards, a sect of rigidly strict French Calvinists.

It is significant that Wieland's murders closely resemble those perpetrated by a religiously insane New York State farmer in the 1790s. Among the many things that the novel tries to do—most of them not worth doing—one is to reveal the ravages that fanaticism can have on a mind prone to excess. Brown carefully shows that there has been madness in two preceding generations in Wieland's family. But be that as it may, Wieland is a victim of more than bad heredity. He is primarily a victim of what Brown considers an irrational theology. Brown, not being of Calvinist background, does not share the undercurrent of sympathy that writers like Hawthorne and Melville had for certain Calvinistic doctrines—predestination among them. Yet, in his very anti-Calvinism, he belongs to a group whose novels drew upon this theology for their themes. Wieland may be the first, but he is not the only, character in American fiction who equates his own will with God's. We have just seen another example in Mary Wilkins Freeman's Deborah Thayer (in *Pembroke*). However, Deborah falls short of outright madness. Her apparent killing of her son, as she performs God's will and hers, is not intentional. Her conscience, not a voice directly from heaven, compels her to beat the catechism into the invalid boy. She is following the dictates of *her* will even though she identifies it with God's.

If one substitutes the devil for God, one finds that Ahab and Chillingworth are seeking revenge, and Mrs. Thayer is trying to save her son's immortal soul. Their monomanias may approach madness—they may even go over the edge at times—but their crimes are not so wanton or monstrous as those of Wieland, who is, of course, totally insane.

But while demonstrating that Wieland was simply insane and that God or any supernatural power had nothing to do with his actions, Brown places him under an equally cogent determinism. A person with a completely deranged will is not accountable for his actions. Brown has substituted pathology for predestination and eternal decrees. Not being responsible for his crime—as Ahab and Chillingworth seem to be for their behavior despite predestination—Wieland is diminished to a mere pawn of circumstances. In him Brown provides the first instance in American literature of what was to be a widespread replacement of predestination by a more rigid determinism. This process is well exemplified in the thought of Oliver Wendell Holmes.

Oliver Wendell Holmes

Elsie Venner

A descendant of a long line of Congregational clergymen, Holmes was deeply interested in his ancestors' beliefs, which he found fascinatingly repellent to his own scientific and Unitarian mind. In an essay on Jonathan Edwards he vigorously attacked Calvinism in general, but especially the doctrine of original sin, which of course underlies the doctrine of election. Without original sin, man would not need to be redeemed. He would not need to be elected to salvation, nor would he need to exercise whatever freedom of will he possesses. For a man who rejected theology, Holmes's interest in theological problems was remarkable. This interest expressed itself in his essays, his novels, and his poetry.

In January 1860 the first installment of *The Professor's Story* appeared in the *Atlantic Monthly*. The professor was Oliver Wendell Holmes, author of the "Breakfast Table" series in the same magazine, and the story is now better known as *Elsie Venner: A Romance of Destiny*, under which title it was published as a book in 1861. As one reads this novel, which is Holmes's best, one is struck by the irony of the author's attempt to establish on a mechanistic basis a determinism even more rigid than the one he was decrying in Calvinism. A "medicated novel," as Holmes calls it, *Elsie Venner* is a forerunner of the highly deterministic biochemical novels of Dreiser. Like Dreiser's work, too, its science is humanized by a sincere and poignant pity for humankind. But unlike Dreiser, Holmes writes whimsically and gracefully, and he commands more than a scientist's wisdom; he possesses a wide-ranging common sense and an understanding that derive from his experience as a physician and his interests as a writer of belles lettres. Holmes was both a better scientist and a better writer than was Dreiser. The almost complete neglect of his wrtings outside the classroom is one of the puzzles in American literature.

The thematic key of *Elsie Venner,* and of much of Holmes's other writing, is the principle of heredity, as it was later in Zola's work. The novel begins with one of the frequent didactic essays that, again like Dreiser except for their superior wit, are liberally interspersed throughout his narrative. This one is on the subject of the intellectual classes of New England. The Brahmin, who is scholarly, sensitive, somewhat delicately built though not necessarily physically weak, is a product of generations of inbreeding and conditioning within the priestly caste of the larger New England towns. The Brahmin is simply different from the rest of the population; heredity and environment have made him so. Through no merit of his own, he stands above his fellows of less specialized heredity. So important did Holmes consider family heritage in forming character that he thought one could judge a man by his heir-looms. A library of volumes going back to the seventeenth century, several portraits by Copley and Stuart on the wall—these were the outward evidences of Brahmin superiority. Holmes has been accused of being a snob, and he was a snob—on scientific grounds. Conscious of his own ancestry, he cor-rectly—according to his own definition—considered himself a Brahmin and, consequently, a better person than most.

The hero of *Elsie Venner,* Bernard Langdon, is a Brahmin who, in financial straits, is forced to teach for a time in a girl's seminary in an up-country town notable mainly for the rattle-snakes on a mountain that overhangs it. Among his pupils is Elsie Venner, a strange but beautiful girl, a misfit who falls in love with him but whose love he is unable to return, even though she saves his life from a huge snake. Elsie's fate is that she herself shares something of the nature of a snake. Her mother had been bitten by one of the reptiles while she was pregnant with Elsie. The poison affected the child's na-ture permanently and incurably. Fantasy, romance—yes. That is precisely what Holmes intends to produce in spinning his yarn from the fibers of such an old wives' tale. He does not expect, of course, that the plot will be taken seriously, but like that other "romancer," Hawthorne, who may well have provided the model for Holmes's approach, Holmes expects that the implied psychology and the ethics will be taken seriously. In his preface he carefully spells out his purpose:

> The real aim of the story was to test the doctrine of "original sin" and human responsibility for the disordered volition coming under that technical denomination. Was Elsie Venner, poisoned by the venom of a crotalus before she was born, morally responsible for the "volitional" aberra-tions, which translated into acts become what is known as sin, and, it may be, what is punished as crime? If, on presen-tation of the evidence, she becomes by the verdict of the human conscience a proper object of divine pity and not of divine wrath, as a subject of moral poisoning, wherein lies the difference between her position at the bar of judg-

ment, human or divine, and that of the unfortunate victim who received a moral poison from a remote ancestor before he drew his first breath?[3]

The symbolism is clear: Elsie is the daughter of Eve, the mother of the human race; the crotalus is Satan, with whom Eve had traffic in Eden; and the taint left on Eve's progeny is "original sin." The problem is: would a just and benevolent God hold human beings responsible for acts arising from a taint of will in their remotest forebears? Within the novel at least one clergyman, the Reverend Doctor Honeywood, radically modifies his theology on the strength of this consideration. He surprises his congregation by preaching a sermon on "that remarkable argument of Abraham's with his Maker in which he boldly appeals to first principles. He took as his text 'Shall not the Judge of all the earth do right?' "[4] The sermon was significantly entitled "On the Obligations of an Infinite Creator to a Finite Creature." The "Oriental hyberboles of self-abasement"[5] of the Calvinists were no longer acceptable in the reverend doctor's church. Instead he rhetorically queries:

> Is not a Creator bound to guard his children against the ruin which inherited ignorance might entail on them? Would it be fair for a parent to put into a child's hands the title-deeds to all its future possessions, and a bunch of matches? Are not men children, nay, babes, in the eye of Omniscience?[6]

So much, then, for a major Christian doctrine—posterity's responsibility for the sins of Adam and Eve. Holmes does not deny the imperfection, the innate weaknesses of man; he does deny the possibility of any God, other than a monster, who would punish man for hereditary weakness.

Holmes, of course, prefers to speak of determinism in scientific rather than in theological terms. Thus, in reference to hereditary influences, he writes, "we are mainly nothing

but the answer to a long sum in addition and subtraction."[7]
Like most scientific determinists, he sees all forms of life,
animal and human, subject to the same laws: "the 'struggle
for life' [that] Mr. Darwin talks about reaches to vertebrates
clad in crinoline, as well as to mollusks in shells. . . ."[8] But
Holmes is not primarily a Darwinist. His determinism is
more far-reaching, even biochemical. Thus, humorously, of
a rigidly doctrinal deacon who had drunk a glass of wine, he
remarks:

> —It is very odd how all a man's philosophy and theology
> are at the mercy of a few drops of a fluid which the chem-
> ists say consists of nothing but C_4, O_2, H_6. The Deacon's
> theology fell off several points towards latitudinarianism
> in the course of the next ten minutes.[9]

So sweepingly deterministic does Holmes become that he
verges on ruling out all responsibility for crimes: "I will tell
you my rule in life, and I think you will find it a good one.
Treat bad men exactly as if they were insane. They are *in-sane*, out
of health, morally [italics Holmes's]."[10]

Holmes was not consistent throughout his life in his views
on freedom of the will. Elsewhere he postulates a significant
amount of such freedom, but in the statement just quoted
from *Elsie Venner* he comes very close to total determinism.
Holmes, however, is not unaware of this inconsistency. When
a minister in the novel objects that the rigid scientific determinism that a doctor has been expounding to him would be
"degrading and dangerous" to humanity since it would cause
individuals to cease to strive—"There is nothing bad men
want to believe so much as that they are govened by necessity"—, the doctor replies:

> . . . all large views of mankind limit our estimate of the
> absolute freedom of the will. But I don't think it degrades
> or endangers us, for this reason, that, while it makes us
> charitable to the rest of mankind, our own sense of freedom,
> whatever it is, is never affected by argument. *Conscience*

won't be reasoned with. We feel that *we* can practically do this or that, and if we choose the wrong, we know we are responsible; but observation teaches us, that this or that other race or individual has not the same practical freedom of choice. [Italics Holmes's][11]

Despite the "proofs" of science, the consciousness of freedom must be reckoned with as a profound reality of our natures and an influence on our lives. An inevitable question results: "If, while the will lies sealed in its fountain, it may be poisoned at its very source, so that it shall flow dark and deadly. . . , who are we that we should judge our fellow creatures. . . ?[12] Like Tolstoy in *Anna Karenina,* Holmes will leave judgment to God: "Vengeance is mine, saith the Lord." The impression conveyed by *Elsie Venner* is indeed suggestive of *Anna Karenina,* though doubtless with less stunning impact. An inevitability hangs over the action of each novel. Dostoevski describes *Anna Karenina* as a dark, inexplicable, yet thoroughly truthful record of the irreversible deterioration of a soul—a record that in men of good will could inspire only forgiveness and pity. In Holmes's novel, the Reverend Doctor Honeywood says much the same thing about Elsie's decline as he preaches at her funeral. In spite of his rejection of orthodoxy, Holmes does not categorically despise organized religion and its ministers, so long as they are not bigots. The physician and the clergyman in this novel perform closely analogous tasks that frequently overlap—the tasks of ministering to sick souls and sick bodies.

The spectacle of Elsie in the clutch of forces that are destroying her and over which she has no control, whatever she may choose to be, fills Holmes with a compassion that enlarges itself to include all humanity. One is reminded of reports of Jonathan Edwards pacing his study and wringing his hands and moaning with pity as he thinks of the innumerable souls damned to perdition by God's decree of reprobation. Indeed, under both the Calvinistic and the naturalistic determinism, man is reduced to a pitiable object. Yet, under

Calvinism, the diminishment is not so complete; struggle still plays a significant part in the process of salvation, and salvation, if achieved, confers on the recipient a glory absent from any naturalistic scheme. In short, to the Calvinist, man is still a major concern of God, and thus whether damned or saved, he enjoys a status unlike that of the rest of nature.

Holmes's comment on a snatch of verse by a certain "E. M."—

> When I am dead and lay'd in dust
> And all my bones are—

is typical of naturalistic pity: "Poor E. M.! Poor everybody that sighs for earthly remembrance in a planet with a core of fire and a crust of fossils!"[13] Holmes, at times, seems almost to fit into the "dark tradition," of which scholars in recent years have made so much as an element in American literature. Some of his passages on the rattlesnakes and their mountain habitat do, in fact, betray an awareness of "the power of blackness" postulated by Melville (the orginator of the term) or by Hawthorne (whose works inspired Melville's use of the term). In speaking of some of the serpents caught by his hero in *Elsie Venner,* the author speculates:

> What did the Creator mean to signify, when he made such shapes of horror, and, as if he had doubly cursed this envenomed wretch, had set a mark upon him and sent him forth, the Cain of the brotherhood of serpents? It was a very curious fact that the first train of thoughts Mr. Bernard's small menagerie suggested to him was the grave, though somewhat worn, subject of the origin of evil. There is now to be seen in a tall glass jar, in the Museum of Comparative Anatomy at Cantabridge, in the territory of the Massachusetts, a huge *crotalus,* of a species which grows to more frightful dimensions than our own, under the hotter skies of South America. Look at it, ye who would know what is the tolerance, the freedom from prejudice, which can suffer such an incarnation of all that is devilish to lie unharmed

in the cradle of Nature! Learn, too, that there are many things in this world which we are warned to shun, and are even suffered to slay, if need be, but which we must not hate, unless we would hate what God loves and cares for.[14]

Yet there is a crucial difference between the feeling generated in *Moby-Dick,* for example, by the terrors of nature, and the feeling conveyed by Holmes and by later naturalistic novelists like Crane and Dreiser. In Melville and Hawthorne, man is more on equal terms with the universe, hostile and dark though it may be. Like Ahab and Chillingworth, he may even contain within himself some of the fearsomeness that lies at the heart of nature; or he may even make war against evil and terror as did the crew of the *Pequod.* But Elsie Venner and many characters in the naturalistic novels are helpless victims (there are exceptions to be noted later), possessing perhaps some of the more unpleasant characteristics of other animals—such as greed or selfishness—but unable either to suppress these traits or to use them for some end that would inspire a beholder with the potential grandeur of man. One can shed tears for Elsie and even for Wieland, but one cannot admire them: for they neither put up a hard fight against the forces that destroy them nor abandon themselves bravely to the doomed course of their lives, nor in their downfall do they inspire wonder and awe. In short, *Elsie Venner* is a sentimental novel; it induces tears or mere shudders, whereas the great novels of Melville and Hawthorne inspire not only pity but also terror and awe in place of tears and shudders. Holmes's plea that we not hate the hideous serpent he has described is similarly sentimental.

"Mechanism in Thought and Morals"

In *Elsie Venner* the human will is reduced to such impotence as to strip man of any meaningful responsibility for his deeds. One is what one's heredity and biochemistry and environment make one, and one's choices and actions are determined by these. This is an extreme position that Holmes does not consistently adhere to. The year before (1859) the appearance of *Elsie Venner,* stung by the accusation that he had "attacked the reality of the self-determining principle,"[15] Holmes explained that he considered the will to be restricted, limited, yet *fluid*—that is, characterized by mobility. Man he describes as a "subcreative centre," a sort of agent of God but yet possessed of an independent will. He quotes one of his own poems to illustrate the lengths he is prepared to go toward a libertarian standpoint. The transcendental influence, by no means negligible in Holmes, is obvious.

> —Thought, conscience, will, to make them all thy own
> He rent a pillar from the eternal throne!
> —Made in His image, thou must nobly dare
> The thorny crown of sovereignty to share.
> —Think not too meanly of thy low estate;
> Thou hast a choice; to choose is to create![16]

That the ideas in this poem do not square with passages either in *Elsie Venner* or in "Mechanism in Thought and Morals," which will be considered next, points up a paradox. Science sees our will and actions as determined by influences largely outside our control; as a scientist Holmes substitutes a mechanism for the old-time Calvinist predestination—in short, he does little to extend the scope of the will's freedom. But as a humanist, Holmes refuses to reject the evidence of his own consciousness, which made him aware of significant personal freedom. Holmes was sufficiently impressed with the complexity of life and man to accept the paradox—to attempt to live with the conflicting testimonies of reason and consciousness. In this acceptance he was unknowingly in agreement with Leo Tolstoy, who a few years earlier had written in *War and Peace:* "To conceive a man having no freedom is impossible except as a man deprived of life." According to Tolstoy, "a mob of ignoramuses" had accepted the findings of physiologists and evolutionists as conclusive evidence that there is no freedom of the human will,

> not at all suspecting that thousands of years ago all religions and all thinkers have admitted—have never, in fact, denied—that same law of necessity, which they are now so strenuously trying to prove by physiology and comparative zoology. They do not see that natural science can do no more in this question than serve to illumine one side of it. . . . It does not advance one hair's-breadth the solution of the question, which has another opposite side, founded on *the consciousness of freedom* [italics added].[17]

In a speech titled "Mechanism in Thought and Morals," delivered before the Harvard Phi Beta Kappa Society in 1870, Holmes provides us with a statement of his thought on the will and on moral responsibility that marks a retreat toward libertarianism from the views expressed in *Elsie Venner*. He begins with a definition: "I call that part of mental and bodily life mechanical which is independent of our volition."[18] The heart-beat, breathing, digestion, and the secretions of the body obviously come under this heading. So do most of our instincts and the changes induced by age and the "unconscious mental action"[19] in the free association of ideas. Creative inspiration is also essentially passive, Holmes thinks; ideas and images well up in us quite independently of the will, though Holmes suggests that we might regulate our creativity by the food we consume: "So much logic, so much beef; so much poetry, so much pudding."[20]

Proceeding to ethics, Holmes states: "The moral universe includes nothing but the exercise of choice: all else is machinery."[21] And the area of choice, he insists, is rather extensive. He admits that necessity (that is, determinism) may be proved logically or scientifically. But strong with him is the consciousness of freedom—"the sense that we are, to a limited extent, self-determining; the sense of effort in willing; the sense of responsibility in view of the future, and the verdict of conscience in review of the past. . ."[22] Holmes's reasons for rejecting the "proofs" of determinism are so close to those of William James that he may well be credited with anticipating James's pragmatic stand on the will.

> For Holmes writes:
>   . . . *nego quia probatum est* . . . I reject, therefore, the mechanical doctrine which makes me the slave of outside influences, whether it work with the logic of Edwards, or the averages of Buckle; whether it come in the shape of the Greek's destiny, or the Mahometan's fatalism; or in that other aspect dear to . . . "The crocodile crew that believe in election."[23]

Holmes, then, is a limited determinist. He recognizes a certain amount of mechanism, or determinism, in human choice and action, but he also recognizes a large area where determinism does not operate. These two areas he demands be kept distinct, and he strongly feels that religion, especially Calvinism, has failed to do this. "Moral chaos begins with the idea of transmissible responsibility."[24] Guilt, or responsibility, Holmes argues, cannot be inherited; we cannot be held morally accountable for the malvolitions of our forefathers. The implication is clear; mankind since the Fall cannot be held responsible for Adam's mistake. Holmes is willing to admit that tendencies to evil may be inherited, but an individual, or a race, should not be held answerable for a bad inheritance that was inflicted on the species long before the birth of any living member of it. Such inheritance "should go to our side of the account, if the books of heaven are kept, as the great Church of Christendom maintains they are, by double entry."[25]

"The pound of flesh," writes Holmes, "I will grant to Nemesis; but, in the name of human nature, not one drop of blood,—not one drop."[26] Holmes readily grants the Calvinists and the scientists a certain degree of determinism, but he will not grant them the right to judge actions resulting from determinism by the same standards suitable for judging actions resulting from free choice. "If we suffer for anything except our own wrong-doing, to call it punishment is like speaking of a yard of veracity or a square inch of magnanimity;"[27] that is, it totally materializes morality, because it removes morality from the sphere of spiritual values, which is the sphere in which free will must operate in its constant choosing between good and evil. And once we have "materialized the whole province of self-determination and its consequences, the next thing is, of course, to materialize the methods of avoiding these consequences."[28] Panaceas, or gimmicks, tend to supplant self-control. "The moment our belief divorces itself from character, the mechanical element begins to gain upon it. . . ."[29]

Could Holmes have foreseen our own age when criminality is attributed to glandular malfunction, and a well-regulated intake of vitamins is warranted to cure everything from bad temper to homicidal mania? The question is more than merely rhetorical, for Holmes, so far as the will is concerned, was walking on a razor's edge. He may have contributed much more than he would have liked to think to the rise of a philosophy of determinism—to the materializing of the erstwhile spiritual values of life—during the latter part of the nineteenth century. That he did not intend to go to this limit is indicated in his essay "Crime and Automatism," in which he states:

> . . . the belief in a power of self-determination, and the idea of possible future remorse connected with it, will still remain with all but the moral incapables,—and the metaphysicians,—and this belief can be effectively appealed to and will furnish a 'strongest motive' readily enough in a great proportion of cases. . . . Society must present such motives of fear to the criminally disposed as are most effective in the long run for its protection.[30]

Harriet Beecher Stowe

Whether Holmes's determinism was of the rather extreme variety developed in *Elsie Venner* or of the limited scope found in "Mechanism in Thought and Morals," he was consistently harsh on Calvinism, because it justified punishment for predestinated offenses or for hereditary guilt, neither of which would be subject to the free action of the offender's will. Holmes's position stimulated the intense interest of another New England writer, Harriet Beecher Stowe, who in 1859, the year preceding the serialization of *Elsie Venner,* had published (also in the *Atlantic Monthly*) *The Minister's Wooing,* a novel critical of her ancestral Calvinism. She had read Holmes's novel as it appeared, and many years later she wrote to Holmes: "All your theology in that book I subscribe to with both hands."[31] What she chiefly approved of was Holmes's contention that one who is "morally *in-sane*"[32] cannot be held accountable for one's actions, whether the ill health be inherited or derived from environment. The reading of *Elsie Venner* marked a turning point in Harriet's spiritual life. So strongly impressed was she that within a decade she left the Congregational Church of her forefathers and joined the Episcopal Church, of which the doctrines on the will and on moral responsibility had become Arminian and libertarian.

The Minister's Wooing

The fact that *Atlantic Monthly* published two theological novels in successive years indicates the interest in religion still present in the nation at the mid-century. The fact that both novels attacked certain Calvinist beliefs indicates that such doctrines were still alive. *The Minister's Wooing* owes its theme to a series of spiritual trials suffered by Harriet and members of her family. It must be realized that the Beechers were the very incarnation of New England orthodox, Edwardsian, and Hopkinsian theology. Lyman Beecher, the father, was one of the great Calvinist preachers of his day. His wife and children shared his total commitment to his church and its teachings, and all were completely and intensely sincere in their commitment.

Too sincere, perhaps. One of Harriet's brothers, after reading Edwards's *Freedom of the Will,* found that if he were honest with himself—and the Beechers were always in the clutch of a deadly honesty in spiritual matters—he could be nothing but a despairing fatalist—certainly not a result that Edwards would have approved of. More critical was the case of Harriet's sister Catharine, whose fiancé, a brilliant divinity student, died of drowning before, it was feared, he had experienced conversion. Catharine investigated the young man's recent life, hoping to find "evidences" of regeneracy. She found nothing to allay her worst fears. Though the youth had struggled, *had chosen,* to undergo conversion, he had apparently not received the essential grace. The only orthodox conclusion was that he was burning in hellfire. Unable to accept this, Catharine took to writing on theology, sometimes not entirely anti-Calvinistically, but eventually arguing herself into Unitarianism.

Harriet's own life had its share of religious crises. Her first conversion, occurring when she was fourteen, proved after several years to have been false, a discovery that caused her intense emotional shock and continuing pain. Her true conversion did not take place until almost twenty years later, after her brother George's death in a shooting accident had thrown her into severe depression. Finally fortified with grace, she was able to take in stride the death by cholera of her year-old son (even Edwards had not believed in infant damnation). But in 1857 came a blow that shook her faith at its foundation. Her son Henry, a student at Dartmouth, drowned in the Connecticut River, apparently unconverted. According to her religion, this son was now condemned to everlasting torture. Subjected to the same test that her sister had endured, she too began to write on theology—not tracts, but in the disguise of fiction—, and within ten years she had become an Episcopalian.

In *The Minister's Wooing,* the first of Harriet's theological novels, a young and devout girl, who is obviously one of the elect, turns down a lover because he cares little for religion, though she loves him. The disappointed lover goes to sea and supposedly dies in a shipwreck, not converted. His former sweetheart and his mother suffer, as Catharine and Harriet had suffered in analogous situations. The girl, in spite of her Calvinism, brings herself to trust in Christ's goodness, but the mother, an intellectual as well as a believer, rebels. Her rantings against the doctrines of predestination and election doubtless reflect Harriet's bitterness in her agonies over her drowned and unconverted son:

> ". . . I cannot, will not, be resigned: . . . to all eternity I will say so! To me there is no goodness, no justice, no mercy in anything! Life seems to me the most tremendous doom that can be inflicted on a helpless being! . . . The number of the elect is so small that we can scarce count them for anything! Think what noble minds, what warm, generous hearts, what splendid natures are wrecked and thown away by thousands and tens of thousands! . . . Dr. Hopkins says that this is all best—better than it would have been in any other possible way,—that God *chose* it because it was for a greater final good,—that He not only chose it, but took means to make it certain,—that He ordains every sin, and does all that is necessary to make it certain,—that He creates the vessels of wrath and fits them for destruction, and that He has an infinite knowledge by which He can do without violating their free agency."[33]

The Dr. Hopkins referred to is none other than the great preacher who carried on the Edwardsian brand of New England theology. A character in this semihistorical novel, he is actually a warm, generous person—which serves only to make some of his beliefs all the more appalling. It is clear that Harriet rebelled mainly against those doctrines of Calvinism that, despite assurances to the contrary, stripped mankind of freedom of will and hence, as Dr. Holmes so insistently argued, of moral responsibility. In *The Minister's Wooing* the supposedly drowned man (he later turns up alive and regenerate, to satisfy the reading tastes of the day) had made no real effort before his shipwreck to become converted. But Catharine Beecher's fiancé and Harriet's son Henry had striven as "free agents" to achieve grace and had failed even in achieving a real "hope." There was no reliable evidence that they ever would be converted. By the definition of free will applying in this study, and surely by Harriet's definition, these unfortunates could hardly be said to enjoy "freedom" of any sort in determining the eternal destiny of their immortal souls. They were helpless, in other words, in what according to their religion was the most important matter in their lives, what was, indeed, the sole reason for their existence.

Oldtown Folks

In another novel, *Oldtown Folks,* written in 1869 shortly after the author abandoned the Congregational Church, the dilemma of the would-be convert is made even more explicit. A "perfectly faultless"[34] and "reverent" girl, conscientious in all personal and religious respects, "had in vain striven to bring herself to the required state of emotion"[35] prerequisite to conversion. Thus

> she judged herself to be, and was judged to be by the theology which her father taught, utterly devoid of virtue or moral excellence of any kind in the sight of God. The theology of the times also taught her that the act of grace which should put an end to this state, and place her in the relation of a forgiven child with her Heavenly Father, was a voluntary one, momently in her power, and that nothing but her own persistent refusal prevented her per-

forming it; yet taught at the same time that, so desperate was the obstinacy of the human heart, no child of Adam ever would, or ever could, perform it without special inter-position of God,—an interposition which might or might not come. Thus the responsibility and the guilt rested upon her. [36]

In the case of this girl, conversion eventually occurs, but it could have failed to come, the writer implies, just as her own dead son's had. Harriet's answer to this Calvinist pre-dicament is to reject the doctrine responsible for it and trust in a loving God. She by no means condemns all Calvinist doctrine, and she feels kindly towards the Calvinist clergy. But for some persons of sensitivity, intelligence, and goodness, much in this religion is too harsh. Thus it cannot represent God's sole or ultimate relationship with His creatures. For those of the laity who can accept and thrive under the harder aspects of Calvinism she has admiration. Such is the grand-mother in *Oldtown Folks,* whose solace is her "Blue Book," a compendium of orthodox theology written in 1750 by the relentless Joseph Bellamy, a colleague of Edwards. In a still later novel, *Poganuc People* (1878), which was mentioned in a previous chapter, she treats humorously but respectfully a type of New England countryman whose will has become as hard as flint under the rigors of the soil, climate, and theol-ogy of the region. The doctrine of predestination can stiffen some wills while it breaks others. For Harriet the strain was too great, and she sought relief in a milder spiritual climate.

Mark Twain

Much less of a libertarian than Oliver Wendell Holmes or Harriet Beecher Stowe is Mark Twain, who also had a Calvinist (Presbyterian) upbringing. Although he rejected the orthodox doctrines of election, original sin, and pre-destination, he replaced them with a much more rigid determinism, in the form of either a stark fatalism, a scientific materialism, or a cynical pessimism. In "The Man That Corrupted Hadleyburg," for the doctrine of original sin he substituted the gloomy conviction that all human beings, even those with the most enviable reputation and record of honesty, are corruptible if subjected to sufficient temptation. The only way in which one may remain blameless is to remain isolated from all opportunity to err—a manifest impossibility in this world. Thus man is of a nature even more sinful than that postulated by the most rigorous of Christian theologies. The idea of redemption, even for a limited number of persons (the elect), is rejected in favor of a dogma of universal and unavoidable depravity. The comforting doctrine of the perseverance of saints fares no better in this tale, for it denies that there are any saints to persevere.

Pudd'nhead Wilson

In *Pudd'nhead Wilson,* Twain specifically satirizes the doctrine of election. When Roxy decides to switch the two infants in their cradles, so that her own "Negro" (one thirty-second black) baby will be brought up as a member of the white family and the white child will be brought up as a slave, she cites, in extenuation of her act, a sermon she had once heard:

> Now I's got it; now I 'member. It was dat ole nigger preacher dat tole it, de time he come over here fum Illinois en preached in de nigger church. He said dey ain't nobody kin save his own self—can't do it by faith, can't do it by works, can't do it no way at all. Free grace is de *on'y* way, en dat don't come fum nobody but jis' de Lord; en . . . *he* don't kyer. He do jis' as he's a mineter. He s'lect out anybody dat suit him, en put another one in his place, en make de fust one happy forever en leave t'other one to burn wid Satan.[37]

Thus Roxy plays the Calvinist God, but without success. Her own boy, brought up as a white child, turns out to be a thief and a murderer, whereas the other baby, in his unconscious role as a slave, is of excellent character, though uncouth. For Roxy's child is fated to an evil and miserable life, and nothing his doting mother can do can save him. Twain seems almost to be supporting the Calvinist doctrine he is satirizing: no human efforts can redeem the unregenerate. The reader is told that Roxy with her secret knowledge of her son's birth glooms "over him like a Fate."[38] She is herself a symbol of his wretched destiny. Appropriately, the final chapter of the book is entitled "Doom," for in it fingerprints—the unalterable stamps of one's individuality—reveal the usurper for what he is and condemn him. Exposed as a murderer, he is not hanged, for he is also revealed to be a slave; and as such he escapes the gallows and is sold down the river. Mere human beings cannot interfere in what the Fates have destined—such seems to be one of Twain's points in the novel. The most orthodox Calvinism could be no more deterministic.

"The Mysterious Stranger"

Twain's fatalism sinks to its gloomiest depths in "The Mysterious Stranger." Man's life, Satan explains in that book, is like the boys' game in which a row of bricks is set on end: when the first brick is knocked over, the rest inevitably follow. "A child's first act knocks over the initial brick."[39] From then on his life follows an undeviating course—not one foreordained by God but set in motion by the unknowing child himself. Elsewhere Twain records his conviction that a similar fatalism was at work in his own life. For example, his becoming a writer followed inexorably from an attack of measles he had as a boy. Twain does not present his arguments for this view very cogently. As a logician and a philosopher he is negligible, although he spent much time and energy in philosophizing. His most ambitious and least successful venture into the realm of abstract thought is undoubtedly his *What Is Man?*—which reduces human beings to soulless and will-less machines.[40] It is true that Twain's most deterministic and most pessimistic works are the products of his later years after he suffered a series of devastating personal misfortunes. In his earlier and best-known works, the fatalism is present mainly as an undercurrent—for instance, Huckleberry Finn's superstition about rattlesnake skins and hair balls, and the murderous snags beneath the placid, sunset-tinted surface of the river as described in *Life on the Mississippi.*

Like Holmes, Twain was interested in the problem of moral responsibility in an agent whose actions are predetermined by forces beyond his control. By asserting that no moral responsibility exists in regard to actions over which the agent does not have a clearly evident power of choice and volition, Holmes violently contradicted the Calvinists, who maintained that despite predestination and original sin man was still accountable for his depravity. As already seen, even in his most libertarian moods, Holmes recognized large areas of human activity that are purely mechanical and hence outside the rather limited confines of moral responsibility. On the other hand, Twain, who substituted for predestination an even harsher mechanical determinism, insisted that man possesses a "Moral Sense,"[41] which endows an agent with a knowledge of right and wrong but which is powerless to direct him with any significant consistency along the paths of righteousness and humaneness. Thus to Twain, mankind in general is in the same plight that the Calvinists presupposed the unregenerate to be in: though knowing the difference between good and evil, human beings unassisted by grace are incapable of willing good. Both the Calvinists and Twain hold man accountable for that over which he has no control.

The difference between the anatomy of the will as presented in the works of the Calvinist-influenced writers discussed in the previous chapter and that presented by the mechanistically inclined Holmes and Twain, as well as by the so-called naturalists of a generation later, is that in the first group's thinking the will is conceived of as playing an ex-

tremely important role in the motivation of characters, while
to the second group the will is simply a cog in the machine
or a chemical in the retort. In the area of human action that
Holmes regards as mechanical, will is really lacking altogether, as it is in such extremely deterministic works of Twain
as "The Mysterious Stranger" and "The Man That Corrupted Hadleyburg." Among the naturalists, who will be discussed in detail later (in chapters 4, 5, and 6), such mediocrely
endowed characters as the "heroines" (really anti-heroines) of
Crane's *Maggie: A Girl of the Streets* and Dreiser's *Sister Carrie*
suffer from abulia. And the gifted ones, like the ruthless
financiers in Dreiser's and Norris's novels, possess wills that
are better described as instincts, since their pressure is more
or less unconscious and certainly infrequently opposed by
anything like conscience. Both the weak and the strong operate as if there were no alternative actions to those they follow.
Choice is lacking, as it is not—even if it is predestinated—in
such authors as Melville and Hawthorne.

The Calvinism-tinged authors—Melville, Hawthorne,
Emily Dickinson, and Mary Wilkins Freeman—regard the
will as a mystery, something that adds to the stature and
dignity of man's life, not something to be explained chem-
ically, physically, or biologically, or brushed aside as simple
chance or fate. Mystery rather than explanation is the key
word of these authors when they deal with human motivation.
Nor do they preclude the possibility of a shift in will as with
Dimmesdale, Barnabas Thayer, or even Wieland. The possibility of increased understanding is also everpresent, as
with Ishmael or Pierre or Captain Delano. And an ancestral
curse, despite its deterministic impact on many lives in many
generations, may be worked out, as in *The House of the Seven
Gables*. Above all, among writers like Hawthorne, Freeman,
and Melville, love—*agape*—functions as a redemptive force,
straightening a warped personality, adding significance to a
wasted life, ushering in new dispensations. The grip of fate
is not a stranglehold down through the ages; it can be broken

by increased understanding, by conversions from hate to love, by something like God's grace operative in a receptive soul.

The Law for Things: Naturalism

"Two Laws Discrete"

In 1847 in his "Ode to W. H. Channing" Emerson summarized one of the intellectual and spiritual dilemmas of his and the ensuing century:

> There are two laws discrete,
> Not reconciled,—
> Law for man, and law for thing;
> The last builds town and fleet,
> But it runs wild,
> And doth the man unking.[1]

Machines—things—build town and fleet; they carry man across the sea and land, through the air, and recently into space. They do, or can do, the bulk of man's manual labor, safeguard his bodily health, and do much of his thinking. They bestow upon him food, clothing, and playthings in unheard-of quantities; but modern man like a spoiled child reaches out his hand for more. Western civilization is engulfed in things; it revels and wallows and sometimes swims for its life in the outpourings of the materialistic cornucopia. Even cultures like those of the Hindus and the Arabs—that for millennia have sung the praises of austerity and simplicity—are being lured by the siren song of material plenty and measure the progress of their societies by such milestones as the successful building of a jet airliner or a hydroelectric

dam. Confucius, Buddha, and Mohammed—not to mention
Jesus, John the Baptist, and Isaiah—though still honored
by service from several billion lips, are no longer the prophets
that guide men's lives. Marx, Ford, Edison, Pavlov, and
Einstein are the truly honored ones, if honor consists of eager
and grateful acceptance of what a supposed benefactor has
to offer.

Yet, for the past two hundred years a doubt—the one which
Emerson sensed—has been clouding the sunny skies of scientific
knowledge: is man himself a machine, subject to the law
of things exactly as are the steam engines and the Atlas rockets
that he has so cleverly made? And if man is a machine—
body, mind, and soul—does this fact diminish his stature
or jeopardize what he had always considered his high rank
in the universal order? Does it "unking" him, as Emerson
asserted it did? And if man is "unkinged," does the resulting
change in his attitude toward himself cause him to behave
in a manner different from his old ways, whether to his benefit or his detriment?

Many answers have been given, none of them conclusive.
These answers may be classified under two extremely general
headings: humanistic and naturalistic. To distinguish between
the two is not easy, but a usable approach is to assay the a-
mounts of determinism and free will present in the philosophy
under scrutiny. Philosophies that are totally libertarian
or totally deterministic are, of course, very rare. But naturalistic philosophies *tend* to play down the element of free
choice and free will in human activity, while humanistic
philosophies tend to emphasize them. These tendencies are
to be expected. The naturalist sees one law in the universe—
the law of nature or of things. As it affects inanimate objects
and all but the most complicated forms of life, this law, until
recently, has been held to be altogether unalterable. The
final step is to assume that the "higher organisms," including
man, are also subject to the same general law, although its
working in the case of intelligent beings—who appear to act

according to their individual volitions—may not be so obvious as in the case of unintelligent matter. Yet the naturalist must ever strive to include all objects and beings in the ironclad dispensation, for he is under the compulsion to establish the cosmos as a monism, a single vast mechanism, with or without a governing power in control of it.

That the naturalist usually does not take the final step toward total determinism is a tribute to his intellectual honesty. As an empiricist, which he usually considers himself to be, he observes an apparent element of freedom in human life, as did Holmes. Yet he is unable to conceive how this may be, or at least he has not been able to until the recent discovery of the "uncertainty principle" in the behavior of the particles of the atom—a discovery which suggests that, after all, chance may play some role in the workings of the universe. If the directions of moving electrons cannot be predicted in each individual case, perhaps man's direction cannot be predicted either. A rigid determinism in human affairs no longer seems quite so inescapable a conclusion. Yet the chance play of electrons and man's free and considered use of his judgment and will in attempts to control his own destiny are not impressively analogous. There has been no gaping breach in the wall of determinism, nor does there promise to be.

The humanist, on the other hand, as Irving Babbitt points out, is a dualist. With Emerson he recognizes "two laws discrete," one for man, and one for things. To him the law for things may be as unyielding as it is to the naturalist. Chemicals combine, amoebas multiply, and the universe, perhaps, expands and contracts according to unchanging patterns. But there remains to man, as the humanist sees him, an area of free action, an area which may be quite confined but which is more extensive than that allowed by the naturalist.

Emile Zola and Claude Bernard

On a nontechnical level philosophies both of free will and, especially, of determinism have found expression in the more serious literature of the past two centuries. The next task, then, is to trace the impact of scientific determinism on the viewpoints of representative American authors, with some consideration of European influences. For the most part the concern will be with belles lettres—fiction, essays, and poetry—but, for the sake of background and clarification, a number of scientists, political theorists, philosophers, and psychologists will have to be glanced at as well.

Naturalism, as it is found in literature, especially in the novel, is a view of life. Though certain literary devices have become associated with it, it is not primarily a technique. For example, naturalistic novels like those of Theodore Dreiser tend to accumulate detail. Yet Stephen Crane's *Maggie: A Girl of the Streets* and *The Red Badge of Courage*, which are philosophically naturalistic in the extreme, are stylistically remarkable for their selective impressionism. Again, the style of the naturalistic novel is reputed to be dispassionate, suggestive of a case report. But actually naturalistic prose is notable for its variety. Some examples are: Jack London's straightforward, vigorous story-telling; Frank Norris's purple passages as lush and dense and interminable as a rain forest; Ernest Hemingway's closely controlled patterns of image and rhythm; and John Steinbeck's amalgam of whimsey and poetry. Nor is naturalism simply an extreme form of realism, as it has sometimes been described. In some respects naturalism is more romantic than realistic, for it imposes a philosophy on life, whereas realism theoretically reports and photographs. Insofar as realism embodies a philosophy—as it did in its early forms from the pens of Henry James and

William Dean Howells—it is humanistic, especially in its insistence on free will and on moderation, or the law of measure, as a followable rule of life; and thus it is diametrically opposed to naturalism.

Naturalism as a movement was fathered by Emile Zola, whose essay *Le Roman Expérimental* is still an important source of naturalistic ideas. Zola himself was inspired by a work entitled *Introduction à la Médicine Expérimentale* by the French physician Claude Bernard. As a scientist, Dr. Bernard, whose book appeared in the middle of the nineteenth century, was of great service to humanity, for his efforts did much to lift medicine from a slough of tradition and conjecture to the level of experimentally tested and established knowledge. Whether Zola's contribution is of equal benefit is questionable. At any rate, Zola displayed an unbounded enthusiasm for Bernard, whose work he read in a state of awe. Zola's procedure in *Le Roman Expérimental* was to quote a passage from Bernard on physiology and then apply this passage to what he was pleased to call the science of novel-writing. For example, Bernard wrote:

> I propose to establish the fact that the science of the phenomena of life can have no other basis than the science of the phenomena of inanimate bodies, and that there are, in this connection, no differences between the principles of biological science and those of physics and chemistry. . . . [The vitalists] consider life as a mysterious and supernatural agent, which acts arbitrarily, free from all determinism, and they condemn as materialists all those who endeavor to trace vital phenomena to definite organic and physico-chemical conditions. These are false ideas. . . .With living beings as well as inanimate, the conditions of the existence of each phenomena are determined in an absolute manner.[2]

Joyfully, Zola improvises on Bernard's text:

> All things hang together; it is necessary to start from the determinism of inanimate bodies in order to arrive at the

determinism of living beings; and since savants like Claude
Bernard demonstrate now that fixed laws govern the human
body, we can easily proclaim. . .the hour in which the
laws of thought and passion will be formulated in their
turn. A like determinism will govern the stones of the
roadway and the brain of man.[3]

Bernard recommended that the physiologist follow the
scientific method; he or she should proceed toward the discovery of truth through observation and experimentation.
Zola sees the novelist's method as the same. Notebook in hand,
he or she should seek out and record his or her data; then as
an experimenter he or she "sets his [sic] characters going in a
certain story so as to show that the succession of facts will be
such as the requirements of the determination of the phenomena under examination call for . . . ."[4] Zola is, of course,
thoroughly unscientific, although he does not seem fully to
realize it. Far from experimenting, he adopts an a priori
approach, interpreting his observations by "laws" arrived
at by others in other sciences:

In fact, the whole operation [of writing a novel] consists
in taking facts in nature, then in studying the mechanism
of these facts, acting upon them, by the modification of
circumstances and surroundings, without deviating from
the laws of nature. Finally, you possess knowledge of man,
scientific knowledge of him, in both his social and individual relations.[5]

A commentator describes Zola's type of naturalism as follows:

The basic thing . . . is the fact that the naturalist has subscribed to the postulate of universal causation, and writes
with the purpose of showing cause to effect relationships
as he conceives them. . . . If he interprets the principle of
physical causation as applying to choice itself, the result
is determinism in the realm of human action, man being
subordinated to nature in such a way as to leave no intel-
ligible grounds for effecting reform, and the result is a

thoroughgoing pessimism.[6]

The naturalistic novelist, Zola insists, is not a mere photographer; rather he manipulates his data as they appear in the lives of his imaginary characters so as to contribute substantially to a scientific understanding of human behavior. To Zola the novel is definitely an experiment in which the novelist professes "to perform scientific experiments on his imaginative characters."[7] Thus allied with the scientists, whom he so admires, Zola speaks contemptuously of the "follies of the poets and the philosophers" who search fruitlessly for the "Why?" of things. Like the men of science, he is concerned only with the "How?"[8]

Obviously there is an inconsistency in Zola's stance—a serious one. Though he is a rampant determinist who believes that "a like determinism will govern the stones of the roadway and the brain of man,"[9] yet he vehemently disclaims being a fatalist, as does indeed Claude Bernard. Bernard, Zola points out, distinguishes between fatalism, which is the "essence of phenomena," (that is, their final, ultimate cause) and determinism, which is the "nearest or determining cause of phenomena . . . the condition essential for the appearance of any phenomenon."[10] In other words, Zola is content that one know the "entire mechanism [determinism] of nature, without troubling one's self for the time being with the origin [fatalism] of the mechanism."[11] The trouble with this distinction is that natural laws by their very definition *presuppose* some higher power, or some overall order of things—in short, a fatalism—that sets them inexorably to work in the universe and in men's lives. One can perhaps logically refuse to try to answer the question "Why?" but the question "How?" demands an answer far more sweeping and profound than a mere recording of apparent surface cause and effect. It demands an answer perhaps in terms like those of the deists' analogy of the universe to a vast clockworks designed and presided over by a master clock-maker.[12]

Zola fell into another inconsistency when he insisted that efforts to reform human nature are not futile. A thoroughgoing determinism precludes the effectiveness of such efforts. Yet Zola contended that once we discover the determining causes of human behavior, we can act upon them and modify them in accordance with the laws of nature, "in such a way as to develop the good and reject the bad, from the point of view of their utility to man." [13] Man can make use of the determinism of nature to alter the conditions of nature insofar as he does not violate the principles by which the mechanism operates. Presumably, in this activity the reformer will be making use of his or her mind; yet Zola, I repeat, believes the brain of man to be subject to as rigid a determinism as the stones of the roadway. Man, according to this doctrine, can never be able to direct his thoughts by anything resembling free choice; any decision he makes as to what is good or bad will be the result of the same unyielding determinism that controls all else. Man's thoughts, choices, and value judgments—indeed, the very theory of determinism—are merely the results of such scientific causes as his own heredity, environment, and biochemistry.

To put it another way, can a machine think about itself? Can it estimate its own value or what is good for itself? Can it redesign itself? Can any part of it think about, appraise, and modify the remainder? For example, can the carburetor of an automobile reconstruct the transmission so as to make the whole machine more efficient? Admittedly, there are, or soon will be, self-repairing machines, but these do not create radically different machines. They work upon the original mechanism. And even so, there is a controlling force outside the mechanism—the mind of man—which can pass judgment on it and change its operation in accordance with some scale of values.

But one point is unmistakable: Zola doggedly asserts that man's body, passions, and mind are subject to an absolute determinism. Thus he and other total naturalists, whether scientific or literary, must be simply parts of the vast machine of the universe and must be helplessly bound by the laws underlying the operation of that machine. As a result, they are as powerless as the carburetor, either in coming to objectively valid conclusions about themselves or about the machine as a whole, or in any way exerting free will (Zola uses the phrase)[14] in improving the machine. The dilemma is inescapable. The rigid naturalist must resign himself or herself to the idea of a "block universe" in which even one's most private thoughts are mechanical, and in which the distinction between good and evil—dependent as it is on the existence of moral agents endowed with freedom of choice—no longer obtains. It is a universe in which any efforts to change the order of things are impossible and irrelevant, since the machine will or will not change itself—including that part of it which is man—according to its own inevitable and uncontrollable laws and in no other way.

Some tough-minded naturalists have accepted just such an inflexible view of things, but Zola is not among them. More tender-minded, he has permitted himself to fall into inconsistencies which permit man to retain a modicum of freedom of choice and action. Thus he excludes from ironclad determinism the mental processes of scientists like himself and Bernard. The scientific mind must be able to deliberate and then act independently of the machine itself. To the extent that he is thus inconsistent, Zola is tinged with humanism. He leans, perhaps unconsciously, toward the idea that man's soul and intellect stand apart from nature in a sort of dualism; he acts upon the principle that, as Emerson said, there are "two laws discrete . . . law for man, and law for thing." Moreover, he likes to think that his novels are highly moral. The naturalistic novelists are "experimental moralists"[15]; that is, they operate on a plane where the distinction between good and evil exists and a choice between them can be made.

To be the master of good and evil, to regulate life, to regulate society, to solve in time all the problems of socialism, above all, to give justice a solid foundation by solving through experiment the questions of criminality—is not this being the most useful and the most moral workers in the human workshop?[16]

This desire to improve the lot of man on earth—and the conviction that improvement is possible—might well be considered humanistic in the classical definition of the term. Also humanistic is the implied assumption that man can be master of his future, of his destiny. Yet, insofar as Zola confines freedom of will to only a few superintellects, he is naturalistic. This latter view is obviously dominant in Zola's thought.

Thomas Malthus

Claude Bernard is but one of many scientists who laid the groundwork for naturalism in European and American literature. Writers, with few exceptions, are not particularly competent as scientists. In the main, their knowledge of science comes from the more or less popular reading of their period. To glance at a few influential nineteenth-century scientific books readable by laymen is the best way to get an idea of the scope and pervasiveness of the materials the naturalistic writer could draw from. Obviously, no detailed summary of any of these germinal books is possible or necessary here. The literary men themselves draw general ideas rather than specific facts from them. Important among the ideas that interested them were those that bore on the problems of the freedom of the will and the existence of good and evil. As we have seen, the naturalists restrict, if they do not eradicate, the freedom of the will and blur the dichotomy of good and evil.

In the following consideration of several basic scientific writings, all that will be examined is the extent to which they contributed to these two pivotal naturalistic attitudes.

Determinism, of course, can be traced back through the world's philosophies—not to mention theologies—to the Greek atomists. In the seventeenth and eighteenth centuries in particular, men like Hobbes, Descartes, and Hume were deeply concerned with the question of the freedom of the will, and these thinkers contributed much to the intellectual atmosphere of the nineteenth century. But literary naturalism began its rise only after the speculations of the philosophers and pure scientists on determinism took a foothold in the social and biological sciences, which would, of course, be of more immediate interest to the belletrists than would be, say, physics or mathematics.

Thomas Malthus's *An Essay on the Principle of Population,* first published in 1798 and drastically revised in many subsequent editions, is the earliest of these germinal works to be considered here. Noting that population grows "in a geometrical ratio" and "the means of subsistence . . . in an arithmetic ratio," Malthus concludes that "the increase of the human species can only be kept down to the level of the means of subsistence by the constant operation of the strong law of necessity. . . ."[17] So rigid is the law that it dominates all human activity. On such a foundation Malthus erects a truly "dismal science," which renders most difficult, though not entirely impossible, any radical improvement in the human condition.

> No improved form of government, no plans of emigration, no benevolent institutions, and no degree or direction of national industry can prevent the continual action of a great check to population in some form or other; it follows that we must submit to it as an inevitable law of nature, and the only inquiry that remains is, how it may take place with the least possible prejudice to the virtue and happiness of human society."[18]

Malthus's basic pessimism concerning man's ability radically to change his lot is typical of naturalistic and deterministic social philosophers and writers down to the present. The reader will become acquainted with many others who equalled or surpassed him in pessimism.

Yet it must be emphasized that Malthus was not a total determinist. A clergyman by profession, he sees the mind of God behind the natural order. Though there is a rigid limit to what we can do to modify the conditions of our lives, there is still something that we can do—certainly enough to keep us, especially as individuals, exerting ourselves to the extent of our admittedly feeble powers. As Malthus points out, there is a purpose in the constant struggle that the circumstances of this world force upon us. That purpose is "the creation and formation of mind; a process necessary, to awaken inert, chaotic matter, into spirit; to sublimate the dust of the earth into soul. . . ."[19] But even this activity of the individual soul comes under a determinism. Malthus finds that the inhabitants of genial climates are less alert and less resourceful than those of harsher regions, where the intellect, with greater demands upon it, is more vigorous. In this supposition he anticipates some of the ideas of the literary naturalist Hippolyte Taine.

Nor does Malthus question the dualism of good and evil. God's purpose in the world, that of transforming matter into mind, is, of course, good. Part of the mind-forming process is the struggle of each of us to achieve what Christians have traditionally regarded as good—love of God and of moral virtue, a sense of the latter being innate in every man. "Evil exists in the world, not to create despair, but activity. We are not patiently to submit to it, but to exert ourselves to avoid it."[20] To the extent that a man is successful in eliminating evil—whether material or spiritual—from his own life and the lives of his fellow beings, "he will probably improve and exalt his own mind"[21] and thus more nearly fulfill the design of the Creator. His reward will be life eternal as promised in the

Gospels. The person who fails to exert himself for personal and social betterment will find death and will return into the clay, untransformed into imperishable spirit.

Malthus, then, is a determinist—a naturalist—on the social level, and a rather thoroughgoing one at that. But the individual, in Malthus's view, enjoys a true control of his or her own destiny; in one's power is a choice between everlasting life and everlasting death, a choice between fulfilling God's purpose for oneself and aborting it.

Karl Marx

Another and stauncher determinist than Malthus is Karl Marx, whose philosophy of dialectical materialism is too well known—or at any rate too involved—to develop here. As with other theorists, Marx's attitude toward human motivation, volition, and action is more important to the understanding of literary naturalism than are the details of his system. His emphasis, of course, is on social laws, which he sees "working with iron necessity towards inevitable results."[22] He is concerned with individuals "only in so far as they are personifications of economic categories, embodiments of particular class-relations and class-interests. [His] stand-point, from which the evolution of the economic order of society is viewed as a process of history, can less than any other make the individual responsible for relations whose creatue he socially remains. . . ."[23] As a Russian critic has pointed out, "Marx treats the social movement as a process of natural history governed by law not only independent of human will, consciousness, and intelligence, but rather, on the contrary, determining that will, consciousness and intelligence."[24]

Thus Marx presents us with a closed system in which individual responsibility, choice, and action are all as mechanical as, say, the chemical phenomenon of oxidation. Oxygen combines with other substances at certain temperatures, releasing heat and creating new compounds in the process. Class struggles are as inevitable as the movement and clash of atoms within the molecule as matter passes from one form into another.

However, this extreme position has not been held to in practice. Many Marxists of today feel, as did Zola, that the laws of society, once studied and understood, can serve as a guide whereby man by his own efforts may better his lot. As one writer puts it, "In any case, the condition of felicitous social action is an harmonious adjustment to the deeper currents whose movements will not be denied."[25] Yet it must be emphasized that present-day Marxists, when they ally themselves to natural law, are exercising a choice that Marx himself considered nonexistent, since, to him, the laws themselves determine "the will, consciousness, and intelligence" and hence, of course, any choice that these may make. Insofar as a Marxist considers himself capable of free choice, he is a deviationist.

Similarly, in its acceptance, in practice, of a distinction between good and evil, most contemporary Marxism falls short of pure naturalism. Most Marxists today subscribe to a definite and quite traditional set of values: good health, economic well-being, the opportunity for individual self-development—whether physical, intellectual, or artistic—brotherly love, and the like. They believe that their system will make available these values to more people than will capitalism or feudalism. Optimistically, they feel that nature, or history, is constantly progressing toward a wider dissemination of the good things. They simply consider themselves wiser than the capitalists in choosing the system that they are convinced nature intends for the fulfillment of her purposes.

Charles Darwin

Though Marx differed from Malthus in many particulars, both thinkers postulated struggle as the underlying condition for historical development. Struggle, in fact, was a component of most nineteenth-century naturalistic thinking. It is most pronounced, of course, in Charles Darwin, who is the strongest single influence on literary naturalism from its beginning down to the present. Darwin's basic theory, that of natural selection, is as simple in its statement as it is revolutionary in its impact:

Owing to this struggle [for life], variations, however slight and from whatever cause proceeding, if they be in any degree profitable to the individuals of a species, in their infinitely complex relations to other organic beings and to their physical conditions of life, will tend to the preservation of such individuals, and will generally be inherited by the offspring. The offspring, also, will thus have a better chance of surviving, for, of the many individuals of any species which are periodically born, but a small number can survive.[26]

Mankind, as well as all other forms of life, has been, and is, subject to this same law.

However, the system is less rigid than that of Marx. Darwin cannot admit of an ineluctable determinism working toward certain ends—"that each particular variation was from the beginning of all time preordained"[27]—because the number of false starts, the redundancy of reproduction, the many injurious as well as beneficial "deviations of structure"[28] all indicate no such eternal purpose, much less a benevolent one.

But Darwin is far from subscribing to the notion of a totally disorderly universe:

The birth both of the species and of the individual are [sic] equally parts of that grand sequence of events, which minds refuse to accept as the result of blind chance. The understanding revolts at such a conclusion whether or not we are able to believe that every slight variation of structure, the union of each pair in marriage, the dissemination of each seed, and other such events, have all been ordained for some special purpose." [29]

As a part of the "grand sequence of events," man's destiny is under a determinism; it is only the multifarious particular episodes in the sequence that refuse to be explained by determinism. Thus man's position is somewhat equivocal. Though man "may be excused for feeling some pride at having risen . . . to the very summit of the organic scale . . . ," [30] yet the rise has not been the result of his own exertions. And with all his "exalted powers" [31]—reason, compassion, brotherly love—man must never forget that he is no more than a part of nature; that he "still bears in his bodily frame the indelible stamp of his lowly origin." [32]

What the literary and philosophical naturalists seized upon in Darwin was his monism, his insistence that "man is the co-descendant with other mammals of a common progenitor." [33] In his final chapter in *The Descent of Man*, Darwin explores the religious and moral implications of his theory. Man, he ever insists, is subject to the same laws as the rest of the organic and inorganic universe. Man's intellect, which differs from that of the animals only in degree and not in kind, is the natural result of the evolutionary process. The development of moral qualities, though more difficult to explain, can be attributed to instincts acquired through natural selection. Conscience Darwin accounts for as the clash of personal desires and passions with those instincts (morals) that are beneficial to the race as a whole. A feeling of dissatisfaction arising from the breach of the social instincts constitutes a pang of conscience. His personal passions having subsided, the individual "resolves to act differently for the future—and this is conscience." [34] Good is defined by Darwin as the happiness of the individual, which can be achieved among a social species only through the greatest happiness of the group.

Hence, by obeying his social instincts, which are the basis for his morals, man is furthering good, that is, furthering the happiness of himself and his species. Struggle, with which so much unhappiness is associated, is necessary for the advance of any species. Thus, as with Malthus, what seems evil actually may be good; Darwin continues the blurring between good and evil begun by other naturalists.

Herbert Spencer

"There should be open competition for all men; and the most able should not be prevented by laws or customs from succeeding best and rearing the largest number of offspring,"[35] wrote Darwin. This became the theme of much of the economic and social theory, and hence of vast quantities of naturalistic writing, of the fifty or seventy-five years following the publication of Darwin's great books.

Evolution is basic to the thought of Herbert Spencer, whose ideas became so influential as to constitute almost a cult. Spencer went far beyond Darwin in attempting to establish a naturalistic monism. All phenomena whatsoever he finds dependent on the principle of what he calls Persistence of Force, that is, the conservation of energy. Knowledge, he concedes, has not yet developed into "an organized aggregate of direct and indirect deductions from the Persistence of Force"[36]; that is an achievement for the remote future. But progess is being made. Meanwhile, Spencer warns against the assumption that his philosophy is essentially materialistic, for it is not. Nor is it spiritualist (to use Spencer's term). Science does not and cannot explain the ultimate nature of reality. All it can do is to provide "an interpretation of the process of things as it presents itself to our limited consciousness; but how this process is related to the actual process, we are unable to conceive, much less to know."[37]

Thus Spencer by no means slams the door on religion,

though his system, rigidly based as it is on Persistence of Force, would leave little room for the exercise of human volition and hence would be inimical to humanism. Certainly he does not postulate "a law for man and a law for things," as does the true libertarian. He is not a materialist. Nor is he a spiritualist, because he refuses to accept any dualism. Matter and spirit, which between them assuredly must include man, are but signs of the one "Unknown Reality which underlies both."[38] The Unknown Reality is, of course, God.

Spencer's popularity in the nineteenth century is not difficult to account for. Having left a God, at least of sorts, in the universe, he next assumes the existence of a cosmic purpose—a concept reassuring even to the clergy. This cosmic purpose works itself out through the evolutionary process—a concept reassuring to scientists—in accord with a "universal and necessary tendency towards supremacy and multiplication of the best."[39] Furthermore, "the struggle for existence has been an indispensable means to evolution."[40] The struggle has brought hardships, even horrors, but it has been necessary in creating our civilization and its values. When Robinson Jeffers in his poem "The Bloody Sire" writes that war has created all the world's values, he is echoing Spencer's statement that war with all its bestialities has contributed to the advance of mankind, which except for the universal antagonisms of nature and of history would still be a race of "feeble types, sheltering in caves and living on wild food."[41]

But always optimistic, Spencer thought that humanity was evolving from a state of perpetual strife to one of equilibrium and harmony—an industrial stage. He makes the assertion, amazingly erroneous in the light of the past fifty years, that man's "limbs, teeth, and nails are but little employed in fight; and his mind is not ordinarily occupied in devising ways of destroying other creatures."[42] Spencer would no doubt be appalled by the sixty-billion-dollar defense budget of the United States alone and by the vast cooperative effort of the sciences in all the major nations to contrive machines of destruction inconceivable in Spencer's time. Spencer was thus the victim of his own, and his century's, oversimplification of man and human history.

Spencer, who attempted to reduce all phenomena to a single vast synthesis, or monism, had specific notions as to the will, and these notions, as might be expected in such a philosophy, were deterministic. He admits that one is at liberty to do, or attempt to do whatever one desires; but he denies

> that every one is at liberty to desire or not to desire, which is the real proposition involved in the dogma of free will. . . . When, after a certain composite mass of emotion and thought has arisen in him, a man performs an action, he commonly asserts that *he* determined to perform the action; and by speaking as though there were a mental self, *present to his consciousness*, yet not included in this composite mass of emotion and thought, he is led to the error of supposing that it was not this composite mass . . . which determined the action. . . . Naturally enough, then, the subject of such psychical changes says that he wills the action.[43]

Actually, however, a person has no control over the components of the mental and emotional state that constitute a motive, or a volition (for the two are virtually synonymous). "Until there is a *motive* (mark the word) there is no Will,"[44] Will is "nothing but the general name given to the special feeling that gains supremacy and determines action."[45] Since the complex state of mind and feeling that makes up a desire or motive or act of willing derives from all the influences in a person's individual, societal, and evolutionary past, any specific volition can hardly be called free. As with Edwards, but for different causes, man is free to do as he chooses but not to choose as he chooses.

The vogue of Spencer was immense, especially in America. This nation was then not yet totally beyond the frontier stage. Huge fortunes were to be had and were struggled for in a multitude of areas from politics to the production of oil, and political and economic freedoms were highly touted national institutions. This nation delightedly accepted a philosophy that saw competition as fundamental to social progress. Individualism was the password of the times.

Emerson had elevated the private man into virtual deity, and had, in fact, sung the praises of business as one of the arenas for individual exertion. But in justification of material success, not only in terms of personal gain in wealth and power but as necessary to the betterment of the race, Emerson offered only a watery potion in comparison to the heady drink of Spencer and other social Darwinists with their clamor about natural selection, survival of the fittest, and free enterprise.

Among the novelists, Norris, Crane, London, and Dreiser studied their Spencer and became more or less his disciples. In the work of these authors we see a superb example of literature harmonizing with and fortifying the spirit of the times, for businessmen, preachers, and philosophers also rallied to the credo of Spencer. John D. Rockefeller, for instance, in a Sunday school address phrased the mystique thus: "The growth of a large business is merely survival of the fittest. . . . This is not an evil tendency in business. It is merely the working-out of a law of nature and a law of God."[46] Similarly, Andrew Carnegie felt that the natural course of events—that is, the working out of the law of natural selection—was so sacred that he expressed shock when a well-known philosopher, a disciple of Herbert Spencer no less, admitted to giving a quarter dollar to a beggar. That gift, Carnegie opined, would "probably work more injury than all the money which its thoughtless donor [would] ever be able to give in true charity [would] do good."[47] True charity, Carnegie explained, consists in giving the community at large "ladders upon which the aspiring can rise."[48] Mere handouts do nothing but block the process of natural selection in eliminating the unfit. Thus Carnegie chose to endow libraries as ladders whereby the naturally superior individual could mount toward self-betterment and the consequent betterment of the race.

William Graham Sumner

Another American Spencerian was William Graham Sumner. Fiercely devout in his faith in the law of the survival of the fittest, he condemned as absurd any efforts to make over society by bypassing this law. He was suspicious of democracy because of its leveling tendencies, which are counter to the whole spirit of evolution. If the race is to progress, great inequalities must exist among individuals. Man-made laws which would erase these inequalities impede the order. "The first instinct of the modern man," Sumner sneers, "is to get a law passed to forbid or prevent what, in his wisdom, he disapproves."[49]

The current fear of, and resentment toward, the captains of industry are unfounded. Social advancement, Sumner says, can be produced only by great forces. The manipulation of forces—steam or electricity, for example—demands men of great capacities. That the capitalists controlling these energies may be motivated directly by lust for wealth and for power is irrelevant.

> If it is said that there are some persons in our time who have become rapidly and in a great degree rich, it is true; if it is said that large aggregations of wealth in the control of individuals is a social danger, it is not true. . . . There are no earnings which are more legitimate or for which greater services are rendered for the whole industrial body.[50]

Sumner, having traveled in Germany for two years with apparent inconvenience, suggests that that nation would "make an excellent bargain"[51] if it put its railroad system into the hands of a Vanderbilt.

Like the Marxists, Sumner feels that "in the economic forces which control the material prosperity of a population lie the real course of its political institutions, its social class-adjustments, its industrial prosperity, its moral code, and its world-philosophy."[52] Sumner takes comfort in the fact that man can do little to bring about change, however ardently he may de-

sire it. Changes are the result of great spontaneous forces—
social and physical. "These causes will make of [the Earth] just
what, in fidelity to them, it ought to be. The men will be
carried along with it and made by it."[53] Again, as the Marxists
believe, man at most can only play along with the cosmic
forces already at work, perhaps modifying or hastening their
action slightly, but never diverting them into a direction
counter to the general tendency of things.

Like so many naturalists, Sumner revels in what is almost
a romantic ecstasy at the spectacle of the universe he has
described. His rhetoric, as he warms up to the subject, smacks
of Byron:

> The great stream of time and earthly things will sweep
> on just the same in spite of us. It bears with it now all the
> errors and follies of the past, the wreckage of all the philos-
> ophies, the fragments of all the civilizations, the wisdom
> of all the abandoned ethical systems, the debris of all the
> institutions, and the penalties of all the mistakes. It is only
> in imagination that we stand by and look at it and criticise
> it, and plan to change it. Every one of us is a child of his age
> and cannot get out of it. He is in the stream and is swept
> along with it. All his sciences and philosophy come to him
> out of it. Therefore the tide will not be changed by us. . . .
> That is why it is the greatest folly of which a man can be
> capable, to sit down with a slate and pencil to plan out a
> new social world.[54]

Henry George and Lester Ward

Sumner's profound pessimism is not uncommon among
naturalists, but it is by no means universal. Malthus, Darwin,
Spencer, and Marx all envisaged life as struggle, and all were
reasonably optimistic concerning the ultimate worthwhileness
of the struggle. Many American reformers found themselves in
harmony with this pleasanter note in evolution. True, they
felt that only by cooperating with natural tendencies much
stronger than puny man could humanity achieve progress; any
attempt to reverse the course of events would result in failure.

But as shown above, the Marxists and Sumner, with totally antagonistic concepts of the goals of society, considered themselves to be on the side of history deterministically conceived.

The differences among the various evolutionists as to the direction in which evolution was going are much narrower. Thus Henry George, whom Sumner branded as a visionary, is basically very much an evolutionist and a Spencerian. He finds a close analogy "between the development of society and the development of species."[55] Both evolve from the homogeneous to the heterogeneous, from the simple to the complex; and with increased complexity, in both the society and the individuals of a species, come increased wants and dangers. "Strong as it may seem, our civilization is evolving destructive forces. . . . Nor should we forget that in civilized man still lurks the savage."[56] But "these dangers, which menace not one country alone, but modern civilization itself, do but show that a higher civilization is strugging to be born. . . ."[57]

The chief of these dangers is the concentration of wealth into the hands of a few. George considers this not the natural state of affairs, as did Sumner, but a maladjustment which the people, the species, can rectify. A redistribution of wealth may be brought about by one simple device, that of the single tax upon land. The very simplicity of the remedy attests to the naturalistic, the mechanistic, view of society entertained by George. The machine has gotten out of repair; one major adjustment and it will be running smoothly again, conveying all mankind to happiness and well-being. Man *can* repair the machine. Man is not helpless; he is not in the grip of a determinism as inexorable as Sumner's.

Another "reforming Darwinist"—that is, one who would consciously apply the principles of evolution to the betterment of society and not wait passively, as would Sumner, for natural laws to operate towards inscrutable ends—was Lester Ward. Ward sees the same evils in contemporary society that George did—evils accruing from undue concentration of wealth. The masses are approachng a condition forecast by Ricardo's "iron law of wages"; they are receiving for their labors only enough barely "to subsist and perpetuate their race."[58]

But the iron of Ricardo's law does not impress Ward as being unmalleable. Man can be freed from its shackles; evolution is tending in that direction. Temporarily the process may be stalled, but man by his conscious efforts will be able to get the mechanism in motion again. Society has thus far evolved through a series of forms: autocracy, aristocracy, democracy, and, recently, plutocracy. Plutocracy will be crushed only by a power stronger than itself, and that power is society. The next form of government will be sociocracy, rule by society, by means of sociological principles consciously applied by society itself. Plutocracy marks the high point of the reign of the individual, in other words, of democracy. This has been good, for after all it has been part of the natural order. The individual has acted in his or her own self-interests and has acted ably and successfully. Rather than being reviled for this, the individual should be applauded.

Society indeed should profit from the example of the individual. It too should act with a will, with intelligence, and with purpose, toward a goal that will benefit itself. This is sociocracy; it differs from democracy in that it emphasizes *social* welfare, rather than individual welfare. "The prevailing democracies of the world," Ward asserts, "are incompetent to deal with problems of social welfare."[59] Sociocracy differs from socialism in that it is less dogmatic, more pragmatic. It will solve its problems as it comes to them, rather than approach them with a panacea. Sociocracy implies a change in the goals of government rather than a change in form.

Finally, the progress toward sociocracy, Ward believes, is more or less inevitable. If it can be shown that society is actually moving toward any ideal, the ultimate substantial realization of that ideal is as good as proved. What Ward means apparently is that the evolution of society cannot be halted, any more than the operation of the law of gravity.

Going to some pains to indicate that there is a ground swell toward evolution into sociocracy, Ward is confident that he has detected a natural process at work, and natural processes cannot be reversed. They can be helped along, or slowed, but never permanently thwarted. Determinism is a part of Ward's outlook, as it is with all the Darwinists.

Hippolyte Taine

This discussion has gotten rather far afield from literary naturalism, though it will be amply evident that naturalistic thought is very much the same whether it stems from the mind of a scientist, a philosopher, or a novelist. This has been seen with Zola, who derived his ideas from the physiologist Bernard. Another Frenchman, Hippolyte Taine, wrote a history of English literature which, scholarly though it may be, is today better known for its theorizing than for its scholarship. In his introduction to this volume, Taine wrote in words now familiar:

> Now-a-days history, like zoology, has found its anatomy. . . . There is a cause for ambition, for courage, for truth, as there is for digestion, for muscular movement, for animal heat. Vice and virtue are products, like vitriol and sugar; and every complex phenomenon has its springs from other more simple phenomena on which it hangs. Let us then seek the simple phenomena for moral qualities, as we seek them for physical qualities.[60]

According to Taine, the three determining influences upon a nation and its culture are race, surroundings, and the epoch. There are variations among mankind just as among animals. From these inherited characteristics, inevitable and uncontrollable, arise the most basic variations among cultures. Milieu or surroundings are of scarcely less importance. For example, the profound differences which are manifest between the German races . . . and the Greek and Latin . . . arise for the most part from the difference between the countries in which they are settled: some in cold moist lands, deep in black marshy forests or on the shores of a wild ocean, caged in by melancholy or violent sensations, prone to drunkenness and gluttony, bent on a fighting, blood-spilling life; others, again, with a lovely landscape, on a bright and laughing sea-coast, enticed to navigation and commerce, exempt from gross cravings of the stomach, inclined from the beginning to social ways, to a settled organisation of the state, to feeling and dispositions such as develop the art of oratory, the talent for enjoyment, the inventions of science, letters, arts.[61]

All this difference arising from climate alone! The historical inaccuracy of such generalizations, it need hardly be said, is blatant. For example, there have never been more gluttonous people than the Greeks and the Romans at certain periods of their history. As for fighting and bloodletting, had Taine never read the bloodiest of epics, the *Iliad*? And the Norsemen were even more famed as navigators, despite the cold, foggy seas of their homelands, than were the Mediterranean peoples. Yet no less astute a thinker and honest an artist than Thomas Mann, in contrasting the Germanic and the Latin races, echoes not only the spirit but at times even the words of Taine (see the chapter "Snow" in *The Magic Mountain* and *Death in Venice*).

The third in Taine's triad of determinants of human destiny—the epoch—is as inexorable as the other two. The development of a people, he finds, resembles that of a plant; each presents "but a mechanical problem."[62] He concludes that

. . . the unknown creations towards which the current of the centuries conducts us, will be raised up and regulated altogether by the three primordial forces; that if these forces could be measured and computed, one might deduce

from them as from a formula the specialties of future civilisation; and that if . . . we try to form some idea of our
general destiny, it is upon examination of these forces that
we must ground our prophecy.[63]

The study of literature to Taine became a science whereby
one "may construct a moral history, and advance toward
the knowledge of psychological laws, from which events may
spring."[64] Like Zola, he expected the literary man to be a
scientist, and he expressed great admiration for Stendhal,
who, he maintains, "first marked the fundamental causes of
nationality, climate, temperament . . . [and] treated of sentiments as they should be treated,—in the manner of the naturalist, namely, and of the natural philosopher, who constructs
classifications and weighs forces."[65]

Sigmund Freud

At the end of the nineteenth century appeared the last of the
great seminal figures in scientific determinism, Sigmund
Freud, whose influence was to be as far-reaching and as prolonged as that of Darwin. Freud did not make an impact on
the first round of naturalistic writers such as Crane, Norris,
London, or even Dreiser (whose career continued until 1945).
But on other writers—for example, Sherwood Anderson,
Eugene O'Neill, and William Faulkner—psychoanalysis,
which within a decade or so after the turn of the century
became a part of the intellectual atmosphere of the times,
exerted a marked effect.

The theories and methods of Freud are too familiar to
warrant the cursory summary which would be all that could
be given of them here. It should be carefully noted, however,
that Freud himself was a determinist of rather typical nineteenth-century rigidity. Thus, in a discussion of the psychology
of errors, he minces no words in answering the person who

would attribute such "inadvertencies" as slips of the tongue to mere accident rather than to the unconscious will:

> Does [the objector] mean to maintain that there are any occurrences so small that they fail to come within the causal sequence of things, that they might as well be other than they are? Anyone thus breaking away from the determination of natural phenomena, at any single point, has thrown over the whole scientific outlook on the world (*Weltanschauung*). One may point out to him how much more consistent is the religious outlook on the world, which emphatically assures us that "not one sparrow shall fall to the ground" except God wills it. [66]

The objector receives a similar scolding when he characterizes as capricious the ideas elicited by free association starting from a dream experience:

> I have already taken the liberty of pointing out to you that there is within you a deeply rooted belief in psychic freedom and choice, that this belief is quite unscientific, and that it must give ground before the claims of a determinism which governs even mental life. I ask you to have some respect for the *fact* that one association, and nothing else, occurs to the dreamer when he is questioned. . . .It can be proved that the association thus given is not a matter of choice, not indeterminate. [67]

Thus, according to Freud, whether we are neurotic or "normal," we choose, and will, and behave as we do, not in freedom but as a consequence of scientifically demonstrable laws of causality. Our conscious wills, far from being free, are determined by unconscious desires over which we have no direct control. As with Calvin's system, conscious volition is predetermined—although, of course, not by divine fiat—and when we think we are acting freely we are actually responding to unsuspected forces. Healthy, or normal, persons will that which makes for their well-being; neurotic persons will that which causes them discomfort or pain in an attempt to achieve psychic balance; but the wills of both have their unconscious causality. Psychoanalytic therapy consists of tracing back one's erring will to the point where it took the wrong fork in the road—that which leads to neurosis or worse. Then by reliving one's life, so to speak, with the therapist as a substitute parent (by transference), one turns one's unconscious will onto the road that leads to health. One does not directly will a return to health, although one must wish strongly for a cure and must open one's conscious mind to the discoveries resulting from the analysis. The redirection of the will over a period of months or years occurs unconsciously. To this extent—and no more—can the volition be controlled.

5

Election and Natural Selection

The Prestige of Naturalism in America

It has been impossible to be a writer, in Western civilization at least, in the last hundred years without in some way taking into account naturalistic modes of thought. Naturalism—the contention that mankind is subject to the same laws as the rest of the organic and inorganic universe—had, by the late nineteenth century, become the temper of the times. In no country did it carry more prestige than in America, with the possible exception of France, whose literature by the mid-century was definitely supplanting that of Britain as a major transatlantic influence.

Like so much in American intellectual life, naturalism was a European import. But why did it find such enthusiastic acceptance in this country? If America is a democracy, as most of her citizens have believed her to be for approximately 200 years, and if democracy exalts the worth and potential of the individual, why did a philosophy which has determinism as its basic tenet take root and flourish so luxuriantly here?

Men are like the other animals; they are like birch trees, amoebas, and the predators of the jungle, say the naturalists. Men's lives and the history of their society follow iron-clad laws. Where, then, is the individual liberty that supposedly underlies a democratic society? According to the naturalists, the individual is caught in the trap exactly as is history. The individual with some special endowment, by heredity or mutation, will prosper; but just as inevitably, the commonplace person will remain undistinguished, gaining no power and leaving no mark on his or her times. The strong and the weak, the stupid and the brilliant are both natural phenomena, and no more, their lives governed by laws not of their own making and certainly not to be abrogated by them. There is no credit in being successful or highly capable, any more than there is discredit in being a failure or mediocre.

American businessmen, the captains of industry, were in the forefront of those who eagerly accepted the new philosophy. For inherent in it was a balm for consciences that might be troubled by certain aspects of business practice not completely in conformity with the old morality. When personal credit and discredit for success or failure vanish, the conventional distinction between right and wrong must vanish as well. To a financier who ruthlessly beat down all competitors in his own rise to the top, Darwin had more comforting words to say than did Jesus. Thus in 1889 Carnegie published the following cleansing of his conscience:

> The price which society pays for the law of competition, like the price it pays for cheap comforts and luxuries, is . . . great; but the advantages of this law are also greater still. . . . But, whether the law be benign or not, we must say of it . . . : It is here; we cannot evade it; no substitutes for it have been found; and while the law may be sometimes hard for the individual, it is best for the race, for it insures the survival of the fittest in every department. We accept and welcome, therefore, [a condition] to which we must accommodate ourselves, great inequality. . . . It is a law, as certain as any of the others named, that men possessed of this peculiar talent for affairs, under the free play of economic forces, must of necessity, soon be in receipt of more revenue than can be judiciously expended upon themselves; and this law is . . . beneficial for the race. . . .
>
> Objections to the foundations upon which society is based are not in order.[1]

According to Carnegie, conscience need not be consulted at all; as a matter of fact, it probably does not even exist, and if it does, it is merely a vestige of an outdated system of folkways. For the rich of necessity (that is, by determinism) must get richer; and the poor must remain poor or rise on the coattails of the rich by the same necessity. Since everything (even the amassing of the Carnegie fortune) must happen by natural law, conscience—which operates only where there are alternatives of action—becomes a meaningless, if not a ridiculous, concept.

But the appeal of naturalism to business entrepreneurs is scarcely a suffcent cause for the wide approbation enjoyed by this outlook in democratic America. The question still remains, with what pervasive undercurrent in American life did this new outlook harmonize? No certain answer can be given. But the sympathetic chord that was struck might have had religion as a component. In the nineteenth century, America was overwhelmingly Protestant, and in Protestantism—whether Lutheran, Calvinistic, or even Anglican—the Augustinian strain of predestination is strong. Predestination is, of course, a form of determinism, for, as has been shown, it is the doctrine that teaches that men are chosen for salvation or damnation by the sovereign whim of God before the beginning of earthly time. The outcome of men's lives in this world is solely dependent on God; their volition is predetermined, as are their actions resulting from the will. Calvinism has gone through many modifications both in America and abroad, but fundamentally it subordinates man's will to that of God; it enhances the grandeur of God and diminishes the stature of man.

Man is dependent on God, say the Calvinists. Man is dependent on natural law, say the naturalists. The passage quoted in chapter 4 from Charles Sumner—in which he waxes lyrical in a description of puny man's helplessness in remedying and controlling his lot as he is driven along on the current of natural evolution—is highly Calvinistic in spirit. It is perhaps significant that Sumner, like Malthus, started life as a clergyman in the Anglican, or Episcopal, Church, whose articles of belief have unmistakable Calvinistic leanings. Let us again quote Article 10 ("Of Free-Will,") which assures the faithful that

> the condition of Man after the fall of Adam is such, that he cannot turn and prepare himself, by his natural strength and good works, to faith, and calling upon God. Wherefore we have no power to do good works pleasant and accept-able to God, without the Grace of God by Christ preventing [anticipating] us, that we may have a good will, and working with us, when we have that good will.[2]

But this is rather moderate Calvinism. To find an utterance more closely analogous to Sumner's unbending determinism, one only need turn to the sermons of the New England Puritans. Typical is a discourse, or Puritan sermon, on "The Sovereign Efficacy of Divine Providence" by Urian Oakes (1631–81), a minister at Cambridge, Massachusetts, and for several years president of Harvard College. The doctrine of Oakes's sermon is

> That the successes and events of undertakings and affairs are not determined infallibly by the greatest sufficiency of men or second causes, but by the counsel and provi-dence of God ordering and governing time and chance ac-cording to his own good pleasure.[3]

Oakes's thesis is interesting, because it deals with a matter central to evolution. His text is Ecclesiastes 9:1: "I returned, and saw under the sun that the race is not to the swift, nor the battle to the strong, neither yet bread to the wise, nor yet riches to men of understanding. . . ."[4] Evolution says, of course, that the race is to the strong. Oakes concurs to a degree: "For the Lord doth most ordinarily award success unto causes of greatest sufficiency rather than disappointment and defeat."[5] That is, the race is *usually* to the swift and the battle *usually* to the strong. But behind these human, or secondary, causes, such as swiftness and strength, is a primary cause, whose efficacy, to use Oakes's terms, is sovereign. "Thus no man hath the absolute command of the issue and success of his own undertakings."[6] In words as ecstatically gloomy as Sumner's, Oakes concludes that man is "a poor dependent, nothing-creature" unable to "move a step, or fetch his next breath . . . without help from God."[7]

The problem of the freedom of the will was as central to Puritan discussion as it was to that of the scientific determinists and their opponents in the nineteenth and twentieth centuries. The adversaries of the Puritans were the Arminians, so called after the Dutch anti-Calvinist theologian Arminius, who declared that man is capable of choosing whether or not to do good works, and upon this choice and the action resulting from it depends man's future state. In other words, man is in control of his own destiny to a very significant extent. The Arminians held somewhat the position of the humanists of our own day in that they emphasized man's capabilities rather than his disabilities.

The impact of Arminianism on the New England mind combined with the Calvinistic insistence on "endeavor" to make individual effort seem more and more important in God's scheme for human salvation. Cotton Mather's *Essays to Do Good*, so influential on Franklin, are evidence of this trend in that they taught the necessity of trying to lead a life not only of reverence for God but of helpfulness to one's fellow beings. Though the doctrine of election still survived as a cornerstone of Calvinistic theology, Presbyterian and Congregationalist ministers more and more preached self-effort. One should try to be converted—that is, to have faith in Christ—even though conversion is a matter of foreordination, entirely outside the control of the individual. One should seek sanctification, which also, as an outgrowth of conversion, is beyond the individual's unaided power of attaining. Striving toward these ends is, of course, in agreement with Calvin's own teaching; but, as Perry Miller has pointed out,[8] the mere act of trying became more and more identified with a state of grace. The struggle to become converted and the struggle to do good works became more and more the earmarks of the Christian life.

To the Calvinist, then, the naturalistic doctrine of struggle as the source of all value—the genetic improvement of the race, industrial and cultural progress, and the social and spiritual advance of man—would not be totally strange. A more or less rigid determinism with an area reserved for individual striving is the essence of each philosophy.

The Fusion of Election and Natural Selection

Election and natural selection thus have much in common. The doctrine of election tells us that God has chosen certain souls for salvation. Except that He wishes to show a modicum of leniency toward the human race despite its disobedience in the Garden of Eden, there is no reason why God does this. There is no accounting for the basis of His choice—his rejection of some and His acceptance of others. Natural selection, a characteristic doctrine of naturalism, teaches that nature (or God, or the Unknowable, through nature) has endowed certain individuals of a species with certain traits which ensure their advancement over their fellows and their survival in this life. Nature's reason for so endowing some and not others is as inscrutable as is God's sovereign whim in electing certain souls to salvation. One may object that natural selection is for survival in this life, while election is for survival in the next life. But this objection is only partly valid. Natural selection entails an immortality of sorts in that the seed of the survivor will carry on his superior traits and thus perpetuate his bloodline. And, according to the Calvinist view, the elected saint, because of the favor he enjoys with God, will probably flourish in this life (although Calvin himself was careful to

stipulate that worldly prosperity is not necessarily a concomitant of regeneration).

Far from being mutually exclusive, then, orthodox Calvinism and orthodox Darwinism tend almost to fortify one
another. The Darwinian, indeed almost any naturalist, says,
"The fittest will flourish on this earth. He cannot help flourish-
ing. It is natural law that he flourish." In Sumner's words,
"The law of survival of the fittest was not made by man and
cannot be abrogated by man."[9] The Calvinist, on the other
hand, says, "The saints, the elect, will persevere." Edwards
states the case forcibly and succinctly:

> If the beginning of true faith and holiness, and man's be-
> coming a true saint at first, don't depend on the self-
> determining power of the will, but on the determining
> efficacious grace of God; it may well be argued, that it is
> so also with respect to men's being continued saints, or
> persevering in faith and holiness. . . . It is absolutely fixed
> in God's decree, that all true saints shall persevere to actual
> eternal salvation.[10]

To be one of the elect and to be one of the naturally selected
are thus rather comparable states of bliss. One advantage that
the "fittest" enjoys over the "saint", however, is a firm certainty of his favored status. If he is winning in the battle of
life, amassing a fortune, wielding great influence, and evincing
great creativity, he can be reasonably certain that nature has
placed him in the vanguard of progress of the human species.
Wealth will continue to flow into his coffers; his power will
grow.

The Calvinist can never be quite so certain of his standing
with God as the Darwinian can be in regard to his place in
nature. Yet wealth, like all other things, comes from God. The
man who succeeds in accumulating wealth may fairly safely
assume that he is in God's special favor—that, indeed, he may
well be one of the elect. But whether or not the Calvinist takes
his personal prosperity as a sign of election—and there were

many who did—there can be no doubt concerning the ultimate source of his wealth. Cotton Mather writes:

> Sirs, you cannot but acknowledge, that it is the sovereign God, who has bestowed upon you the *riches* which distinguish you. A *devil* himself, when he saw a *rich* man, could not but make this acknowledgment unto the God of heaven: "Thou hast blessed the work of his hands, and his substance is increased in the land."[11]

Elsewhere Mather quotes Deuteronomy 8:18: "Thou shalt remember the Lord thy God; for it is he that gives thee Power to get wealth." Mather delimits rather graphically the function of mere human effort or will in the acquisition of riches: "In our *Occupation* we spread our *Nets*; but it is God who brings into our *Nets* all that comes into them."[12]

The Calvinist, of course, sees the same hand of providence behind all successful living, not solely in the winning of wealth. John Cotton in a seventeenth-century sermon entitled "Christian Calling" points out that "faith draws the heart of a Christian to live in some warrantable calling."[13] The choice of calling should not be a matter of whim; it should be determined by what the individual conceives to be God's providence for himself or herself. Has providence endowed the individual with talents suitable for a particular occupation? Does a person feel providence "leading him [*sic*] to it"?[14] Is the choice of the calling based on selfish desires or on the desire to do God's work? Once the choice has been made, one must depend further on "God for the quickening and sharpening of his [*sic*] gifts in that calling,"[15] not upon one's own efforts. Nor should one fear any dangers arising in the pursuit of one's calling; if God has destined one for this occupation, God will see one through. Naturally, any success one achieves must be attributed solely to God. In no stage, either in the choice or in the doing of one's life's work, is one on one's own. One is merely acting out God's will.

Responsibilities of the Elect and of the Fittest

Basic to these concepts is the idea of stewardship, and it is just as basic in Darwinian naturalism as in Calvinism. In each, the successful person is serving something larger than himself or herself—either God, or nature, or the species—and has been specially endowed and inexorably led into this function. "The problem of our age," writes Andrew Carnegie in the *North American Review* of June, 1889, "is the proper administration of wealth, so that the ties of brotherhood may still bind together the rich and poor in harmonious relationship."[16] He goes on to deplore the hoarding of huge sums with no regard to their possible usefulness to the community. The superior individual gets rich through "the Law of Accumulation of Wealth, and the Law of Competition."[17] Actually, the rich cannot avoid getting rich; it is the result of nature's fiat. But nature favors the race more than the individual. She works through the individual for the betterment of the race, and the individual must act accordingly. Similarly, among the Puritans John Cotton warns that we must "not only aim at our own, but at the public good."[18] And Cotton Mather recommends "some *Settled Business*, wherein a Christian should for the most part spend most of his [*sic*] time and this, that so, he may glorify God, by doing of *Good* for *others* and getting of *Good* for *himself*."[19]

The view among religious persons that God's chosen ones will prosper and thus help fulfill God's plans for mankind was not confined to Puritan times. It exists in Protestant thinking down to the present, though frequently its statement is mingled with Darwinian terms—another indication that Calvinistic Protestantism and naturalism are in harmony in some of their outlooks. A notorious example of the fusion of the two doctrines is an article by the Episcopalian Bishop William Lawrence. In "The Relation of Wealth to Morals," written in January 1901, Lawrence quotes Emerson's statement that man is "born to be rich."[20] The bishop seems as fond of finding natural laws as the most confirmed Spencerian. Dismissing the Bible with the assurance that it actually does not categorically condemn riches, he asserts that "man draws to himself material wealth as surely, as naturally, and as necessarily as the oak draws the elements into itself from the earth."[21] The words "naturally" and "necessarily" imply a determinism as rigid as that of that other Episcopalian clergyman, William Sumner. Lawrence's argument continues in naturalistic terms. Those "who seek for and earn wealth" are of a "natural, vigorous, and strong character."[22] As firmly as Dreiser and more firmly than Urian Oakes he believes the race is to the spiritually strong. "Godliness is in league with riches."[23] Lawrence continues:

> Put two men in adjoining fields, one man strong and normal, the other weak and listless. One picks up his spade, turns over the earth, and works till sunset. The other turns over a few clods, gets a drink from the spring, takes a nap, and loafs back to his work. In a few years one will be rich for his needs, and the other a pauper dependent on the first, and growling at his prosperity.[24]

Strength and normality, the two attributes of the successful person, according to Bishop Lawrence, are synonymous with morality—an idea quite divergent from unchristianized Darwinism. Yet in other respects the bishop's viewpoint is in accord both with social Darwinism and with Calvinism. Why are certain individuals strong, normal, and hence moral, whereas others are weak, abnormal, lazy, and hence immoral? Whether the difference is accounted for by God's election or nature's selection matters little, nor is the bishop ever clear as to what he thinks on the point. At any rate, there is no question in his mind as to the usefulness of these strong, moral individuals to God and to society.

I have in mind now a man of wealth . . . who lives handsomely and entertains; he has everything that purveys to his health and comfort. All these things are tributary to what? To the man's efficiency in his complete devotion to the social, educational, and charitable interests to which he gives his life. He is Christ's as much as was St. Paul, he is consecrated as was St. Francis of Assisi; and in recognition of the bounty with which God has blessed him he does not sell all that he has, but he uses all that he has, and, as he believes, in the wisest way, for the relief of the poor, the upbuilding of social standards.[25]

Sumner, of course, and the other Spencerians would be unenthusiastic about helping the poor; that would be tampering with the law of the survival of the fittest. Yet in the main, Bishop Lawrence and the Spencerians would be in agreement: certain persons are so endowed temperamentally that they will almost automatically accumulate wealth, and in this fact lies an immense benefit for the race of men. As for the masses not so endowed, they must submit. Grumbling against the divine or natural order is irrational or sacrilegious or both.

Thus Andrew Carnegie, among the devoutest of Spencerians, writes: "The millionaire will be but a trustee for the poor; intrusted for a season with a great part of the increased wealth of the community, but administering it for the community far better than it could or would have done for itself."[26] This is a part of Nature's "fearful symmetry." There are weak and strong, poor and wealthy; the two exist but to serve each other. Inequalities among people, the stratification of classes, are but nature's way—or God's way, if like the Puritans or like the medieval churchmen one believes that nature—to use Chaucer's words—is the vicar general of God:

> For he that is the former principal
> Hath maked me [Nature] his vicaire general. . . .
> My lord and I ben ful of oon accord.
> > "Physician's Tale," lines 19–25.

The same principle applies to political as well as to financial and industrial leaders. Governor Winthrop of Massachusetts Bay Colony used to warn his fellow citizens that once they chose their magistrates they were bound to obey them, for the magistrates' authority came directly from God, who ordained some to obey and some to rule. That the rulers supposed themselves to be of the elect, and hence peculiarly suited to rule, is obvious. As the chosen of God, they ruled according to God's revealed word—indeed it was a theocracy. The people's electing the rulers was merely God's manner of putting them in power.

The idea was a favorite one among early New England Calvinists. William Hubbard, minister at Ipswich, makes the point very clear in an election sermon of 1676:

> And hath not the same Almighty Creator and Disposer of all things made some of the sons of man as far differing in height of body one from the other, as Saul from the rest of the people? And are not some advanced as high above others in dignity and power as much as the cedars of Lebanon the low shrubs of the valley? It is not then the result of time or chance that some are mounted on horseback while others are left to travel on foot, that some have with the Centurion power to command while others are required to obey. . . . And herein hath [God] as well consulted the good of human nature as the glory of His own wisdom and power, those of the superior rank but making a supply of what is wanting in the other. . . . Is it not found by experience that the greatest part of mankind are but as tools and instruments for others to work by, rather than any proper agents to effect anything of themselves?[27]

The same note is sounded during a coal strike in 1902 by the railroad president, George F. Baer: "The rights and interests of the laboring man will be protected and cared for, not by the labor agitators, but by the Christian men to whom God in His infinite wisdom, has given control of the property interests of the country."[28]

Religious Fervor of the Social Darwinists

The Calvinistic and the naturalistic attitudes toward the achievement of success do, indeed, seem almost interchangeable. Both remove ultimate responsibility for success from the individual and thus exonerate him or her from the primary responsibility for the less fortunate lots of others. All that is asked by both Calvinist and Darwinist is that those slated for leadership bear in mind that they serve a larger function than the stuffing of their own pocketbooks—though this latter is a legitimate part of their ordained role. They must recognize their favored place in the divine or natural order, accept it with some humility, and act accordingly. To some, Darwinism was simply contributory to their own Protestant Christianity; such were Bishop Lawrence and Henry Ward Beecher. To others, Darwinism, especially as interpreted by Spencer, was a religion in itself, to which one could be converted with all the enthusiasm and emotion with which one would turn to Christ. Thus Carnegie writes of his own embracing of Darwinian doctrine:

> I remember that light came as in a flood and all was clear. Not only had I got rid of theology and the supernatural, but I had found the truth of evolution. "All is well since all grows better," became my motto, my true source of comfort. Man was not created with an instinct for his own degradation, but from the lower he had risen to the higher forms. . . . Humanity is an organism, inherently rejecting all that is deleterious . . . and absorbing after trial what is beneficial.[29]

To Carnegie, evolution was the law of the survival of the fittest. Many people have not found this to be a beautiful doctrine; in fact, to many sensitive minds it has seemed brutal and disheartening. Similarly, the Calvinist doctrine of election has been repugnant to many persons endowed with compassion and a sense of justice. Conversion to either of these beliefs must be an emotional experience strong enough to override very compelling objections of the heart and the head. Carnegie's emotions upon espousing the evolutionary faith are exactly paralleled in Edwards's feelings, at the time of his conversion, in regard to the doctrine of election:

> It used to appear like a horrible doctrine to me. But I remember the time very well, when I seemed to be convinced, and fully satisfied, as to this sovereignty of God, and his justice in thus eternally disposing of men, according to his sovereign pleasure. But [I] never could give an account, how, or by what means, I was thus convinced. . . . The doctrine [since then] has often appeared exceedingly pleasant, bright, and sweet. Absolute sovereignty is what I love to ascribe to God. But my first conviction was not so.[30]

America as a Destined Nation

Carnegie's faith in the inevitability of progress—"All is well since all grows better"—suggests another common ground shared by social Darwinism and early American Calvinism. Though Carnegie doubtless felt that the tendency for all to grow better was worldwide, he took the United States as the bellwether of progress, as indeed did many other Americans of the nineteenth century. Walt Whitman, himself strongly influenced by evolutionary thought, stated the case as well as any one:

> As the greatest lessons of Nature through the universe are perhaps the lessons of variety and freedom, the same present the greatest lessons also in New World politics and progress. . . . America, filling the present with greatest deeds and problems, cheerfully accepting the past, including feudalism . . . counts, as I reckon, for her justification and success, (for who, as yet, dare claim success?) almost entirely on the future.[31]

Whitman felt that the United States had already advanced through two of the stages necessary to its development into a superlative culture: these were the establishment of sound and just institutions of government and the accumulation of vast material wealth. The third and most important stage would be a spiritual flowering which would utilize to the utmost the opportunities provided by the first two stages.

Whitman was, actually, something of a determinist. To be sure, in *Democratic Vistas* he does not rule out the possibility of America's faltering; success was far from certain. Yet in other places—especially in his poems—Whitman envisaged America's triumphant destiny as inevitable:

> I assert that all past days were what they must have been,
> And that they could no-how have been better than they
> were,
> And that to-day is what it must be, and that America is,
> And that to-day and America could no-how be better
> than they are.[32]

The present, thus, is the sum of the past and contains in itself the seeds of an inevitable future. A melioristic evolution is a certainty—

> (As a projectile form'd, impell'd, passing a certain line,
> still keeps on,
> So the present, utterly form'd, impell'd by the past.)[33]

As will be seen with Emerson, the type of monism that Whitman espoused leads unavoidably into some sort of determinism. Usually with Whitman it is a beneficent determinism, but at times it is fraught with gloom—for example, in "As I Ebb'd with the Ocean of Life," in which he compares human lives to the debris cast up by the sea of eternity at the feet of God.

> We, capricious, brought hither we know not whence,
>   spread out before you,
> You up there walking or sitting,
> Whoever you are, we too lie in drifts at your feet.[34]

In any event, to Whitman man's will, insofar as it exists sep-
arately, is a reflection of something far vaster than the individual, an expression of "occult deep volitions"[35] that flow
through and motivate all humanity.

Others in addition to Whitman saw the same bright future
for America or all of Anglo-Saxondom as the almost certain
goal of evolution on an international scale (not the least of
these optimists being Theodore Roosevelt). Here again history
and evolution were deemed to be on America's side; one
need only flow along with the natural course of events and
America's dominance would be assured. These happy auguries
were reminiscent of the utterances of the early settlers in New
England. Calvin had written that nations, just as individuals,
may be elected by God to fulfill His great designs. In sermons
and histories and tracts by the early Puritans this theme
is harped on: New England was under a special providence;
she had been singled out by the Almighty to be a light to
all people—a city on a hill, a New Jerusalem. As a single example from myriads of others, one may read the statement by
William Stoughton in an election sermon delivered in 1668:

> This we must know, that the Lord's promises and expec-
> tations of great things have singled out New England, and
> all sorts and ranks of men among us, above any nation or
> people in the world. . . . Whom hath the Lord more signally
> exalted than His people in the wilderness?[36]

For nations to feel themselves under the particular destiny
of God is, of course, not unusual in world history. Vergil's
Aeneid deals with the manifest destiny of Rome; and the Fates
(the Roman form of determinism) play no small part in the
matter—in fact, they make Rome's supremacy inevitable. The

nineteenth and twentieth centuries have their doctrines of the White Man's Burden, Aryanism, Pan-Slavism, and Zionism. For nations to feel themselves directed by a destiny is commonplace, especially in recent times.

In America the switch from Calvinistic to Darwinistic determinism in the affairs of nations was so painless as to go unnoticed. Even Whitman, certainly no Calvinist, employed Calvinist terminology when in *Democratic Vistas* he referred to America's *justification*, which signifies the divine forgiveness and freeing from the consequences of guilt as promised in the Covenant of Grace. When Whitman coupled justification with "success,"[37] he was making a conjunction inevitable in both Calvinistic and Darwinistic logic.

6

Four Deterministic Novelists

It is evident that in all the naturalistic thinkers discussed in the previous chapter determinism looms prominently. To a greater or lesser extent, each envisages man and his society as being in the clutch of natural forces, both interior and exterior to the human organism, over which at best only a limited control is possible. So much a part of naturalism is determinism that the two terms are almost synonymous, as will become amply clear in the following examination of four American deterministic novelists.

The first major literary expression of naturalism in America occurred in a group of novelists—Stephen Crane, Frank Norris, and Jack London—writing about the turn of the century, when the tide of scientific naturalism was at its highest. None of these three novelists, as naturalists, attained the stature of Theodore Dreiser, who began his career slightly later, but a consideration of their work is useful as an introduction to Dreiser's more voluminous and, on the whole, more thoughtful output.

Stephen Crane

Some will object to the placing of Crane in a position equal to Dreiser's, but it is only as a naturalist that he is so placed here; beyond a doubt, Crane is the more skillful artist of the two. At any rate, Crane's *Maggie: a Girl of the Streets* is the first self-consciously naturalistic piece of extended fiction in American literature. A student of the sciences, a reader of Zola, and above all a close observer of city life, Crane incorporated into his novel so many departures from convention that the indignant public refused to buy or read it. The language in the dialogue was coarse, the male characters were mainly bums, the heroine was a prostitute, and, perhaps most shocking in the era that produced *Little Lord Fauntleroy* and *Little Women*, the children were presented as little demons rather than little angels. An example is this passage from *Maggie:* " 'Naw,' responded Jimmie with a valiant roar, 'dese mugs can't make me run.' "[1]

Maggie is primarily a study of the deterministic effects of environment, as Crane himself stated in an inscription in a first edition copy.[2] Maggie is a victim of the slums, which drive her first to prostitution and finally to suicide in the East River. A flower blossoming in a mud puddle, as Crane puts it, she is surrounded not only by the sordidness of the Bowery but by drunkenness and brutality in her home. She flowers but soon withers and dies. But the Bowery is more than merely a mud puddle, a place of filth and dilapidation. It is a true Darwinian jungle, a seedbed for throwback traits, or atavisms. Scattered liberally throughout the book are street fights and barroom brawls, staples of the naturalistic novel down to the present day.

The naturalistic elements in *The Red Badge of Courage* are too well known to need discussion. War is, of course, a favorite topic of naturalists because it brings out the "jungle" instincts of man, supplants personal will and choice with the rigidity of army discipline, and subjugates the reason to the emotions of fear and hate. The "Youth" who is the hero of the novel is enclosed in the "moving box"[3] of his regiment and succumbs alternately to the "throat-grappling instinct"[4] and the instinct of self-preservation.

In Crane's short stories the same instinctual and environmental forces propel the characters along undesired courses.

The most powerful of all the stories, although it lacks the drama of "The Blue Hotel" or of "The Open Boat," is "An Experiment in Misery," in which environmental determinism—the most interesting to Crane—works weirdly upon a reporter who has dressed himself as a derelict and gone to live in the Bowery for twenty-four hours to collect material for an article. At the end of the "experiment" the reporter, who has lived the Bowery life too fully, finds himself on a bench in City Hall Park unable to muster the energy to go back to his flat and divest himself of his derelict's attire. Twenty-four hours of living like a derelict have clamped upon him the outlook, the inertia, and the will-lessness of a derelict.

Frank Norris

Contemporary with Crane and more doctrinaire as a naturalist is Frank Norris, an admirer of Zola and at least a casual student of the economic and biological theories of the day. A lesser artist than Crane, his style suffers from a bombast that makes the outpourings of Thomas Wolfe seem restrained. Worse, his tone frequently lapses into bathos and melodrama.

Among novels that have received serious attention from students of American literature, Norris's early opus *McTeague* is doubtless one of the most overwritten, unconvincing, and unintentionally laughable. Yet the book is an interesting showcase of naturalistic attitudes and conventions. McTeague, a moronic dentist with the strength of an elephant, is a walking—or lumbering—embodiment of every atavistic trait a Darwinian could think up, even including a fantastic, animal-like "sixth-sense" that enables the brainless protagonist to *feel* the presence of danger miles away. The reader is escorted through scenes of lust, fighting (including the inevitable barroom brawl), murder, and pursuit. The spectacle of McTeague, in flight from the sheriff, sniffing the mountain air like a moose and sensing the presence of the posse in the next county is surpassed in silliness only by the final scene in which McTeague is left to die in Death Valley handcuffed to the corpse of his captor, whom he slew at the moment of his arrest. The question of free will or free choice hardly arises in *McTeague*. Virtually without reasoning ability, McTeague functions entirely on the level of instinct. He exerts no intelligent control over his actions.

Much stronger because more controlled are *The Pit* and *The Octopus*, the two books of a projected trilogy on the production, distribution, and consumption of wheat—a project that death prevented Norris from completing. The theme of the novels is a deterministic one: the natural law of supply and demand is stronger than the efforts of any one individual or corporation that may attempt to tamper with it for private motives. In the case of wheat, those who place obstacles in the way of its production and its distribution to the hungry masses of the world are toying with their own destruction. Thus, in *The Octopus* a would-be impeder of the normal flow of the commodity is buried alive beneath the Niagara of grain flowing from an elevator into the hold of a ship bound for the famine-stricken Orient. His death symbolizes the futility of the efforts of railroad companies and speculators to divert the natural flow of foodstuffs for their own selfish ends. Norris envisages man and nature working in an ironbound partnership. Responding to the labors of the ranchers, the wheatfields burst forth in a nourishing growth that Norris describes in the ecstatic words of a mystic. This gift of the soil then proceeds on its way to the hungry masses of Europe and Asia, and woe to anyone who willfully stands in its way.

In *The Pit* the meddling with natural law actually has the unintended result of stimulating the operation of the law. The financier Curtis Jadwin attempts to corner the world wheat market on the Chicago Board of Trade, "the Pit." After a near success he is ultimately ruined. Had he succeeded, the supply of wheat in the world markets would have been seriously curtailed. But Jadwin's manipulations have the effect only of increasing the supply of wheat by providing the farmers with a price incentive to plant more and more. Jadwin's frantic buying of futures has created a demand that the soil and the farmers are all too ready not only to meet but to exceed. The resulting surfeit ruins Jadwin. Economic law is too big for any one man to handle; Jadwin has been only a tool in the economic process.

Jadwin, however, is a man of great strength, a Darwinian sport, a superman. His shrewdness, his energy, and his vaulting ambition make him a crushing force on the Board of Trade. Norris exploits the obvious metaphor of the bears and the bulls grappling in the Pit; jungle law, atavism, survival of the fittest—the whole panoply of naturalism is there with banners flying. Many a small investor and many a small—and large—speculator is ruined as the forces fight to the finish. Jadwin—a type to be limelighted later, and more convincingly, by Dreiser—is presented as a man of destiny, a Napoleon of finance. He commands a slavishly faithful following of lesser men; he fascinates the most desirable women. He possesses, like McTeague, a special sixth sense that warns and prompts him as he battles his way through the brawling Pit. But mighty and ruthless as the man is, we are informed that he has been all along in the clutches of a power far greater than the human will.

"You think I am willfully doing this!" he cries to his wife. "You don't know, you haven't a guess. I corner the wheat! Great heavens, it is the wheat that has cornered me!. . .I happened to stand between two sets of circumstances, and they have made me do what I've done."[5] Indeed, all along Jadwin has felt himself to be fated to engage in mighty projects; he has sensed an inevitable destiny awaiting him. Norris makes it very clear that Jadwin's powers of choice had nothing to do with his launching an assault upon the wheat market. To be sure, he exerted superhuman efforts of will in his attempts, but not only was the will frustrated but it had been planted in him by apparently external natural agencies.

The fact is that no one in *The Pit* is master of his own fate, even to the smallest degree. The big and the small are swept along on the flood of wheat. The entire natural order, which to Norris includes human society, is geared to just one purpose: the production and distribution of grain. Individual whims and ambitions count for nothing. In this process Norris sees high romance. Indeed, he is one of the few naturalists to admit that naturalism is a romantic outlook rather than a realistic one. The book opens with Jadwin and others attending an Italian opera in Chicago—a ludicrous and jejune entertainment, as described by Norris. But upon leaving the opera, these men and women see before them the gigantic monolith of the Board of Trade Building looming out of the mist that enshrouds the city, and to the more sensitive of them this grim edifice, rather than the silly posturings of the opera singers, becomes associated with romance. Norris is perhaps unique among writers of prose and poetry in being able to discern in the economic law of supply and demand subjects for lyric outbreaks:

> And all the while above the din upon the floor, above the tramplings and the shoutings in the Pit, there seemed to thrill and swell that appalling roar of the Wheat itself coming in, coming on like a tidal wave, bursting through, dashing barriers aside, rolling like a measureless, almighty river, from the farms of Iowa and the ranches of California, on to the East—to the bakeshops and hungry mouths of Europe.[6]

Jack London

Jack London also became obsessed with the idea of the superman—or superorganism, for he deals with animals as well as with men. In fact, as has been the case with so many naturalists from Crane to Steinbeck, London found the demarcation between animals and human beings to be far from clear. The epitome of London's thinking about evolution is contained in *The Call of the Wild,* the popularity of which from the time of its publication in the *Saturday Evening Post* attests to the acceptability of its theme if not to its literary merit. For there never was a story more fraught with theme, albeit an obvious and perhaps ridiculous one. *The Call of the Wild* is, indeed, allegory. A domesticated dog with all the debilities attributable to civilization finds himself, by a series of unlikely circumstances, a member of a dog team in the Yukon. As with men who take to the wilderness, the dog promptly sloughs off his civilization and becomes a fierce fighter, a veritable wolf—in short, a perfect demonstration of atavism. The coating of domesticity is a mere film; beneath it lurks the savage beast.

As the story progresses, another Darwinian assumption is demonstrated: the dog not only goes native but proves himself to be a specimen of uncommon strength, courage, and sagacity. The law of the survival of the fittest is now seen in action as this extraordinary beast takes over the leadership of the sled team and finally, when cut off completely from human influence, he heads up a wolf pack and is last heard howling through the Arctic night, a canine terror of the Northwest. In the motif of leadership is apparent also a degradation of the philosophy of Nietzsche, which was a favorite of London's though never fully digested by him. A superdog has taken control of a team of commonplace dogs and a pack of wolves. The destiny of the superior being has been fulfilled. Needless to say, there is no question of free will or choice in all this. The better animal instinctively fights his way to the head of the pack. He does so as inevitably as the seasons change or the rain falls.

It is only a very short step from the dog-story of *The Call of the Wild* to the man-story in *The Sea-Wolf.* As his very name implies, Wolf Larsen, skipper of the sealing schooner *Ghost,* is himself a beast in human shape. As the dog rules his pack with his fangs, Larsen rules his crew with his fists. According to Larsen himself, he possesses the potential for a bigger role.

But his *destiny* is otherwise. He confides to Van Weyden, the center of intelligence in the book, "No man makes opportunity. All the great men ever did was to know it when it came to them. The Corsican knew. . . .I should have known the opportunity, but it never came. The thorns sprung up and choked me."[7] To this extent Larsen is the victim of an unfriendly fate. But he has actually come quite far in the world as a result of what seem to be his own efforts. Born of illiterate "peasants of the sea" in Norway, he has made his way to the captaincy of the sealing schooner and he has acquired an education of sorts entirely on his own. Among the books shelved in his cabin are volumes by Shakespeare, Tennyson, Poe, De Quincy, and, more significantly, by Tyndall, Proctor, and Darwin.

His views on life are drawn from his reading in the natural and social sciences. He states:

> I believe that life is a mess. . . .It is like a yeast, a ferment, a thing that moves and may move for a minute, an hour, a year, or a hundred years, but that in the end will cease to move. . . .The strong eat the weak that they may retain their strength. The lucky eat the most and move the longest, that is all.[8]

The question of moral responsibility, of course, never enters into Larsen's reasoning. So outside the world of conventional ethics is he that Van Weyden is prompted to explain: "He was a magnificent atavism, a man so purely primitive that he was of the type that came into the world before the development of the moral nature. He was not immoral, but merely unmoral."[9] Thus Larsen is essentially only a very remarkable animal, an especially complicated bundle of biochemistry; and as such he may be considered subject to a determinism that unfolds his character and controls his actions, just as he is subject to the whims of fate that deny him a larger theater in which to function. His paralysis and eventual death from brain cancer are entirely in accord with the logic of the book.

Wolf Larsen, the amoral blond beast preying upon the weak who exist only so that the strong may put them to use, is again a vulgarized embodiment of the Nietzschean superman. *Martin Eden*, published in 1909 (five years after *The Sea-Wolf*), shows an even stronger influence from Nietzsche. In the course of the book, Martin, who is in part London's self-portrait, emerges as a literary artist and hence a person gifted far beyond the general run of humanity. Martin himself makes it very clear that he does not consider his talent, or genius, to be of his own making. Before the beauty and power of his compositions, "he bowed down and marvelled, knowing that they were beyond the deliberate creation of any man,"[10]— a posture ironically like that of the Calvinist giving God the credit for his good fortune. Alluding to Spencer, Martin is forced to regard himself as "but a bit of the. . . .nonunderstandable fabric, twisted of sunshine and star-dust and wonder."[11] In fact, throughout this book Martin expresses gratitude to Spencer, who has provided him with the "masterkey of life, evolution. . . ."[12] Thanks to Nietzsche and Spencer, indeed, Martin can say of himself that he is one of the few individualists in Oakland. Attending a meeting of socialists, he launches into a violent attack on their philosophy:

> As for me, I am an inveterate opponent of socialism just as I am an inveterate opponent of your own mongrel democracy. . . .I am the only individualist in this room. I look to the state for nothing. I look only to the strong man, the man on horseback, to save the state from its own rotten futility. . . .Nietzsche was right. . . .The world belongs to the strong. . . .to the great blond beasts, to the noncompromisers, to the "yes-sayers." And they will eat you up, you socialists who are afraid of socialism and who think yourselves individualists. Your slave-morality of the meek and lowly will never save you.[13]

How this "individualism" squares with London's later espousal of socialism need not concern us here. The important point is that Martin, like the dog Buck and like Wolf Larsen, is one of nature's sports, a fulfillment of nature's inscrutable purpose, of which his will is the tool. This will is, basically, the will to live—to live life in its fullest and most intense form. It blazes up in Martin's marvelous outbursts of creativity and in his love for a woman. But a time of satiety comes. He loses his will for life, and in its place arises a will for death, which is but feebly combatted by the instinct of self-preservation. In its clutches Martin sails forth into the Pacific, and one night he leaps overboard, endowed now with a "will strong enough that with one last exertion it could destroy itself and cease to be."[14] Whence came this will, as inexplicable as his former will to create? Is it, as with Kirilov in Dostoevski's *The Possessed*, an ultimate assertion of the same volitions that set him apart from the rest of humanity as a creative artist? Was it a final assertion of ego, establishing itself on a footing even with God, who can give and take away life? London gives no definite answer, but he succeeds in making us feel a logic in Martin's switch from life to death—an unanswerable determinism directing him in either case. As he sinks towards the bottom of the Pacific, Martin hopes that the sharks may not strike him too savagely, for the pain might make him struggle to survive—and this he does not desire. But the sharks are kind to him; they strike only once, and with unwavering will Martin plummets out of the world.

Theodore Dreiser

Of all American literary naturalists, Theodore Dreiser is doubtless the most complex, the most thoughtful, and the most influential. In his writings are exhibited all of the major themes and techniques of the naturalist school. Dreiser's naturalism had its inevitable roots in the nineteenth-century scientists—Darwin, Huxley, and Haeckel. His reading of Spencer's *First Principles* crystalized his views: man is subject to the same natural laws as the rest of the organic and inorganic universe. Man's actions in given circumstances may be predicted with accuracy in accordance with those laws. Moral responsibility goes out the window because freedom of choice between good and evil does not exist, and, in fact, the distinction between good and evil has to be discarded. One must study and accept things as they are without making value judgments upon them—at least in terms of anything resembling the Judaeo-Christian system of ethics. All that is permitted us is the famous Dreiserian pity for the ineffective, broken-down machine that the average human being is or becomes. That there is an Unknown Cause for all that happens and exists in the universe—an author of natural laws—Dreiser is willing to concede, along with Spencer. But the very Unknowability of this Cause makes it more or less irrelevant. We may hope to know the Unknowable's laws, which are pretty much all that concern us, but we cannot and need not know the Unknowable Itself.

A vast amount of commentary, much of it of great merit, has been written on Dreiser, who has rightly been taken as the spokesman of a major group of writers—including Crane, Norris, London, and Upton Sinclair, and not excluding Hemingway, Steinbeck and even Faulkner. All that will be done here is to take a reasonably close look at his attitudes towards the human will and its freedom or bondage as expressed in several of his many books.

Sister Carrie

The question of the degree of moral responsibility possessed by man is central to Dreiser's first novel, *Sister Carrie* (1900), as it is to most of his others. Never loath to resort to author's commentary, he has devoted pages to direct discussion of the problem in *Sister Carrie*.

Among the forces which sweep and play throughout the universe, untutored man is but a wisp in the wind. Our civilisation is still in the middle stage, scarcely beast, in that it is no longer wholly guided by instinct; scarcely human, in that it is not yet wholly guided by reason. On the tiger no responsibility rests. We see him aligned by nature with the forces of life—he is born into their keeping and without thought he is protected. We see man far removed from the lairs of the jungles, his innate instincts dulled by too near an approach to free-will, his free-will not sufficiently developed to replace his instincts and afford him perfect guidance. . . .In this intermediate stage he wavers—neither drawn in harmony with nature by his instincts nor yet wisely putting himself into harmony by his free-will. He is even as a wisp in the wind, moved by every breath of passion, acting now by his will and now by his instincts. . . .We have the consolation of knowing that evolution is ever in action.[15]

No one can be wholly a determinist or wholly a libertarian, of course. In this passage Dreiser allows for a modicum of "free-will," which may increase, he believes, through the evolutionary process; for even the archpessimist Dreiser is occasionally touched by nineteenth-century optimism. In the actual presentation of his characters in action, however, he is a more thoroughgoing determinist than the passage just quoted would indicate. To begin with, in *Sister Carrie*—as in other novels, notably *An American Tragedy*—Dreiser musters a cast of characters chosen deliberately for their commonplace education and ability. This intentional focusing upon the dull general average is in the spirit of the naturalistic school, which pretended to deal with life as it is. An excellent earlier example is Crane's *Red Badge of Courage*, an epic of the common private soldier. Since mediocrity is the lot of most mankind, the naturalist must concern himself with mediocrity, though not to the exclusion of the minority made up of evolutionary sports or superior specimens of the race —with whom, as shown above, Norris and London dealt and whom Dreiser treats in a number of novels.

Sister Carrie herself, then, is a very average young woman

from slightly lower than the middle ranks of society. She has, to be sure, several somewhat distinctive qualities, as might be expected of any average person. Carrie is prettier than most, she has a modest flair for acting (for even rather stupid persons can be good mimics), and she is a bit heavily endowed with a directionless ambition. But her decisions, her choices, and her major acts are sparked by instinct rather than by anything resembling free will. With the love of animal similes that naturalists from Zola to Steinbeck revel in, Dreiser compares Carrie both to a sheep and to a chipmunk in the same paragraph. Like these unintellectual creatures, she is equipped with an instinct of self-preservation that guides her through the dangers with which a young and single girl from the country must cope in Chicago.

This basic instinct is, in fact, Carrie's guide throughout her life. When winter approaches, she goes to live with Drouet, for, like all animals, she must make provision for the long season of deprivation. Dreiser implies that in early summer she would not have succumbed to Drouet. When a more dominant, wealthier male—Hurstwood—comes on the scene, Carrie allows herself to be appropriated by him, for he has more security to offer. Later, when Hurstwood ceases to be reliable, she deserts him. That she is never satisfied—that she is always longing for some indefinite fulfillment in the future, as she sits in her famous rocking chair by the window—is nothing more than the evolutionary restlessness of the species, an impulse that sporadically prods the race toward some ill-defined goal. It is a querulous discontent, totally normal, in no way reflecting an iota of superiority in Carrie's abilities or character.

The element of free will—rational choice or decision—is virtually nonexistent in Carrie. So it is also in the other major characters in the novel. The salesman Drouet is dominated by his itch for copulation; he uses, and is used by, Carrie to their mutual advantage. Carrie's sister and brother-in-law are crushed by the drudgery of mere survival in the slums of Chicago. But more than any other character, even more than Carrie, Hurstwood is the puppet of inner and outer forces beyond his ken and hence beyond his control. To many readers, Hurstwood is the most convincing person in the book. His plausibility is in part the result of the success with which Dreiser has shown him performing the most critical action of his life—the theft of his employers' money from a safe that has been accidentally left open.

Dreiser's most effective writing, in fact, is in scenes in which he translates into crucial action the tenets of his deterministic philosophy. In Hurstwood the motivation, most of it unconscious, has been carefully prepared over many preceding pages. Hurstwood, still in the prime of his life, has been rejected by a termagant wife; he is frustrated sexually and is emotionally starved at home. In Dreiser's thinking, the sexual instinct is among the most uncontrollable; thus Hurstwood's meeting with the attractive Carrie can have only one result, an overwhelming impulse to possess her. But Hurstwood lacks the money necessary to establish himself with Carrie, since his wife has put herself in control of his assets. Furthermore, Hurstwood's moderate drinking on the night of his crime clouds what little perception of right and wrong—or of prudent and imprudent, from the point of view of self-survival—that he ever commanded. The ingredients— lust, monetary need, and alcohol—have now been set up for one of Dreiser's "chemisms." Hurstwood is about to react with the same will-lessness and inevitability with which, under prescribed conditions, oxygen and hydrogen combine to produce water.

Zola believed that every novel should constitute a scientific experiment. *Sister Carrie* is a good example of what he meant. Given a man conditioned as is Hurstwood, what will be his action when confronted with such and such a situation? Notice that the situation that confronts Hurstwood as he closes his bar that evening has resulted from chance, over which human volition and reason have no control. The safe door, usually closed by the owners, has been left ajar, and only on observing this fact does Hurstwood experience the impulse to steal.

> To those who have never wavered in conscience, the predicament of the individual whose mind is less strongly constituted and who trembles in the balance between duty and desire is scarcely appreciable, unless graphically portrayed. . . .The wavering of a mind under such circumstances is an almost inexplicable thing, and yet it is absolutely true. Hurstwood could not bring himself to act definitely. [16]

The merit of Dreiser's writing in this and similar scenes in other novels is that he does "graphically portray" the failure of the will, or its nullification, as implied in the words: "Hurstwood could not bring himself to act definitely." Several times Hurstwood withdraws the money from the safe only to restore it. But once, "while the money was in his hand the lock clicked. It had sprung! Did he do it? He grabbed at the knob and pulled vigorously. It had closed. Heavens! he was in for it now, sure enough." [17]

As shown above, in writers such as Brockden Brown, Hawthorne, and Melville, the determinism takes the form of an overpowering desire inclined so exclusively in one direction as to preclude the possibility of any other direction. With the characters created by these writers—Ahab, for example—there is liberty to act in accordance with one's will but not to choose what one wills. But with Dreiser's characters—other than the geniuses that appear in a number of his books—the will is almost totally in abeyance and never so much so as at the most critical moments of their lives. Did Hurstwood perhaps nudge the safe door shut? He honestly does not know, nor does Dreiser. Did he steal the money—that is, as a morally responsible agent would steal it? Did the wine he had drunk, his lust for Carrie, and his hatred for his wife so overwhelm his responses that he was little better than an automaton?

All that can be answered is that the act seems to have been the consequence—predictable by a discerning analyst—of a combination of biological, economic, and biochemical (alcohol affecting the mind) forces, and mere chance. It was most emphatically not the result of singleness of purpose or of a well-laid plan on Hurstwood's part.

After this willy-nilly act, Hurstwood commands enough strength and vitality to possess Carrie for several years in New York. But other forces, even more inexorable than those that made a criminal of him, are at work within his body. As he passes middle age, certain destructive chemicals are released in his bloodstream as the result of changes in metabolism. In Dreiser's words, the balance of anastates and katastates is upset in favor of the latter. His vigor, his initiative, and his courage decline.

The fatal change, which occurs, according to Dreiser, in all human beings and has an ineluctable and adverse effect on one's prosperity in this life, is translated in Hurstwood's case into a dismal chain of occurrences, each one of which brings him a step closer to annihilation. His partner forces him out of business; he becomes morbidly preoccupied with the miseries and catastrophes recorded in the daily newspapers; he becomes a victim of self-pity and its concomitant self-justification; he quarrels with Carrie; he complains of the weather and uses it as an excuse for staying idly at home; he takes over the housework while Carrie becomes the breadwinner; he becomes careless in his dress, as Carrie loses her respect for him; he tries to make money in gambling and, of course, loses; he bluntly asks Carrie for full financial support; he runs into debt for groceries; in a last frantic effort to get on his feet, he hires out as a scab in a trolley-car strike and is beaten in a riot; Carrie deserts him, leaving him a few dollars; he becomes a derelict, a Bowery bum; he dies a suicide in a sordid flophouse room.

The detailed, unremitting, step-by-step account of Hurstwood's decline is justly considered as some of the most powerful writing Dreiser has done. Again, as in the theft scene, he has translated the thesis—that of rigid determinism—into events in a man's life. The strength of the narrative does not lie in conflict, for there is no conflict worth speaking about. Hurstwood's struggles are negligible, pitiable; he exerts no appreciable power of will against the deadly bio-chemistry that has him in its grip. The flopping of a fish in a net can scarcely be called a conflict. The interest is that of scientific demonstration; the appeal is to our sense of pity at the spectacle of human beings so helplessly victimized by a ruthless universal order. The ultimate power of the account results doubtless from Dreiser's utter conviction of the rightness of his interpretation of human life.

An American Tragedy

The best gauges of the degree of Dreiser's determinism are the climaxes of his novels. Another climax worth considering is that of *An American Tragedy*, the story of a youth of mediocre abilities who is destroyed by his environment and his inner drives. The critical event in Clyde Griffith's life is his murder of his pregnant sweetheart, Roberta Alden. Clyde is a commonplace boy from a shabby background; his values are sterile, his sole ambition being acceptance in the country-club set in the factory town where he has a wretched little job in a mill owned by rich relatives. He sees his chance for attaining his goal when a socially prominent girl seems sufficiently attracted to him to wish to marry him. But if he is ever to make his vision a reality, he must get rid of his pregnant girl friend, a mere mill hand. This he hopes to do by drowning her in a canoe "accident" on an Adirondack lake.

The drowning, which is closely based on a real-life murder case of the early part of the century, occurs. But as with Hurstwood's theft, it is never clear to the reader, to Dreiser, or, above all, to Clyde himself whether he actually caused the death. Dreiser's skill in presenting this scene is uncanny. Not only does it exhibit a confusion of motivation in this particular murder, but it prompts the reader to wonder—as Dreiser surely intended—about individual responsibility in all murders, at least those perpetrated by amateur criminals.

What is it that happens on the lake when Roberta loses her life? One thing is certain: Clyde has taken her there with the full intention of destroying her. His plans are elaborate and quite ingenious for a youth of limited intelligence. But it is equally certain that when the stage is set for the murder, Clyde totally loses his nerve. Unassisted by chance, he would never have accomplished his purpose. He would have returned with Roberta, probably married her, and gradually abandoned his ambitions for social success. What paralyzes Clyde in the canoe at the moment when he attempts to execute the murder is not a sense of right and wrong; it is

> "a balanced combat between fear (a chemic revulsion against death or murderous brutality that would bring death) and a harried and restless and yet self-repressed desire to do—to do—to do—yet temporarily unbreakable here and now—a static between a powerful compulsion to do and yet not to do." [18]

Alarmed by Clyde's appearance in this state, Roberta moves forward in the canoe to help him; as she reaches him, he flings "out at her, but not even then with any intention to do other than free himself of her—her touch—her pleading—consoling sympathy—her presence forever—God!" [19] But the vehemence of his push throws Roberta off balance. The canoe capsizes, the gunwale striking the girl's head as she sinks. She flails about in the water, half-stunned, crying for help. Slightly apart from her, swimming, Clyde hears a "voice at his ear," the voice of his desires:

> But this—this—is not this that which you have been thinking and wishing for this while—you in your great need? And

behold! For despite your fear, your cowardice, this—this—has been done for you. An accident. . .an unintentional blow on your part is now saving you the labor of what you sought, and yet did not have the courage to do! But will you now. . . by going to her rescue, once more plunge yourself in the horror of that defeat and failure which has so tortured you and from which this now releases you? You might save her. But again you might not!. . .She herself is unable to save herself and by her erratic terror, if you draw near her now may bring about your own death also. But you desire to live![20]

So Clyde swims "heavily, gloomily and darkly to shore"[21] with "the cry of that devilish bird upon that dead limb—the weir-weir—" rasping in his ears and with "the thought that, after all, he had not really killed"[22] his sweetheart assuaging his fears. Yet even at that moment, Clyde is not sure whether he is guilty or not, any more than he is sure months later in the death-house as he converses with a clergyman who has taken more than a perfunctory interest in him and in his case. The minister, a Presbyterian, motivated perhaps by a remnant of Calvinistic concern with predestination, probes from every angle but can come to no conclusion.

"But you did rise to save her."
"Yes, afterwards, I got up. I meant to catch her after she fell back. That was what upset the boat."
"And you did really want to catch her?"
"I don't know. At the moment I guess I did. Anyhow, I felt sorry, I think."
"But can you say now truly and positively, as your Creator sees you, that you were sorry—or that you wanted to save her then?"
"It all happened so quick, you see. . .that I'm just not sure."[23]

The minister's questions are interesting in that they are directed toward finding whether Clyde had any will at all at the moment of the capsizing and, if he had a will, whether it indicated he was in a state of unredeemed evil—that is, one of the damned—or whether it showed him as enjoying some modicum of God's grace—that is, as being one of the elect and hence capable of good impulses. In any event, the reader's conclusion must be that Clyde is little more than a puppet. The voice that figuratively prompts him to desert the drowning Roberta is the equivalent of the hallucinatory voice that commands Wieland in Brockden Brown's novel to slaughter his wife and children. Neither Clyde nor Wieland is a free moral agent, acting by free choice. But there is this difference: Wieland is overwhelmed by will, not of his own choosing but too strong to be withstood, whereas Clyde is stripped of any will at all and acts mechanically. Wieland's case exemplifies the Calvinistic concept of determinism—a will unwaveringly directed toward one goal. Clyde's case exemplifies the naturalistic concept of determinism insofar as it applies to commonplace persons—a determinism manifesting itself not as fierce willpower but as a complex of reflexes and instincts pulling the agent this way and that as if he were on strings.

The Financier

But the naturalistic theory as it applies to extraordinary persons—evolutionary sports—converges with the Calvinistic. In *The Genius* Dreiser explores the will of a creative artist; in the Cowperwood series—*The Financier, The Titan,* and *The Stoic*—he examines the will of a great capitalist. Of these books most attention will be given to *The Financier.*

This mammoth novel begins and ends with descriptions of marine life—the sea apparently representing to Dreiser nature in its most primitive form. In the first pages of the book, the boy Cowperwood watches a battle to the death between a squid and a lobster in a tank in a fish-store window. When the lobster finally wins and devours the squid, the boy experiences the illumination of a youthful saint having been vouchsafed his first vision of the angels. A revelation of eternal truth has been granted: the lobster won because it was the quicker, the wilier—in short, the better endowed by nature. The theme of the book is the simple Darwinian one: survival of the fittest. But the lobster did not make itself fitter than the squid. It has benefited from an act of nature beyond its choosing, and its utilization of this advantage is again beyond its choice. It acts like a lobster because it is a lobster. The boy Cowperwood is quick to apply this lesson to mankind. Lobsters prey on squids; men prey on other men. Strong men will devour weak men. That is the scheme of things; that is the summary of the law.

On the last pages of the novel, another marine creature is presented—the mycteroperca bonaci, or black grouper, a 250-pound terror of the sea, whose chief advantage in the struggle for survival lies in its chameleon quality of changing its skin color to fit whatever environment it may be in. With this advantage—purely photochemical—the creature can dominate most of its enemies.

Cowperwood, a fictionalized portrait of that buccaneer of finance, Charles Tyson Yerkes, is assuredly the black grouper of the financial world. Hampered by no more sense of pity or conventional morality than his piscine counterpart, he exerts his superlative shrewdnes to fulfill the overwhelming drive of his will to power. Cowperwood could neither stifle this craving nor forgo the use of his exceptional abilities, any more than the black grouper could refrain from changing its colors. He is in the clutch of something bigger than himself:

Something—he could not say what—it was the only metaphysics he bothered about—was doing something for him. It had always helped him. It made things come out right at times. It put excellent opportunities in his way. Why had he been given so fine a mind?. . . . He had not deserved it—earned it. Accident, perhaps, but somehow the thought that he would always be protected—these intuitions, the "hunches" to act which he frequently had—could not be so easily explained. Life was a dark, insoluble mystery.[24]

Yet Cowperwood is not always merely a ruthless aggressor, created by the evolutionary process to further some inscrutable cosmic purpose. He is this—but he is more, for he sometimes realizes his special position in the order of things. Paradoxical as it may seem, there is in Dreiser's writing a leaven of mysticism, or transcendentalism, that becomes more and more noticeable in his later years. Even Sister Carrie, as she sits in her rocking chair, has moments of something resembling spiritual illumination—though these are indeed faint glimmerings that serve only to make her long for a stronger light.

But with Cowperwood, the quasi-mystical sense of his place in the universe and of the meaning of his life is an impressive, if infrequent, experience. Indeed, Cowperwood may be said to be a man with a religion, the cardinal article in which is a belief "in himself, and himself only," whence springs "his courage to think"[25] as he pleases. Realizing that no one "can overcome or even assist the Providence that shapes our ends, rough hew them as we may,"[26] he flings himself into his destiny with the abandon of a saint consigning his life to the guidance of God. At times his vision of the universe goes even beyond himself and his predestinated function in it. His need for, love of, and profound comprehension of beauty as manifested in art and women raise his life occasionally to a spiritual level. His awe and wonder concerning the stars, the mystery of which struck him as he watched them from a prison window, and his haunting sense of kinship with them are genuinely religious feelings, suggestive of Emerson's experience of ecstacy while "crossing a bare common" as described in *Nature*.

Yet such moments are comparatively rare in Cowperwood's life. For the most part he careens on towards financial dominance, the most common diversions from his path being the result of the "chemic" urge that prompts him to capture for his pleasure women like the spirited, vital Aileen, a fitting mate for this superman whose previous marriage to a common-place woman hindered his new amours not a jot.

Clyde Griffith manages to destroy a girl who stands in the way of his petty ambition, but he does this clumsily, more or less accidentally, without benefit of overwhelming purpose. Cowperwood destroys hundreds of rivals—friends or enemies—and he does so in the grip of a purpose inborn and uncontrollable, though it never occurs to him to try to control it. Neither one is worried about conventional morality, but Clyde fears the consequences of his acts or succumbs to instinctual fears that are foreign to the superman Cowperwood.

What is the function of the Clydes and kindred mediocrities—the Carries and the Hurstwoods—on the one hand, and of the Cowperwoods on the other? Insofar as they blunder through their own lives with their petty conflicts and hopes and failures, the mediocrities serve no particular end, unless perhaps it is to propagate the race. But in *The Financier* and *The Titan* Dreiser makes it clear that the mediocrities are legitimate prey for the supermen, who feed on them as suits their purposes.

Hey Rub-A-Dub-Dub

What end does the cannibalism of a man like Cowperwood serve? Dreiser was never one to leave his views ambiguous—a rather refreshing trait in an age, like ours, when ambiguity is regarded as an artistic virtue. In a book of essays, *Hey Rub-A-Dub-Dub*, which is as complete a compendium of naturalistic theory as one is likely to find, there is a piece entitled "The American Financier," which makes clear anything which might have been in doubt. In fact, the essay summarizes views expounded by Dreiser during an interview on the novel *The Financier*. To begin with, Dreiser, as an evolutionist, states that the race is always "to the swift, the battle to the strong; chemical and physical laws not being easily upset by fiats of government."[27]

It is of interest that three centuries earlier the Puritan pastor Urian Oakes had used the same text with only slightly different conclusions: the race is usually to the swift and the battle usually to the strong, "for the Lord doth most ordinarily award success unto causes of greatest sufficiency rather than disappointment and defeat."[28] The main difference between the views, other than the premises from which they start, is that the Puritan Oakes is somewhat less dogmatic than Dreiser the naturalist. Closely paralleling the thought of that other archdogmatist, Charles Sumner, Dreiser cites the example of Vanderbilt, among other ruthless financiers, as fulfilling a need at a certain period in history, though he readily grants that such men are "suggestive of sharks and we of sniveling bluefish. . . .Are they not [the financiers] specialized machines sent here for a purpose?"[29] If we are "to have a Woolworth building, a transcontinental railroad, a Panama Canal, a flying machine, to say nothing of literature and art. . .we must endure a man who is dull, greedy, vain, ridiculous in many ways or even an advocate of every conceivable vice. . . ."[30]

Those who would reform the ways of these creatures are, of course, daft. Again like Sumner, Dreiser finds that "the great aim of all reformers—that of permanently reforming man in his social as well as his religious ways"[31]—is nothing short of ridiculous. A reformer he defines as a person who flies in the face of natural law. When a reformer does accomplish something, the results are due not to his own efforts but to some necessity inherent in the historical process. Thus, "St. Francis was little more than a chemical reaction against a too-heavy materialism that enveloped Europe—nothing more, truly."[32]

Dreiser's naturalism, in fact, is so radical as to amount to a nihilism as thoroughgoing as that found in Russian intellectual life in the 1860s. One can think only of Turgenev's Bazarov or of certain characters in Dostoesky's *The Possessed* when one reads a passage like the following:

> . . . it would seem advisable that man as a whole throw over as swiftly as possible all his old-time religious and moral conceptions, his restraining conventions, taboos and the like, and re-examine for himself the data concerning which, accidentally or otherwise, he now finds himself capable of cerebrating. . . . One of the greatest achievements, of course, would be to rid the human mind of all vain illusion concerning things spiritual, to get it to see, if it were possible, that man is not necessarily an enduring spiritual creature endowed—for who can know?—with an enduring and progressive soul, but . . . an implement or tool in the hands of something else which is creating or using him as, for example, the vine does the leaf, yet which itself may be of no great import in Nature.[33]

Man must learn to regard himself as "a fragment of the chemical whole."[34] Man must resign himself to believing that there are many things that he cannot do, however hard he tries. It is as foolish to think of atoms as achieving success and fame and the like by themselves as to think of our reaching these goals by our own unaided efforts (shades again of Calvin). Honest enough to ask if such a life be worth living, Dreiser is also honest enough to say he does not know. One thing only is he sure of: the religious have neither the answers to the eternal questions nor the key to happiness; they inspire, he believes, only fear. To Dreiser, at this time in his life, the only spiritual satisfaction lies in a courageous attitude— "a healthy, if skeptical, seeking."[35] He would rather be a defiant Prometheus shackled to his rock than "a crawling worm or whimpering slave praying for some endless Nirvana."[36]

The Bulwark

As is well known, Dreiser's naturalism underwent modifications as he grew older. Eventually he became a Communist, thus substituting Marxism for the social Darwinism of his earlier years. For the struggle of the individual to survive he substituted the class struggle with its supposedly inevitable ultimate victory for the proletariat. Simultaneously with his interest in Marxism, Dreiser—remarkably enough—was becoming interested in the philosophies of the Quakers John Woolman and Elais Hicks, both of them mystics imbued with the notion of a God of love who through the Inner Light communicates directly with mankind. No two philosophies could be farther apart in their conclusions than Dreiser's biochemical Darwinism—or, for that matter, his Marxism—and the kindly views of these Friends. Yet the two outlooks have one thing in common: monism.

The enormous physicochemical machine that Dreiser thought the universe to be had no room for dualisms like that of good and evil. Nor could the love-dominated universe of the Quakers share much aside from the love with which God drenches His creation. This is not to say that Quakers necessarily deny the existence of evil, but that they find it to be a much less appalling force than do adherents of certain other religions. A mind like Dreiser's, however, once it has decided that goodness lies at the foundation of the cosmos, would be strongly tempted to the next step, the denial of evil. This is what happened to the transcendentalists, even to Whitman, who was himself strongly under the Quaker spell. All things are immersed in a sea of spirit, that is, in God. The demarcation between good and evil becomes blurred to the vanishing point; the will of many, itself an expression of the all-pervasive spirit, can hardly will that which is harmful for it. It is possible to argue that Solon Barnes, a philosophizing Quaker in Dreiser's novel *The Bulwark,* is entirely fictional and does not represent the author in any way. Yet it is a biographical fact that Dreiser had developed a strong interest in Quakerism and considered it the most acceptable religion he had ever encountered.

Significantly, Solon Barnes, the protagonist of *The Bulwark,* finds peace—spiritual renewal—by allowing his will to merge with that of the divine. In short, he undergoes an abnegation of personal volition perhaps as complete as that entailed in the supposition that man is a mere blob of organic matter in the physical universe. At any rate, the key to Solon's rebirth is a passage from John Woolman's journals: "Then the mystery was opened and I perceived there was joy in Heaven over a sinner who had repented, and that the language *John Woolman is dead,* meant no more than the death of my own will. My natural understanding now returned as before."[37] Previously Solon has become aware of a "great Creative spirit" to whom he finds it constructive to pray. He has had an experience in his garden with a puff adder which he speaks to and shows an interest in, so that, rather than retreating, the reptile crawls across Solon's toe. Solon interprets the event as an instance of the power of love. "And now," Solon tells his daughter, "I thank God for this revelation of His universal presence and His good intent toward all things—all His created world. For otherwise how would [the snake] understand me, and I it, if we were not both part of Himself?"[38] And Dreiser adds: "In this love and unity with all nature . . . there was nothing fitful or changing or disappointing. . . . This love was rather as constant as nature itself, everywhere the same. . . . It was an intimate relation to the very heart of being."[39]

Dreiser worked on *The Bulwark* sporadically for thirty years or so, completing it shortly before his death. The parts of it just examined reflect his final thinking and his strong tendency toward mysticism. Matter by this time had ceased to be the sole reality to Dreiser; rather it was but one manifestation of the mystery of the universe. But it must be emphasized that this new aspect of his thought left no more room for freedom of the will than did his earlier very thoroughgoing materialism. Man, he had come to believe, "is not really and truly living and thinking, but on the contrary is being lived and thought by that which has produced him."[40] Man was an expression of and a part of a universal mind, which in turn "was a kind of ubiquitous electro-physical force."[41] In the final pages of the third novel in the Cowperwood series, *The Stoic,* on which he was working the night he died, it is not surprising to find Dreiser presenting as ultimate truth the Hindu doctrines concerning Brahma and Atma. Electrophysical energy and spirit had become equated under the name "creative force," a term suggestive of Bergson's *élan vital,* used to designate the ultimate energy that informs and creates the universe. But the "creative force" leaves no room for individual choices and volitions; it includes all these within its vast monism of matter and spirit. Dreiser had come to believe that it directed his own artistic efforts, over which he felt less and less personal control. He was merely an outlet for the All which from time to time expressed itself through him. Indeed one is not even free to commit suicide meaningfully, for "an individual death [is] simply part of the life of the universal mind, which [is] therein expressing itself."[42] And in the last chapter of *The Stoic,* he quotes from Emily Bronte's "No Coward Soul Is Mine," the last stanza of which, like Emerson's "Brahma," denies death:

> There is not room for Death,
> Nor atom that His might can render void,
> Thou, Thou art Being and Breath,
> And what Thou art can never be destoyed.

Denying man the option even of terminating his own life, Dreiser has not moved toward a belief in freedom of will as a result of his flirtations with Quakerism and mysticism. If one were looking for a single typical statement of his views on the will, the following, made in 1929, would serve as well as any:

For, as I have personally observed life, man responds quite mechanically, and only so, to all such stimuli as he is prepared, or rather constructed to receive—and no more and no less; . . . this constitutes the sum and substance of his free will and intelligence—responding to these stimuli which are neither more nor less than the call bells of chemical, or perhaps better yet, electrophysical states which require certain other electrophysical or chemical atoms to keep them in the forms in which they chance to be.[43]

As to Dreiser the "creative force" is electrophysical by nature, this definition is inclusive of his earlier as well as of his latest thought on the will. In his later years Dreiser's fondest dream was to be able to effect a philosophical synthesis of spirit and matter; he thought that his concept of electrophysical creative force had put him within reach of that goal.

Ellen Glasgow and William Faulkner: Vestigial Calvinism and Naturalism Combined

Two Southern novelists, Ellen Glasgow and William Faulkner, prolong the influence of Calvinism into twentieth-century American literature. Neither author, of course, was personally of orthodox persuasion. In Faulkner, the Calvinist emphases upon destiny and upon transmissibility of guilt are reflected in his treatment of the old wrong of slavery and its effects on later generations. Faulkner also presents a gallery of religious fanatics tinted in Calvinist hues. As a depicter of the abnormalities fostered by the traditional theology and as a perpetuator of several of its basic attitudes, without himself espousing the dogma, he much resembles Hawthorne, as critics have frequently pointed out. Ellen Glasgow presents numerous orthodox Presbyterians who are free of neurotic abnormality, and she seems to have been imbued with the Calvinist views on predestination but not with those on guilt. What she most admired in her Scotch-Irish ancestors was their strong sense of purpose—their fortitude, their power of endurance against the worst odds. Both authors, of course, were deeply influenced by the sciences and scientific philosophies of the day, such as Darwinism and psychoanalysis, and thus their works are strongly tinged with naturalistic determinism. Finally, each is characterized by a strain of what might be called a geographical mysticism—a strong sense of place, in their case the Southern countryside, and a conviction that those who live close to the land are affected in character and spirit by its distinctive features. With both, this feeling about the land has, at times, transcendental overtones.

Ellen Glasgow: Barren Ground

In 1939 in a volume of personal credos edited by Clifton Fadiman under the title *I Believe,* Miss Glasgow wrote three seemingly contradictory statements on one page:

> I have no recollection that I ever truly believed either in the God of the Shorter Catechism or in the God of the Thirty-nine Articles. . . . The longer I observe experience, the greater emphasis I place on determinism both in our beliefs and in our bodies. Regarding the freedom of the will, and regarding that doctrine alone, I suppose I may call myself more or less of a pragmatist. Indefensible in theory, no doubt, that exalted error—if it be an error—appears necessary to the order of civilized man, and seems to justify, on higher grounds, its long record of service as a moral utility. But certainly every consequence, whether material or immaterial, must follow a cause . . .[1]

Though rejecting her father's Presbyterianism and her mother's Episcopalianism, Miss Glasgow (if we read her statement correctly) as a convinced determinist has not strayed very far from the predestinarianism of the two religious documents whose influence upon her she denies. Having proclaimed herself a determinist, she states that pragmatically, at least, she believes in the freedom of the will, though she considers this "indefensible in theory." Her dilemma is that of the Calvinists: how to reconcile determinism or predestination with a freedom of the will necessary to any acceptable system of ethics. One questions whether the Shorter Catechism and the Thirty-nine Articles have not left their mark on her.

Elsewhere Miss Glasgow wrote: "The book that influenced

my mind most profoundly in youth was *The Origin of Species;*
and it was in response to this benign and powerful inspiration that I conceived my first novels."[2] So strong was her admiration for Darwin that on a visit to Westminster Abbey
she laid a rose upon his tomb. Yet in *The Woman Within—*
a spiritual autobiography that would not be out of place on a
shelf beside Tolstoy's *My Confession* and Woolman's *Journals—*
she states that her knowledge of Darwin and other scientific
writers forbidden by her rigidly Presbyterian father gave
her no "more than a wider intellectual horizon and a longer
perspective."[3] Thus, far from succeeding in totally discarding
Calvinism—as she seems systematically and fervently to have
struggled to do—she was under its influence to a greater extent than she was for many years willing to admit. Her revulsion
was against the person of the Calvinist God, who "permitted
pain to exist, and the Prince of darkness to roam the earth in
search of whom he might devour,"[4] but paradoxically not so
much against the theology premised on such a deity, and
not at all against the strength of purpose and character that
this theology nurtured in its more intelligent adherents.
Frederick McDowell wrote, "If anything, the Calvinist heritage was to dominate her,"[5] and Miss Glasgow comes close to
confessing as much in her discussion of *Vein of Iron* in *A Certain
Measure:*

> "Not in vain had my Aunt Rebecca instructed me, on the
> Sabbath, in the Shorter Catechism and the Westminster
> Confession. . . . I had learned my lesson well and long,
> though I thought I had forgotten it. Nothing remained for
> me to do but to set the scene and attempt to analyze the
> primary elements that composed the Presbyterian spirit
> and the Presbyterian theology. And the chief of these ele-
> ments, or so it appeared in my examination, was the sub-
> stance of fortitude."[6]

As a character in *Barren Ground* says, "Once a Presbyterian,
always a Presbyterian."[7]

Barren Ground

In *Barren Ground,* which she regarded as her finest novel and which she described as having been "gathered up, as a rich harvest, from the whole of my life,"[8] Miss Glasgow has subjected the Calvinist will and conscience to the most searching analysis she was ever to give them. This novel, too, is remarkable for its synthesis of Calvinist predestination, scientific determinism, and a transcendentalism that was derived from Plotinus, the religions of the East, and German philosophy. These three strands—so important both singly and in combination in the life of the American mind and soul—are brought together in *Barren Ground* with a plausibility seldom equaled in American literature.

A favorite phrase of Miss Glasgow's is "vein of iron" which, before she used it as the title of a novel, frequently appeared in her writing and notably in *Barren Ground.*[9] As synonyms she employed, among other phrases, "the spirit of fortitude"[10] and "the vital principle of survival"[11]—the first suggestive of the grace of God which enables the elect to endure life's catastrophes,[12] and the second suggestive of the Darwinian concept of natural selection. Election and natural selection thus merge and become two aspects of the same principle in the concept of the vein of iron, which Miss Glasgow regards as enabling "races and individuals to withstand the destructive forces of nature and of civilization."[13] This close and apparently conscious fusion of Darwinism and Calvinism is an outstanding feature of *Barren Ground.* Other novelists, as shown above, have provided examples of supplanting the doctrine of predestination with that of natural selection; the financial novels of Norris and Dreiser, with their chief characters Jadwin and Cowperwood, come readily to mind. But unlike such "orthodox" naturalist novelists, Miss Glasgow is one of only two or three during her lifetime able to combine these two strains into an inseparable amalgam.

What is the "vein of iron?" It is that which in certain characters will "never bend," will "never break," will "never melt completely in any furnace."[14] Darwinistically conceived, it is the result of heredity, as Miss Glasgow herself implies. But Calvinistically conceived, it is the gift of divine grace, corresponding to the doctrine of the perseverance of saints. As the Westminster Confession puts it,

> "they whom God hath accepted in his Beloved, effectually called and sanctified by his Spirit, can neither totally nor finally fall away from the state of grace: but shall certainly persevere therein, and be eternally saved.
> This perseverance of the saints depends not on their own free-will, but upon the immutability of the decree of election.[15]

Just as the elect "may in this life be certainly assured that they are in a state of grace,"[16] so do the possessors of the vein of iron know in their hearts that they will never be crushed.

In *Barren Ground* the protagonist, Dorinda Oakley, is endowed with the vein of iron. From the point of view of heredity, she has behind her a line of Scotch-Irish pioneers of inflexible will and inexhaustible endurance. The Darwinist in Ellen Glasgow could assert that from such a background an occasional Dorinda is bound to emerge. But the fact is that Miss Glasgow emphasizes the Calvinism in Dorinda's background much more than she does any hereditary trait. Indeed, their Calvinism rather than their bloodlines made Dorinda's forebears successful in an unfriendly land. "The Presbyterian faith sprang up and blossomed like a Scotch thistle in barren ground."[17] Furthermore, the main difference between the maternal branch of Dorinda's lineage, Presbyterian Abernathys and the paternal "poor white" Oakleys, is the intensity of their religion. Though the poor whites, according to Ellen Glasgow, are notable for sloth, lack of endurance, and weak wills, they originally stemmed from the same ethnic and religious stock before succumbing to the Southern disease (Miss Glasgow's diagnosis) of fecklessness. As a matter of fact, two of

Dorinda's brothers are totally her inferiors, one being a mere clod and the other a murderer. Even among those who are not poor whites there are chasmal differences. The Greylocks, once prosperous landowners, have sunk into alcoholic decay, while the Ellgoods are thriving, though rather stolid, farmers.

Such differences within families and among members of the same homogeneous community may be explained, of course, in terms of the chance combining of genes, but Miss Glasgow does not put forward this explanation. In fact, for the most part she offers no explanation at all, with the exception of definitely tracing young Dr. Greylock's drunkenness to a similar propensity in his father. A Calvinist explanation, indeed, though not acceptable either to Miss Glasgow or to most contemporary readers, would fit perfectly. By the "double decree" of Calvinism, Dorinda is elected for salvation, and her murderer brother and the Greylocks are predestinated to damnation. Miss Glasgow, a rebel against Presbyterianism since childhood, has willy-nilly created a situation that accurately reflects much of the rejected theology. Any substitution of Darwinism or other determinism, scientific or not, has been made, if at all, mainly by tacit implication. Insofar as this may have occurred—and it is impossible to gauge the extent—it represents the unconscious ease with which in American thought and attitudes predestination and natural selection could merge into a single and identical determinism.

In commenting on the aftermath of a mystical experience she had in the Alps, Miss Glasgow wrote: "Emotionally, I was a believer; intellectually, I was a skeptic." [18] This was apparently a lifelong contradiction in her mental and emotional life. She never was entirely able to rid her feelings of her ancestral Calvinism, no matter how urgently her reason prompted her to purge her soul of its influence. In fact, even intellectually she respected the metaphysical toughness of the Confession of Faith and the Larger Catechism.

Starting with the premise that Dorinda is one of the elect

or naturally selected, we find many uncanny parallels between the old theology and the new science. Several of these
have already been touched on: Dorinda's drive toward success corresponds both with the doctrine of the perseverance of
saints and with the theory of the survival of the fittest. Her
confidence in her unbreakable will reflects not only the Calvinistic "assurance of salvation" but the necessary and inevitable state of mind of that member of a species selected by
nature to prevail through all trials and hardships. Along with
this assurance, furthermore, goes a certain arrogance of character, as one sees in Dreiser's *The Financier* and *The Genius.* Miss
Glasgow alludes a number of times to Dorinda's "strong and
rather arrogant nature"[19]; and certainly in her dealings with
many of her neighbors, especially the Greylocks, she is arrogant to the point of ruthlessness.

However, for the most part, Dorinda's life after her return
from New York is characterized by good works, which not
only are beneficial to herself and others (for example, her
helpfulness to her servants), but which also demonstrate her
superiority over most citizens of her home village, Pedlar's
Mill. To the evolutionist or social Darwinist, of course, the
naturally superior person will prove of great benefit to society
as well as to himself or herself. He or she will build railroads,
produce great works of art, establish stable governments, or
make scientific discoveries. To the Calvinist, in the words of
the Westminster Confession, "these good works . . . are the
fruits and evidences of a true and lively faith: and by them
believers manifest their thankfulness, strengthen their assurance, edify their brethren . . . [and] stop the mouths of the
adversaries."[20] Dorinda's good works do not manifest thankfulness, for she is not particularly thankful in any religious
sense; nor do they illuminate orthodox faith, which she has
long since abandoned. But her success is edifying to her fellow
farmers in that it provides an example; and certainly it si-
lences and humiliates her adversaries.

Under Calvinism, indeed, the elect as they pursue their

good works must have a sense of mission, a sense of God's approval and encouragement of their activities, for these activities proceed from His spirit. Surely, among American Calvinists at least, this conviction of being used as an instrument to achieve God's purposes on earth is extraordinarily intense. In the Oakley family the sense of mission manifests itself in the mother's obsessive desire to convert souls in the Congo, and it appears in Dorinda's ferocious singleness of purpose.

> In a changed form her mother's frustrated passion to redeem the world was finding concrete expression. . . . The farm belonged to [Dorinda], and the knowledge aroused a fierce sense of possession. To protect, to lift up, rebuild and restore, these impulses formed the deepest obligations her nature could feel.[21]

Along with the sense of mission went a willingness to take chances. She would push on with the project of redeeming the land despite the obstacles and despite her feeling that her chances of success were poor indeed. One who is under the assurance of being of the elect or of the Darwinian select can afford to take chances; God or nature is on one's side. Dorinda's efforts with the land are comparable to those of Curtis Jadwin, the superman hero of Frank Norris's *The Pit*, who feels himself mysteriously called to a high destiny. History tells us that similar feelings were the rule among, for example, the New England Puritans—who were Calvinists embarked on dangerous adventures.

The most characteristic and the most formidable source of strength for the elect and the select is an unbreakable will, which is roughly the equivalent of Ellen Glasgow's principle of endurance or vein of iron. Far from belittling the will, Calvinism, as we have seen, glorified it, making it an instrument of God's purpose. True, one was chosen either for damnation or salvation and one's unaided efforts could in no way alter the divine decree. The unredeemed would be incapable of willing good and hence by their own wills would effect their downfall. The redeemed, once they were filled with grace, would be empowered to will good and would persevere in so willing—but not effortlessly. To the end of their lives the struggle to will good would persist, and the struggle was exacting. God did not make the road to salvation easy, even though salvation was assured. It was rough, narrow, and steep, and to attain its end was a supreme test of endurance and willpower. And if this was true of the elect, it was equally true, in the Darwinian's thinking, of the biological sports, the mutations, who were envisaged as leading the masses along the road of progress. We find it not only, say, in *Pilgrim's Progress* but in the Darwinian novels of Dreiser and Norris.

What are the obstacles that test the endurance, the will to survive, of these chosen ones? Not the least are facets of their own characters—their instincts, their emotions, an unruliness of spirit. Dorinda is almost destroyed by her sex impulses, and her mother by aberrations in her nature that express themselves in visions of black babies being thrown to crocodiles in the Congo River. The wild, unruly element in the human makeup must be eradicated, just as the broomsedge must be torn from the Virginia farmland if productivity is to be achieved. The Calvinists, of course, warned of "a continual and irreconcilable war, the flesh lusting against the Spirit, and the Spirit against the flesh," [22] in which the elect would be unceasingly engaged. Just as the superior human beings in Dreiser's and Norris's novels must guard their superiority against much that is typically human or animal in them and must combat the results of mistakes in their own past, so Dorinda is never able entirely to expunge the devastating memory of yielding to Jason, though "all the strength of her spirit rebelled against the . . . burden of a physical fact, which she dragged after her like a dead fish in a net." [23]

Exterior forces, too, obstruct the progress of the elect.

Natural objects, like the broomsedge, the insects, and the sterile soil in *Barren Ground* must be overcome, as also must be the stupidity, unreliability, or sheer laziness and indifference of the commonality of mankind. "There were times when it seemed to Dorinda that this instinct to slight was indigenous to the soil of the South."[24] More difficult to cope with are the blows of sheer chance. To Dorinda it seemed "that it was always the little things, not the big ones, that influenced destiny; the fortuitous occurrence instead of the memorable occasion."[25] In her own life her first chance meeting with her seducer, Jason; her poor aim when she tried to shoot him; the accident in New York which resulted in the miscarriage of her illegitimate baby; and the train wreck that killed her husband, Nathan Pedlar—these events seemingly changed the course of her life, but they did not atrophy her will. Although she is not one of those people to whom, as Willa Cather puts it, only fortunate accidents occur, she is one whom no accident could put completely out of the running.

Dorinda contemplates with awe these events and their effect on the people involved. This is awe fostered no doubt by the Presbyterian doctrine of predestination which she may have intellectually rejected but which her emotions still half accepted: "God from all eternity did by the most wise and holy counsel of his own will, freely and unchangeably ordain whatsoever comes to pass; yet so as thereby neither is God the author of sin; nor is violence offered to the will of the creatures."[26] The will of the elect or superiorly endowed is not paralyzed by chance happenings, but is strengthened. From the viewpoint of scientific determinism, the mediocre person, like Hurstwood in *Sister Carrie* or the Greylocks in *Barren Ground,* will be destroyed by a series of unlucky events. But the uncommon persons, the Darwinian sports, or Calvinistic elect, not only survive misfortunes but even benefit from them. As Dreiser says of Cowperwood, they have a sense of a befriending destiny.

Dreiser, insofar as he offers an explanation, gives the Dar-

winian one: Cowperwood is Nature's instrument in the evolution of the human race. A Calvinist—were it not for Cowperwood's amorality—would ascribe his success to the grace of
God. Dorinda, though not amoral, enjoys Cowperwood's
ability to surmount difficulties that crush such commonplace
persons as her father, her brothers, and her onetime lover.
Ellen Glasgow is forced to invent a new concept to account
for Dorinda's survival and prosperity—the vein of iron. Had
Miss Glasgow not renounced Calvinism in her mind, she
would have used the old term—grace of God. Ultimately,
whether one uses the terminology of the church, that of
science, or Miss Glasgow's special vocabulary, the result is
the same. Some persons are slated for survival and prosperity
and others for defeat. Pragmatically, Dreiser's chemisms and
instincts, Miss Glasgow's vein of iron, and Calvin's grace of
God are identical, and none dispels the inscrutability of
ultimate cause. But Miss Glasgow's phraseology, being less
scientifically specific, is closer to Calvin's than to Dreiser's,
as is probably her thinking, despite her rejection of the church.

The greatest of all Dorinda's obstacles is her recurrent
sense of futility and despair. Until she is fifty years old, when
the novel ends, she undergoes periods in which "not pain, not
disappointment, but the futility of all things was crushing
her spirit. She knew not the passive despair of maturity. . . ."[27]
It is the same feeling of woe that makes Dorinda's mother, a
lifelong believer in the Presbyterian God, exclaim as death
approaches, "It doesn't seem just right that we have to be
born. It ain't worth all the trouble that we go through."[28]
But with Dorinda "the spirit of fortitude [triumphs] over the
sense of futility,"[29] as it does over lesser obstacles.

In the Westminster Confession it is stated that the elect,
though they "may have the assurance of their salvation divers
ways shaken," yet they "are supported from utter despair."[30]
Similarly the naturalist's Darwinian hero can never wholly
give way to hopelessness. Cowperwood even while in prison at
the end of *The Financier* shook off his moods of pessimism, for

in the depth of his being he felt that "there was no more escaping the greatness that was inherent in him than there was for so many others the littleness that was in them."[31] And in Norris's *The Pit* we get the notion that the temporarily defeated superman Jadwin "will make two or three more fortunes in the next few years"[32] as he transfers the scene of his activities to the Far West.

Periods of near despair in Dorinda's existence alternate with periods of ecstasy, or "assurance," to use the religious term. In fact, spiritual exaltation roughly equivalent to that supposedly felt in "conversion" plays an important role in her life. We are told that as a girl she actually underwent conversion to the Presbyterian faith—accompanied by "a softly glowing ecstasy, which flooded her soul and made her feel that she had entered into the permanent blessedness of the redeemed."[33] But this state did not last. It was followed by the ecstasy of love for Jason Greylock, which vanished when he betrayed her.

But other visitations of ecstasy—stronger ones—occur throughout her life. Dorinda's great-grandfather averred that "he didn't come to Christ till he had thirsted for blood."[34] It is only after she has thirsted for Jason's blood and tried to kill him that Dorinda undergoes a conversion-like change that carries her forward unerringly for the next thirty years. The spiritual change, although beginning at that time, is completed only after a year's time, during which Dorinda has been living in New York. At a concert with a young admirer she is so overcome by the music that she once again experiences an ecstasy, which is described as at first "tearing her vitals . . . destroying the hidden roots of her life."[35] But later, it seems to her while walking "in the blue twilight" of Central Park, "that the music had released some imprisoned force in the depths of her being, and that this force was spreading out over the world. . . . With a shock of joy, she realized that she was no longer benumbed, that she had come to life again."[36] Death and resurrection—death of the old being and birth of a new—this is conversion. The words with which the Westminster Confession describes the effective calling of the elect to God by His grace apply perfectly to Dorinda's experience: her mind is enlightened "spiritually and savingly, to understand the things of God"; her "heart of stone" is replaced by "an heart of flesh," and her will is renewed.[37]

This experience is indeed a turning point, a conversion, in Dorinda's life. After it her purpose quickly forms and hardens: she will return to Virginia and farm the land by new and scientific principles. She will take her chances, grave ones, and will devote her life to her goal. She will not always be sure of success—the elect are not continuously sure of their calling—but she will persist, endure, *persevere*. And along the road, interspersed with seasons of discouragement, there will be moments, and longer, when the feelings of oneness return— oneness with the land, which is her destiny. Constantly, "the spirit of the land was flowing into her, and her own spirit, strengthened and refreshed, was flowing out again, toward life. This was the permanent self, she knew."[38] There was in her life a thread of "unforgettable ecstasy [that] came back to her in her dreams."[39] Again comes to mind the Dreiserian superman, Frank Cowperwood, whose self-assurance may occasionally ebb but never for long, and who is never so strong as shortly after a setback (a sentence to jail or a financial failure)—so that he is never defeated but is, indeed, undefeatable.

Transcendental Strain in Ellen Glasgow's Novels.

In *A Certain Measure,* Miss Glasgow writes:

As Dorinda conquered the land, which was, for her, the symbol of fate, so Jason surrendered through inherited weakness. The slow seasons, the blighted crops, the long droughts, the sudden frosts—all this impotence of nature had afflicted his mind and body, as if it were the symptom of a mortal informity. His breed, unlike Dorinda's, held no immunity from the fatal germ of resignation.[40]

This is assuredly a nod in the direction of determinism through environment and heredity, but, as we have seen, Miss Glasgow makes little of this approach. If she did, she would have too much to account for in her depiction of so many of Dorinda's closest relatives as weaklings. Heredity and environment simply do not sufficiently explain the differences among characters as Miss Glasgow has presented them in *Barren Ground,* as well as in other novels.

Yet we must conclude that upon Miss Glasgow's characters two types of determinism are exerted. The determinism of natural forces—of economics, of the social order, of race, of religion, and of politics, as well as of their own innate inadequacies—heavily afflicts the commonplace, the unredeemed, characters. The exceptional characters, the sports or the redeemed, prevail against these forces to a remarkable extent and hence appear to be relatively free. But they are products of another sort of determinism; superiority is theirs by no choice of their own or credit to themselves. To this extent they are the products of determinism or blind chance as are their less generously endowed brethren. The world has many Jasons for each Dorinda; many Hurstwoods—victims of biochemistry and outer circumstances—for each Cowperwood or Eugene Witla. Just as Calvin said the elect could take no credit for their state of grace, the scientific determinist can assign no personal merit to the successful sports of evolution.

What sets Dorinda apart most fundamentally from other characters is her tendency toward mysticism, which is in no way the result of her own conscious choice or volition; in other words, it, too, is the unaccountable, unpredictable result of determinism. This tendency is of additional interest for two reasons. It reflects a strong mystical strain, already commented on, in Miss Glasgow's own spiritual and emotional life, and it is consonant with the transcendental element in American literature, philosophy, and religion. In these two respects it has the same significance as the mysticism in Dreiser's two posthumous novels, *The Bulwark* and *The Stoic.*

True, it may be argued that Dorinda never achieves the complete mystical union described by William James in *Varieties of Religious Experience*. But she approaches it as again and again she is visited "by the feeling that the moment [is] significant if only she could discover the meaning of it before it eluded her. Strange how often that sensation returned to her. . . ."[41] There are times when "the earth and air and her own being [are] purified and exalted into some frigid zone of the spirit,"[42] or when she is overwhelmed by the recognition of "a deep profounder than the deeps of experience."[43] These feelings come to Dorinda most frequently when she is contemplating the vast, impersonal landscape on which she has lived most of her life. She feels herself a part of the landscape, yes, but she senses that both she and the countryside may conceal a meaning of incredible significance. Her experiences are in fact akin to that reported by Emerson in *Nature* (1836), while he is "crossing a bare common, in snow puddles, at twilight, under a clouded sky."[44] Dorinda does not become "a transparent eye-ball,"[45] nor do "the currents of the Universal Being circulate through"[46] her as vigorously as through Emerson; hers is a less complete revelation, but it is a revelation nevertheless.

Significantly, like Emerson, Ellen Glasgow studied and absorbed the teachings of Plotinus, and she always expressed a profound interest in the *Bhagavad-Gita,* although she asserts that transcendental philosophy was only a passing phase with her. Passing phase or not, her own life was touched by experiences similar to those of the more mystical of the transcendentalists. At least once, in Switzerland, she experienced a true mystical transport in which she "knew, or felt, or beheld, a union deeper than knowledge, deeper than sense, deeper than vision,"[47] and ever afterward she believed "matter to be only a single aspect or manifestation of that mystery"[48] in which man has his being. Just as she was more of a Calvinist than she thought, Miss Glasgow was also more of a transcendentalist than she seemed willing to admit.

In a later book, *Vein of Iron* (1935), the transcendentalism is more explicit. The novel, as its title implies, has as its main purpose the celebration of "the living pulse of endurance, of that deep instinct for survival which has enabled man to outlast not only catastrophe, but even happiness, even hope."[49] This is, of course, a trait most commonly found among Presbyterians, Miss Glasgow would have us believe. Thus, in *Vein of Iron*, Grandmother Fincastle—the oldest living member of the family with which the novel deals—is the connecting link with past generations of Scotch-Irish forebears of Calvinist persuasion. The grandmother alone remains a faithful Calvinist, as ready as Jonathan Edwards to suffer hellfire for the greater glory of God. Her son John had started life in the Presbyterian clergy, but had abandoned the old doctrine for an idealism based on the philosophy of Plotinus. Consequently he has been unfrocked and, as the novel begins, is living with his mother and wife and child Ada in the ancestral mansion at Ironsides in the heart of the Virginia mountains. Reduced to penury, the family gets along on the slight proceeds from a little school that John keeps in his house. His important work is his vegetable garden and the multivolumed philosophical tract *God as Idea* that he is writing. In this manner the family manages to create an "island of happiness" surrounded by "the ebb and flow of a treacherous universe."[50] In an age of shoddy values, objectless except for happiness-hunting, an age "distraught, chaotic, grotesque . . . of cruelty without moral indignation, of catastrophe without courage,"[51] the Fincastles were building "a home in the wilderness of the machines as their forefathers had cleared the ground and built a home in the wilderness of the trees."[52]

As in *Barren Ground*, the spirit that makes possible their survival is in itself a deterministic force; it corresponds to the Calvinist drive of will, God-given, that carries the elect to inevitable triumph through the evils and miseries of life. "The vein of iron . . . *could* not yield . . . *could* not be broken."[53] (Italics added.) Partly, the spirit of fortitude is the gift of a tradition—

"the strong fibers, the closely knit generations."[54] One can rely on this heritage in moments of adversity. But partly it is something God-given to man, for one can reject the doctrine of election without rejecting God.

At any rate, in the words of John Fincastle, Ellen Glasgow (one may assume) is herself rejecting the materialist forms of determinism: "It is possible that God is more than motion. It is even possible that modern man is more than glandular maladjustment."[55] The frontier, Miss Glasgow asserts, occasionally produces persons who can rise above destiny. It is not possible without the vein of iron, which cannot yield, cannot be broken. When one of Miss Glasgow's protagonists— usually a woman—is in deep trouble, the vein of iron asserts itself and, like a *deus ex machina,* provides an escape from despair.

William Faulkner

In his Nobel Prize acceptance speech, William Faulkner, like Ellen Glasgow, stated his conviction that motivation and character are more than functions of the glands. The proper subject for the novelist, he said, is the human heart in conflict with itself. By the heart he means, perhaps among other things, the will, the desires. But the heart, he finds, is not totally free. It is directed by its own determinisms, though not primarily by biochemical ones. In *The Sound and the Fury* the idiot Benjy is, of course, deprived of even the slightest semblance of free will. With him glands, or whatever body chemistry causes idiocy, is in complete control. But with other characters in the book we find something quite suggestive of Calvinism: the heart in the clutch of overwhelming desires that it carries out freely in accordance with its own sometimes perverted logic. Quentin is incapable of willing anything but his own destruction; the greed-and-hate-dominated Jason wills revenge upon his sister and more profits from his speculations in cotton. It would be difficult to imagine either of these characters acting other than as presented in the book. They are embodiments of more or less destructive desires over which they seemingly have no control and which they are unable to displace by other desires.

How, then, can Faulkner disclaim naturalistic determinism, as he appears to be doing in the Nobel Prize speech? Some very competent critics have regarded that speech as mere rhetoric, high-sounding sentiments, having no connection with the realities of Faulkner's own writing. However, by a Calvinistic line of reasoning an explanation can be reached. All the major characters other than Benjy in *The Sound and the Fury* are so free to follow their wills that they achieve their goals, ruinous though they may be, with great success. Some human beings willfully direct their lives toward destruction. Such disparate figures as Calvin, Dostoevski, and Freud are agreed upon this. And to Dostoevski and Calvin, at least, freedom to achieve these ends is freedom of the will.

What is the source of these perversions of the will? Original sin, the inscrutable soul of man, and faulty childhood up-bringing are three of the many origins postulated. In none of these cases does the agent have much to say about the nature of his will, and to this extent his will is not free. Each thinking person will have his own notions as to what such circumscribed freedom really is worth. To most the bondage will not seem so great as that presented in a strictly naturalistic novel where the characters are the playthings of environment and bio-chemistry to the extent of being automatons. Whatever the degree of his determinism, Faulkner's viewpoint squares more closely with Calvinism than with naturalism. The ex-istence in his novels of such liberated characters as Dilsey and Lucas Beauchamp—who seem very much in control of their own destinies and are not dominated by a one-track will—places him farther on the Calvinist side. Such characters correspond to the elect, the redeemed who are free to do con-structive deeds, while the Candaces, the Quentins, and the

Jasons are the damned. A strict naturalist cannot logically create characters like Dilsey and Lucas, for everything in their lives is contradictory to what one would expect from the conditioning of their environment.

The most compelling echo of Calvinism in Faulkner's major novels is the impression they convey of a destiny being worked out on a plane broader and loftier than that occupied by mere individuals. In these novels there is always a strong sense of the past—usually a sinful past—which exerts an evil influence on the present and, like the original sin of Adam, must be expiated, or redeemed. Indeed if the orthodox Christian ascribes the perverted will of man to the sin in the Garden of Eden, Faulkner relates the sorry plight of his doomed characters to family histories of violence and crime. To Faulkner the original sin in Yoknapatawpha County—and in the whole South—was the white man's exploitation of the black man as his chattel and the black woman not only as a slave but as a concubine whose children by him he disowned and condemned to bondage. One way of explaining the misdirected wills of the Compsons and others is that they are reaping the evil sown by their fathers. At any rate, where a race or a society has fallen, redemption becomes imperative. Faulkner's South still awaits redemption, although in *Intruder in the Dust, The Bear,* and *Light in August* Faulkner shows the beginnings of redemptive operations.

Light in August

In *Light in August* the sense of destiny is the strongest, as the echoings of Calvinism are the most persistent. On one level we have everyday life—the life principle itself—embodied in Lena Grove as she trudges across Alabama and Mississippi in search of the father of the child that has swollen her belly. Lena herself, to be sure, is the victim of a one-track will directed toward the survival of her child and the establishment of a family for it. There is, moreover, something mechanical about her movement as she rides along on the monotonously rumbling farm wagons of the countrymen who give her lifts on her journey. Her will is so single-purposed that she seems will-less, a machine. But Faulkner takes pains to blend her into the landscape so that she appears as a part of the purpose of nature; her mechanical motion is a delusion fostered by the harmony of desires with those of nature. People like her and Byron Bunch, who marries her after her lover deserts her, represent what Hawthorne was fond of calling the great warm heart of humanity. They are the true mothers and fathers of the human race, and redemption, if it occurs, must be for them and their progeny rather than for the tragic, haunted figures who play out the roles of expiation.

Other major figures of *Light in August* are indeed haunted— by their own past and by that of their families and of their region. Not one of them is a free agent in the sense of having the ability to break out of the fated groove of his will; all are doomed to pursue destinies which they *desire* obsessively to achieve. Most monomaniacal of all is "Doc" Hines, Joe Christmas's grandfather, in whom we have a modern equivalent of Brockden Brown's Wieland— a man who commits the most hideous atrocities because he believes they are God's will. "Doc" Hines is convinced that he is God's "chosen instrument"[56] to serve His foreordained will. God's will, as Hines understands it, is to eradicate "abomination"[57] and "bitchery"[58] from the world and to slaughter all Negroes. When his daughter has sexual relations with a dark-skinned circus roustabout who might be either a Mexican or a Negro, Hines, assuming the man is a Negro, shoots him in the back and permits his daughter to die in childbirth while he forcibly keeps the doctor from her bedside. After taking the child to a white orphanage one Christmas Eve (thus the child, later the protagonist of the novel, is named Joe Christmas), Hines himself takes a job in the institution as a janitor, not revealing his identity. For a number of years he observes the child, becoming more and more convinced of his Negroness. When

Joe is adopted by a white farmer, Hines loses track of him. But years later he learns that the murderer of the white woman Joanna Burden is his grandson, and he does his best to incite a mob to lynch him.

Hines is, of course, the victim of religious dementia and, as such, affords a clear-cut example of a will trapped beyond all hope of release. Yet his delusion that he is God's instrument is a perversion of the Calvinist theology of the time and place, as his murderous hatred of Negroes is an exaggerated instance of a well-known prejudice. One would never say that Hines is responsible for his actions, but neither would one say he did not pursue his diseased volition with considerable freedom and success. And, psychotic though Hines may be, his actions as Faulkner presents them seem part of the logical, inevitable working out of the destiny of the South. They have a significance that the mere aberrations of a crazed mind seldom have.

Less dangerous but scarcely less completely obsessed is the Presbyterian minister, the Reverend Gail Hightower. His entire awareness is focused on the supposedly glorious death of his grandfather, an officer in the Confederate Army. Hightower sought his appointment to the church in Jefferson (the major scene of the novel) because it was there that the grandfather's martyrdom occurred (actually the grandfather was shot while robbing a chicken coop). So far gone is Hightower that he suffers from hallucinations, hearing the thunder of the raiding cavalry's hoofbeats as he muses in his easy chair. Needless to say, his ministry suffers from this preoccupation; and when his wife also goes mad, mainly from living with him, and dies violently, he is dismissed. He lives on in Jefferson, listening to the hoofbeats, until the time of the chief events of the novel.

As a man dominated by an obsession, Hightower cannot be said to enjoy much freedom of the will, though he does have the satisfaction of gratifying the obsession at the cost of every other value in life. Unlike Hines, he is also able to understand the causes of human cruelty and to feel compassion not only for its victims, but, more importantly, for its perpetrators. He himself is whipped by a mob because he keeps a Negro woman in his house after the loss of his wife. Yet typical of him is the exclamation: "Poor man. Poor mankind"[59]; and of the impending lynching of Joe Christmas, he says: "And they will do it gladly. . . . Since to pity him would be to admit self doubt and to hope for and need pity themselves. They will do it gladly, gladly. That's why it is so terrible, terrible, terrible."[60] The killing about to take place he considers a crucifixion—of the people themselves as well as of their victim.

As a minister, Hightower is strong on the idea of redemption; everything in life must be paid for; "there is a price for being good the same as for being bad."[61] When he delivers Lena's baby, Hightower pays for some of the selfishness in his life—as if the night riders had not long ago exacted full payment with their whips. When he lies to the lynchers in an effort to save Christmas, he further redeems his past but at the same time risks the exaction of additional retribution by the mob. His good act will thus be paid for in suffering. But the façt is that Hightower is capable of redemptive action outside the narrow channel of his obsession, and to this extent he may be considered a free agent.

The notion of redemption, so emphatically voiced by Hightower, lies at the heart of the novel and is most fully manifest in the life and death of the main character, Joe Christmas. To begin with, Joe's destiny is presented in such a way as to suggest a parallel with that of Jesus. The import of his last name is obvious; his first name, Hines points out, is that of Mary's husband, the head of the family in which Jesus lived. Joe is first introduced into the white world when his grandfather leaves him on the steps of an orphanage on Christmas Eve. Since Hines, according to his own demented mind, is not only God's instrument but sometimes God Himself ("Don't lie to me, to the Lord God,"[62] he admonishes an employee in the orphanage), we can say that in terms of this delusion Joe's advent, like that of Christ, was part of the divine plan for the universe. Joe's growing up, his youth and his manhood till the time the story begins bear little resemblance to the life of Christ, but in his last days parallels are discernible again. Joe feels himself to be acting out a special destiny, albeit a criminal one; to this destiny his life is devoted and he will not betray it. But after he commits the murder, he himself is betrayed for reward money by his Judas-like disciple Brown. In the thirty-third year of his life, approximately the same age as Jesus at the time of his passion, Joe suffers a violent death—repeatedly referred to as a crucifixion—at the hands of a lynch mob headed by the citizen soldier Peter Grimes.

It would be possible to explain Joe's disastrous life in psychoanalytic or sociological terms. But Faulkner, who repudiates scientific determinism in accounting for human action, has apparently superimposed the Christ legend upon Joe's story in order to lend the latter more significance than a straight case history would have. One should not, however, totally reject the psychoanalytic and sociological determinants, but should accept them as offering only a partial illumination of Joe's motivation. Joe's career had its inception—perhaps was given its lifelong direction—in an episode that occurred in his babyhood at the orphanage. Sneaking into the dietician's room to eat her toothpaste, he unintentionally witnessed an act of coitus between her and a young intern. Becoming actively sick from the toothpaste, he is discovered by the dietician, who calls him a "little nigger bastard."[63] Nausea, sex, and Negroness combine into a complex that undoubtedly influences all Joe's subsequent actions. The close association of the three makes him disgusted with the sex act, though he indulges in it often, and antagonizes him towards his own identity as, supposedly, a part Negro. But none of this is sufficient to account for the feeling that Joe has from earliest childhood, that he has been chosen for some special destiny. When his grandfather abducts him from the orphange (he is soon returned), Faulkner writes: "[Joe] might have thought *He hates me enough even to try to prevent something that is about to happen to me coming to pass.*"[64]

When he is adopted by the McEacherns, a strict Presbyterian couple, the husband of which, like Mrs. Thayer in Mary Wilkins Freeman's *Pembroke*, attempts to beat the Westminster Catechism into the boy's brain with a whip, Joe's sense of participating in a predestined drama grows upon him. There is something mechanical in all his movements, as if directed by a will outside himself. Thus when he is fleeing from his foster parent, he runs straight to McEachern's horse "with something of the adopted father's complete faith in an infallibility in events,"[65] though he is far from certain where the beast is tied. Later, when he first establishes himself as Joanna Burden's lover, he finds that his feet, quite outside his own volition, carry him there with a sensation of effortless floating. In his whole relationship with Miss Burden, he is more like an automaton than a self-directed being. Joe is in fact at times disturbed at what he finds himself doing. "[This was not the] lonely street he had chosen of his own will. . . . *This is not my life. I don't belong here.*"[66] Yet this lonely street— that of a man who is neither white nor Negro—is not, apparently, his destiny, though he believes it to be. His being sidetracked from it, and his consequent martyrdom, is more likely the great event for which his life is predestined. What he thinks he has chosen for himself is unattainable, and his days are hurtling onwards toward a very different end.

But he fights for what he thinks is his chosen direction: "If I give in now [by marrying Joanna], I will deny all the thirty years that I have lived to make me what I chose to be."[67] However, all along, his chosen life as a lone wolf outside the law has been fraught with "bewilderment and perhaps foreboding and fatality."[68] Before he enters Joanna's house on the night of the murder, the foreboding has grown to a certainty: "*Something is going to happen. Something is going to happen to me.*"[69] At this point, "he believed with calm paradox that he was

the volitionless servant of the fatality in which he believed that
he did not believe. He was saying to himself *I had to do it* already
in the past tense; *I had to do it. She said so herself*[.]."[70] What he
had to do was murder Joanna, go through the motions of
fleeing from the law, and suffer the inevitable capture and
death by lynching. The events after the murder, however, need
not concern us here. They proceed with a mathematical exacti-
tude and certainty. Events, forces outside his immediate choice
or control have made a sacrificial victim of Joe. Lest his life
be taken as merely a sociological phenomenon, Faulkner
has seen fit to present it within a framework of destiny—as part
of some purpose larger than the series of happenings which
it includes.

If this drama of destiny is to be understood at all, Joanna
Burden's role in it must be examined. Joe Christmas murders
Joanna because she blocks the lonely road that he has chosen
to follow—the road traveled by those who are neither Negro
nor white. Were he to settle down with her, he would no
longer be alone. Furthermore, Joanna has offered to help him
get an education and make a place for him in life, and Joe
has always violently rejected any help that well-meaning
persons have offered him. Like Captain Snegirov in *The
Brothers Karamazov*, he is one of the humiliated in whom hu-
miliation has engendered a fierce and destructive pride. From
the days when Mrs. McEachern tried to treat Joe like a son,
his pride has not allowed him to accept kindness. In summary,
Joanna is a threat because in connection with the race problem
she has chosen the approach of love, and Joe is dominated by
hate.

But one must not be sentimental about Joanna. Her work
in improving the lot of the Negro is based on a fanaticism as
strong as that of the lynchers. Joanna's heritage is one of New
England Calvinism. Her father and grandfather came to
Mississippi right after the Civil War with government com-
missions to help the freedmen. Not long afterward the grandfather and Joanna' halfbrother—she was not born until four-

teen years after his death—were shot by a former Confederate general in a quarrel over Negro voting rights. Joanna's father did not avenge the death of his kinsmen because, being part French (as Joanna explains), he respected "anybody's love for the land where he and his people were born" and understood "that a man would have to act as the land where he was born had trained him to act."[71] The same respect and understanding for the South, whose people (in Jefferson at least) incidentally maintained an unflagging hostility toward her, prompted Joanna to remain there and carry on the work her family had begun. These qualities in her stamped her with the mark of Faulkner's approbation.

The motive of the first Burdens in helping the Negroes was entirely theological, albeit weirdly so, and the traces of theology are present in Joanna's rationale for her activities. Joanna's father summarizes for her, as a girl, the Burden mystique:

> Your grandfather and brother are lying there, murdered not by one white man but the curse which God put on a whole race. . . . A race doomed and cursed to be forever and ever a part of the white race's doom and curse for its sins. Remember that. His doom and his curse. Forever and ever. Mine. Your mother's. Yours, even though you are a child. . . . None can escape it.[72]

These words, Joanna says, had a powerful influence on her. Previously she had taken Negroes for granted, simply as creatures who inhabited the same world into which she was born. But now she saw them as a "black shadow in the shape of a cross"[73] falling across the lives of the whole white race, past, present, and future. The shadow terrified her and she had nightmares about it. She told her father she must escape the shadow or she would die. But he told her she could not escape it:

> You must struggle, rise. But in order to rise, you must raise

the shadow with you. But you can never lift it to your level. I see that now, which I did not see until I came down here. But escape it you cannot. The curse of the black race is God's curse. But the curse of the white race is the black man who will be forever God's chosen one because He once cursed him. [*sic*][74]

The Burdens' view and "Doc" Hines's view are similar in that each presupposes that the Negro is accursed. But Hines would exterminate the Negro while the Burdens would attempt to "improve" him. In neither view is there brotherliness; rather there is fear mingled with anger. For the Negro who has accepted the white man's notion of what is the good life, Joanna's efforts to "lift" him to the white man's level are certainly more acceptable than Hines's murderous hostility. In fact, as has been stated, Joanna's labors are doubtless leavened with love. But for Joe Christmas, the outcast from either race, Joanna's way is as objectionable as Hines's. Men like Joe, inevitable products of an ethnic situation like that in America, seem doomed to be crushed, either by death or by life. By paralleling Joe's advent and death with Christ's, Faulkner would suggest that there is some redemptive value in suffering like his, that men outraged as he has been die not entirely without making some impression in the spiritual evolution of man. And to Faulkner, the racial problem is basically a spiritual one. Its sociological aspects are secondary.

Thus in *Light in August*, as in many other Faulkner novels, the protagonists are endowed with wills the directions of which are determined by forces other than the agents' free choice. In short, we have an applicaton of the Calvinist formula. Nor with Faulkner's characters is the direction of the will wholly determined by "scientific" laws. Freudian, environmental, and historical forces do play a part. But there is something more than these: something closely resembling predestination Calvinistically conceived. Calvinistic predestination and naturalistic determinism have been fused into an amalgam.

8

Libertarian Philosophies Opposed to Predestination and Naturalistic Determinism

Arminianism

The transition from Calvinistic predestination to naturalistic determinism, as shown above, was an easy one. Equally easy, and taking place much earlier was the step from liberalized religion, in which predestination and election had either been dropped or come to be virtually ignored, to a full-fledged humanism in which the will was believed to be firmly in control of its own destiny. The first force to exert influence in this direction was Arminianism, which has been an issue of controversy since the seventeenth century.

Arminianism consists of the views of the Dutch Reformed theologian, Jacob Arminius (1560–1609). As set forth in a document of 1610, Arminianism rejects the Calvinistic doctrines of predestination, including election; of limited atonement, whereby Christ is held to have died only for the elect; of irresistible grace; and of the perseverance of saints. According to Arminianism, salvation is attainable by all who believe in Jesus Christ, though one may reject grace when offered. As with Calvinism, salvation is dependent on God's grace, but this grace is accessible to all persons of genuine faith. To the Arminian, life is a testing and training ground where man, born with a capacity for righteousness as well as for evil, can by his own efforts cast off the guilt incurred by Adam and achieve redemption.

Needless to say, Arminianism allowed for a much wider scope of freedom of choice and of will than did Calvinism. Even within the Calvinist churches, the drift toward Arminianism was strong and unceasing. By the time Cotton Mather started writing his *Bonifacius: An Essay upon the Good*, the efficacy of good works—the Covenant of Works, as the idea was loosely called—in winning one's salvation was on the verge of general acceptance. It was against this tendency in the New England churches that Jonathan Edwards leveled the polemic of his famous treatise on the will.

In most theological controversy of the seventeenth, eighteenth, and early nineteenth centuries, the question of the freedom of the will was pivotal. As William James has pointed out, philosophies and religious sects stand or fall according to the solutions they present for this knotty problem. Our lives, James reminds us, are passed in a continuous expenditure of effort to one end or another. Whether this effort is free or not—that is, whether it is under our own relatively autonomous direction or not—is obviously a matter of the utmost importance in shaping our attitudes toward existence and our more formal philosophies and theologies. In an eloquent passage at the end of the chapter on "Will" in *Psychology*, James affirms the critical place of effort in our lives and in our estimates of our own worth:

> Thus not only our morality but our religion, so far as the latter is deliberate, depend on the effort which we can make. *"Will you or won't you have it so?"* is the most probing question we are ever asked; we are asked it every hour of the day, and about the largest as well as the smallest, the most theoretical as well as the most practical, things. We answer by *consents or non-consents* and not by words. What wonder that these dumb responses should seem our deepest organs of communication with the nature of things! What wonder if

the effort demanded by them be the measure of our worth as men! What wonder if the amount which we accord of it were the one strictly underived and original contribution which we make to the world![1]

Competing with Calvinism were other organized religions that were markedly libertarian without being self-consciously Arminian. Among these was Quakerism, with its emphasis upon humane action as pleasing to God and its assumption that salvation is open to all who permit the always available love and light of God to flow freely through them. The following passage from John Woolman's *Journals* states the Quaker view:

> Our own real good and the good of our posterity in some measure depend on the part we act. . . . Such are the different rewards of the just and unjust in a future state that to attend diligently to the dictates of the spirit of Christ, to devote ourselves to His service and to engage fervently in His cause during our short stay in this world is a choice well becoming a free, intelligent creature.[2]

Quaker belief was, and is, strongly weighted toward the Covenant of Works.

Anglicanism, though paying lip service to Calvinistic ideas on predestination and election, was essentially Arminian in the eighteenth century and has remained so ever since. Most notable among the Anglican thinkers in colonial America was Samuel Johnson of Connecticut. A Congregational minister in his youth and an instructor at Yale College, where Edwards was his pupil, Johnson was later converted to the Anglican Church, in which he took orders. The first president of King's College (now Columbia) in New York, and a good friend of Benjamin Franklin, he was prominent in the intellectual life of the times. His pronouncements on the subjects of predestination and free will are diametrically opposed to those of the Calvinists, against whom he carried on an unrelenting war of words.

> Indeed that [God] should, without any voluntary fault of
> mine, put me into a condition that is, in the whole, worse
> than not to be; or that He should, in giving me my being,
> lay me under an absolute necessity of being finally sin-
> ful and miserable: this would be a very hard case indeed:
> But this I must think utterly impossible, as being what I
> cannot think consistent with His wisdom, holiness, justice
> and goodness. . . . If now I should ask, why hath God made
> me at all peccable, or capable of sin? This would be the
> same as to ask, why hath He made me capable of duty?
> Or, why hath He made me a free agent? But this would be
> a strange question; for without liberty I should be destitute
> of one of the chief excellencies of my rational nature, and
> should not be capable of either duty or sin, properly speak-
> ing; for a sin consists in a free and willing disobedience to
> the known Will of God. So that without a power of liberty or
> free agency, there could have been no such thing as either
> virture or vice, praise or blame. . . .[3]

Finally, beginning in the latter half of the eighteenth century, Unitarianism—a schism from the Calvinistic churches
in New England—hammered away at such orthodox doctrines
as that of irresistible grace. A passage from William Ellery
Channing's famous discourse, *Unitarian Christianity*, is sufficient illustration.

> We believe that all virtue has its foundation in the moral
> nature of man, that is, in conscience or his sense of duty,
> and in the power of forming his temper and life according
> to conscience. We believe that these moral faculties are
> the grounds of responsibility and the highest distinctions of
> human nature, and that no act is praiseworthy any further
> than it springs from their exertion. We believe that no
> dispositions infused into us without our own moral activity
> are of the nature of virtue, and therefore, we reject the doc-
> trine of irresistible divine influence on the human mind,
> moulding it into goodness as marble is hewn into a stat-
> ue. . . .[4]

Deism

Among most deists the shift to good works as the basis for a religious life was complete. Benjamin Franklin, brought up as a Calvinist, speaks with impatience of sermons on predestination to which he was subjected in his early years. Though he himself, in *A Dissertation on Liberty and Necessity, Pleasure and Pain* (1725), argued for a deterministic universe, he quickly abandoned this view. Such matters, indeed, seemed of no importance to him; they had no bearing on the affairs of everyday life. Useful work—useful to one's fellows as well as to oneself—was Franklin's idea of activity pleasing to God. Admitting his debt to Cotton Mather's *Bonifacius: An Essay upon the Good*, he retained the ethical side of Puritan teaching but rejected Calvinist theology. The ideal of self-improvement, making the best out of what one has, found its chief expression in his famous plan for attaining moral perfection. The inevitable self-analysis, the soul-searching that went into the diaries of Puritans examining the evidences of their conversion, took its form with Franklin in the account book reckonings that he made of his daily deviations from a carefully preplanned set of rules of behavior. As for man's very considerable control over his personal and collective destiny, Franklin and the deists had very little doubt. They believed that by the use of reason and good will mankind could achieve happiness and a nearly perfect society on this earth. They believed in an afterlife in which the individual receives a reward or a punishment in accordance with his actions during his years in the world. Election, or the Covenant of Grace, was discarded.

Thus Thomas Jefferson, born an Anglican but in later life a deist, considered Calvin an atheist, for "the Being described in [Calvin's] five points, is not . . . the Creator and benevolent Governor of the world; but a daemon of malignant spirit."[5] Jefferson would have been in full agreement with Elihu Palmer, in whose draft of the "Principles of the Deistical

Society of New York" is the statement "that man is possessed of moral and intellectual faculties sufficient for the improvement of his nature, and the acquisition of happiness."[6]

As outspoken as Jefferson in the assault upon Calvinsim is Ethan Allen, who, in his *Reason the Only Oracle of Man*, holds up to ridicule the Edwardsian argument that in following out the foreordained bent of one's will one actually enjoys a measure of freedom:

> Some advocates for the doctrine of fate will also maintain that we are free agents, notwithstanding they tell us there has been a concatenation of causes and events, which has reached from God down to this time, and which will eternally be continued; that has and will controul [*sic*] and bring about every action of our lives, though there is not anything in nature more certain than that we cannot act necessarily and freely, in the same action, and at the same time, yet it is hard for such persons, who have verily believed that they are elected (and thus by a predetermination of God become his special favorites) to give up their notion of a predetermination of all events, upon which system their election and everlasting happiness is nonsensically founded.[7]

The consciousness of freedom was strong in the eighteenth century, which was indeed a century of social and individual liberation. Vernon Parrington argues that Calvinism with its sense of destiny—the assurance that it imparts to the elect that God directs their every step—was a system of thought made to order for settlers in a hostile wilderness. If this is true, then the libertarianism of the eighteenth century was no less appropriate to an age that contained the American and French Revolutions. The fact that in America the masses were still adherents to the older, more orthodox religions—which in many cases meant Calvinism—does not alter the case. The leaders, who were for the most part deists and hence libertarians, were not in the least averse to making an appeal to the orthodoxy of the people. Deists are by very definition tolerant of other religions.

Even Thomas Paine, the least tolerant of the deists, inserts into *Common Sense* many Biblical statements that he supposes support his cause, though in *The Age of Reason* he characterizes most of the Bible as a compendium of superstition and falsehood. In eighteenth-century America reference to the Bible to bolster one's argument was sound debate; it swayed men's minds when pure reason would not. Similarly, Paine appealed to the sense of destiny that had been a facet of the American mass mood since the Puritans first convinced themselves that they were God's instruments in founding a New Jerusalem. Thus Paine writes: "The authority of Great Britain over this continent, is a form of government which sooner or later must have an end. . . . It is not in the power of Britain or of Europe to conquer America, if she does not conquer herself by *delay* and *timidity.*"[8] Yet in general, *Common Sense* is overwhelmingly an appeal to reason rather than to religious sentiment. It assumes, as do Paine's more deistic utterances, that man has his future in his own hands. He can make of his life what he wishes. He can be a slave or a free man; the choice is his.

The antipathies aroused by Calvinism in the eighteenth and early nineteenth centuries cannot be exaggerated. Among its attackers and detractors two states of mind prevailed: an outraged sense of justice and an outraged sense of logic. We have already noted the indignation aroused in Jefferson. His reaction was commonplace. Jonathan Mayhew, an early religious liberal, bluntly stated that the doctrine of reprobation whereby God arbitrarily condemns some souls to hell regardless of their efforts to win salvation "is horrible to the last degree and blasphemous against . . . God."[9] Even W. E. Channing, normally a mild man, found that the Calvinist system filled his mind "with horror which we want words to express."[10] These same writers, of course, also attacked Calvinism on grounds of logic and common sense, with results wittily, though perhaps exaggeratedly, described by Oliver Wendell Holmes in "The Deacon's Masterpiece," which was directed specifically against the theology of Edwards:

> The poor old chaise in a heap or mound,
> As if it had been to the mill and ground!
> You see, of course, if you're not a dunce,
> How it went to pieces all at once,—
> All at once, and nothing first—
> Just as bubbles do when they burst.
> End of the wonderful one-hoss shay,
> Logic is logic. That's all I say.[11]

What outraged and shocked all these critics is the degradation of both God and man that they saw resulting from the
deterministic basis of Calvinism. Of God they thought it
made a merciless, irrational, immoral tyrant; of man, a puppet
to be played with or smashed at the whim of its maker. That
Calvinism as preached and practiced was not usually so bad as
these critics implied goes without saying. As Harriet Beecher
Stowe repeatedly pointed out, the Calvinist ministers were,
more often than not, rather mild and humane men. Every
sermon was not on the subject of election or predestination.
The Christian virtues were encouraged and observed to an
impressive extent. Yet an age that was supposedly devoting
itself to the political liberation of mankind could hardly be
expected to favor a religion whose God had certain unmistakable resemblances to King George III. There is no advantage to freeing oneself from the rule of an earthly despot,
if the ruler of the whole universe is equally oppressive. A
consciousness of freedom is essential if we are to seek freedom.

Transcendentalism

Many of the more radical Unitarian ministers who later
became associated with what is loosely called the transcendental movement combated not only Calvinism but any
system that tended to reduce man to a mechanism. Thus
Theodore Parker writes heatedly against the "sensational

school," by which he apparently means those philosophies derived from John Locke:

> The sensationalist knows no first truths in morals; the source of maxims in morals is experience; in experience there is no absolute right. Absolute justice, absolute right, were never in the senses, so not in the intellect; only whimsies, words in the mouth. The will is not free, but wholly conditioned, in bondage; character made always for you, not by you. The intellect is a smooth table; the moral power a smooth table; and experience writes there what she will. [12]

In opposition, Parker places "the transcendental school," or those philosophies which ascribe to man "faculties which transcend the senses." [13]

In the realm of ethics, that is, of personal conduct, "transcendentalism affirms," according to Parker,

> that man has moral faculties that lead him to justice and right, and by his own nature can find out what is right and just, and can know it and be certain of it. . . . Conscience transcends experience, and not explains but anticipates that, and the transcendental system of morals is to be founded on human nature and absolute justice. . . . The will of man is free; not absolutely free as God's, but partially free, and capable of progress to yet higher degrees of freedom. [14]

American transcendentalism, of which Parker was a major voice, marked a high point of reaction against determinism, whether of Calvinist or other origin. But paradoxically, transcendentalism contained within itself the seeds of another determinism, that of naturalism. In considering any phase of transcendentalism, one's chief attention must be paid to the works of Emerson. Not only was Emerson the most influential expounder of this philosophy, but he was one of the generally most influential writers and thinkers that America has produced. His essays have been standard reading in colleges and high schools for a hundred years; with many people his writings are associated in importance with such basic

American documents as the Constitution, Washington's Farewell Address, and Lincoln's Gettysburg Address.

In Emerson's essays one gets the ultimate among statements of individualism, of the potential dignity and godlike qualities of man. And one gets comfort from the essays, if one believes them. For if man is as Emerson says he is—a sharer in the Oversoul, a possessor of a spark of the Divine—then democracy must be the best form of government, and its success is insured. Man by his very divine nature should be his own governor. No longer is he subject to a remote or tyrannical monarch, whether earthly or heavenly. Even the sense of destiny, of fulfilling God's will, becomes supplanted by an exhilarating sense of man's own competence to attain whatever ends he sets himself. "There is a great responsible Thinker and Actor working wherever a man works. . . . A true man belongs to no other time or place, but is the centre of things."[15]

Emerson was keenly aware of the problem of the freedom of the will, and he grappled with it on a number of occasions. That his efforts never produced a dogmatic answer is a tribute to his honesty. One would naturally expect that a philosophy that exalts man into a participant in divinity itself would strive to endow him with a will that is divine in its liberty and ability to achieve its ends. Such seems to be the burden of the concluding passage of "Self-Reliance." After asserting that power and good come to us from within ourselves, not from outside, he deals with that most puzzling of exterior forces—fortune. "Most men gamble with her, and gain all, and lose all, as her wheel rolls. But do thou leave as unlawful these winnings, and deal with Cause and Effect, the chancellors of God. In the Will work and acquire, and thou hast chained the wheel of Chance. . . ."[16] The will of God and the will of man are one, Emerson would say. Through sequences of cause and effect God carries out His will. Godlike man can similarly use the laws of cause and effect to his own ends. Could there be a bolder statement of man's essential divinity? Could there be a more blasphemous doctrine, from the orthodox view?

In his essay "Fate" in *The Conduct of Life*, Emerson presents his most careful treatment of the problem of the will. He begins by describing fate—the uncontrollable, deterministic forces in life—as graphically and as uncompromisingly as any one has ever done. "We must see that the world is rough and surly, and will not mind a drowning man or a woman, but swallows your ship like a grain of dust."[17] Hereditary taints, natural disasters, accidents of birth—"no picture of life can have any veracity that does not admit the odious facts."[18] Everywhere and at all times man is beset by "Nature . . . the tyrannous circumstance, the thick skull, the sheathed snake, the ponderous rock-like jaw. . . . The book of Nature is the book of Fate."[19] None of the deterministic implications of science escapes Emerson: geology, phrenology, and biology, and the shackles that they seem to lock upon the will and the actions of the individual—all these he takes into account.

But having said all this, Emerson asks the same question that Tolstoy asks at the end of *War and Peace*: whence comes the consciousness of freedom?

> We must respect Fate as natural history, but there is more than natural history. For who and what is this criticism that pries into the matter? Man is not order of nature, sack and sack, belly and members, link in a chain, nor any ignominious baggage; but a stupendous antagonism, a dragging together of the poles of the Universe. . . .
> Nor can he blink at freewill [*sic*]. To hazard the contradiction,—freedom is necessary. . . . Forever wells up the impulse of choosing and acting in the soul. Intellect annuls Fate. So far as man thinks, he is free.[20]

Emerson's argument in the rest of the essay is the familiar Platonic or transcendental one found at the end of "Self-Reliance." It can be summarized as follows: mind infuses and informs matter; matter is the manifestation of mind and thus is subject to it. Man shares in the eternal mind (the Oversoul); thus man's mind controls matter. But the individual's particle of the Oversoul must be in accord with the entire cosmic Oversoul, which is obviously self-governing. The individual, then, works out the will of the Oversoul of which his spirit is a part. Man is free, therefore, to do the Oversoul's will, his own will, God's will. God's will, of course, is good. Emerson's conclusion, then, is essentially that of Augustine: true freedom lies in the inability to do evil.

> He who sees through the design, presides over it, and must will that which must be. We sit and rule, and though we sleep, our dream will come to pass. Our thought, though it were only an hour old, affirms an oldest necessity, not to be separated from thought, and not to be separated from will. They must always have coexisted. . . . It is not mine or thine, but the will of all mind. It is poured into the souls of all men, as the soul itself which constitutes them men. . . . A breath of will blows eternally through the universe of souls in the direction of the Right and Necessary.[21]

In addition to their similarity to Augustine's definition of true freedom, Emerson's remarks hauntingly echo the arguments of Edwards. One "must will that which must be" sounds suspiciously Calvinistic. So do the following comments of Emerson: "The soul contains the event that shall befall it,"[22] and, "The tendency of every man to enact all that is in his constitution is expressed in the old belief that the efforts which we make to escape from our destiny only serve to lead us into it."[23] Translated into Calvinist terms, these remarks say simply that the saints, come what may, will persevere to their salvation, for which they have been "elected." Everything they do will work toward that glorious destiny. Similarly, those not elected for salvation will inevitably bring about their own damnation; any efforts they make to escape will serve only to lead them to their fated end. And finally, Emerson's dictum in this same essay that a "man's fortunes are the fruit of his character"[24] echoes the Calvinist assumption that the elect will prosper materially as well as spiritually. "I have noticed," writes Emerson, "that a man likes better to be complimented on his position, as the proof of the last or total excellence, than on his merits."[25]

Emerson postulates in man a certain passiveness inappropriate to a creature endowed with thoroughgoing freedom of choice and action. "We lie in the lap of immense intelligence, which makes us receivers of its truth and organs of its activity."[26] This is the mystic's position, and mysticism, as practiced in the West at least, is basically a matter of allowing forces greater than ourselves to play through us and to find expression in our experience. The vast intelligence, the Oversoul, will do our choosing, our work, for us, provided we surrender ourselves to its influence. Certainly this surrender is not automatic, according to Emerson; in itself it is an act requiring power of the will. It involves sloughing off all the encrustations of custom, the spurious claims of society; it involves a complete return to one's self, this self being the world spirit, the Oversoul, the atman. "If any one imagines that this law is lax, let him keep its commandment one day."[27] But is not the ability to keep the commandment something akin to Calvin's saving grace?

At any rate, once one has abided by the commandment, the Oversoul will do the rest. This is the basis of most human accomplishment, Emerson believes, whether military, political, or artistic. It is well illustrated by his theory of aesthetic creativity: "The condition of true naming [poetry], on the poet's part, is his resigning himself to the divine *aura* which breathes through forms, and accompanying that."[28] Poetic insight, he argues, is not the result of intellectual effort, but of the mind's merging with the universal mind that informs all things. Artistic creation is thus a passive process. Inspiration will or will not come. One cannot force it; nor can, nor should, one control it when it does come. Vivian Hopkins in her book on Emerson's aesthetic theory, *Spires of Form*, has pointed out the analogies with Calvinism:

The need for individual submission, as Emerson interprets

it, carries a religious emphasis that implies obedient trust in Divine power. Emerson's conviction of the necessity for the soul's submission springs from his own experience and is reinforced by his awareness . . . of Calvinistic theory. . . . Edwards' speculation may well have assisted Emerson in shaping his theory of the submissive creative will.[29]

The Edwardsian influence here is perhaps less that of *Freedom of the Will*, with which Emerson was acquainted, than that of his sermon "A Divine and Supernatural Light." The "doctrine" of the latter is, "That there is such a thing as a Spiritual and Divine Light, immediately imparted to the soul by God, of a different Nature from any that is obtained by natural means."[30] This light is actually a feeling (not an intellectual conviction, but something much stronger) of the excellence of God and His revelations in the Scriptures. Like the individual's awareness of the Oversoul, the experience of such light may be considered mystical; in neither case is there a conscious effort of the will. Yet Edwards's idea implies a dualism: God working on the spirit of man. Emerson's is a monism: man is the Oversoul, or a part of it. Man's will is God's will.

Emerson's dilemma was that at heart he was a humanist and a monist at the same time. Humanism is essentially dualistic, or perhaps pluralistic: men and nature are separate; God and man are separate. In Emerson's own words,

> There are two laws discrete. . . .
> Law for man, and law for thing.[31]

It is only as a humanist, indeed, that Emerson is an indeterminist; but humanism is an extremely important, probably the most important, side of Emerson. A comparison of a great humanistic passage from Sophocles with a typical utterance of Emerson well illustrates this aspect of his philosophy. By Sophocles man is shown to be subject to certain divine laws which he is free to transgress, but at his own peril. But man himself in turn has dominion over God's other creatures:

Wonders are many, and none is more wonderful than man; the power that crosses the white sea, driven by the stormy south-wind, making a path under surges that threaten to engulf him; and Earth, the eldest of the Gods, the immortal, the unwearied, doth he wear, turning the soil with the offspring of horses, as the ploughs go to and fro from year to year.

And the light-hearted race of birds, and the tribes of savage beasts, and the sea-brood of the deep, he snares in the meshes of his woven toils, he leads captive, man excellent in wit.

And speech, and wind-swift thought, and all the moods that mould a state, hath he taught himself; and how to flee the arrows of the frost, when 'tis hard lodging under the clear sky, and the arrows of the rushing rain; yea, he hath resource for all. . . .[32]

Is Emerson in the following passage from "Fate" paraphrasing Sophocles?

The mischievous torrent is taught to drudge for man; the wild beasts he makes useful for food, or dress, or labor; the chemic explosions are controlled like his watch. These are now the steeds on which he rides. Man moves in all modes, by legs of horses, by wings of wind, by steam, by gas of balloon, by electricity, and stands on tiptoe threatening to hunt the eagle in his own element. There's nothing he will not make his carrier.[33]

And like a true humanist, Emerson deplored attitudes of mind that might paralyze the will of man. "They who talk much of destiny, their birth-star, etc., are in a lower dangerous plane, and invite the evils they fear."[34] Thus Emerson should be ranked among the humanists, among those who have faith in man's ability to shape his destiny. Emerson's monism does not constitute a closed system—or at least he was not willing to accept it as such—as does Spencer's reduction of all phenomena to manifestations of the law of conservation of energy, or Henry Adams's interpretation of history in terms of the second law of thermodynamics. In the final analysis, we must credit Emerson with strong libertarian convictions. It is no small thing to equate man's will with God's and not to subordinate one helplessly to the other, as was the Calvinists' wont. And it is the opposite of the spirit of scientific determinism to envisage man—as did Emerson—as endowed with an innate sense of right and wrong. Emerson wrote of laws, true,—laws of human psychology, such as his law of compensation, by which a seeming calamity is neutralized by a beneficent factor arising from it, or his law of evolution toward perfection: "The direction of the whole and of the parts is toward benefit. . . ."[35] But these laws are not deterministic.

Transcendentalism and Naturalism

Between transcendentalism and naturalism, however, there are definite links—there is transition rather than cleavage. The unity, the monism, that the transcendentalists were always trying to establish is certainly not alien to the monism that is the goal of science: the reduction of all phenomena to as few principles as possible and eventually and ideally to one. Transcendentalists, indeed, usually welcomed any advance of science toward unity. It was not tolerance but a feeling of spiritual kinship that made Whitman proclaim himself the poet of science. Also, the passive tendency in transcendentalism could easily blend into the determinism of science. Submissiveness to God, or to the Oversoul, is, after all, analogous to submissiveness to nature, of which we are a part.

These two aspects of transcendentalism are plainly present in Emerson, but they are more prominent in Henry David Thoreau. Emerson believed that nature exists as a manifestation of spirit and has, perhaps, no existence otherwise. Hence the Oversoul and the spirit of man (which is part of the Oversoul) contain nature within themselves. Thoreau similarly, as a transcendentalist, regarded spirit as the ultimate reality and held material nature to be the incarnation of spirit. Yet he did not differentiate so sharply between nature and spirit as Emerson did. To Thoreau, the spiritual reality and the material illusion were more closely identified as modes of one and the same unity. Thoreau felt keenly a oneness with the spirit which lies behind, or encompasses, nature, but he equally felt a oneness with nature herself. Nature is absorbed in the spirit, and man is absorbed in nature as well as in the spirit. In the words of St. Theresa, "the fish is in the sea and the sea is in the fish." God is in nature and nature is in God; and, to the transcendentalist, man as God and nature combined is in both.

The difference between Thoreau's view, as outlined above, and that of Emerson is one of degree, but it is appreciable. Emerson could not have said as Thoreau did in *Walden*: "I go and come with a strange liberty in nature, a part of herself. . . . Shall I not have intelligence with the earth? Am I not partly leaves and vegetable mould myself?"[36] All of Thoreau's writings are, in a sense, a plea for us to attune ourselves to nature, for to do so is to attune ourselves to the Oversoul that informs all nature. "I wish to speak a word for Nature, for absolute freedom and wildness, as contrasted with a freedom and culture merely civil,—to regard man as an inhabitant, or a part and parcel of Nature, rather than a member of society."[37] Thus does Thoreau begin his essay on "Walking," published in the *Atlantic Monthly* in 1862. On the surface, this is simply another essay on nature, its beauties and its revivifying effects on man. But from the beginning, the religious implications are obvious. The saunterer (a word that Thoreau derives from the French *Sainte-Terre* and thus meaning a *Holy-Lander*) is as much a pilgrim as were those who of old walked across Europe to Jerusalem, "For every walk is a sort of crusade, preached by some Peter the Hermit in us, to go forth, and reconquer the Holy Land from the hands of the Infidels."[38]

But the walker must be passive, must submit himself to nature. Thoreau meant this quite literally. When he himself issued from his house for a walk with no destination in view, he found that invariably he would head toward the west. This westward gravitation he finds to be a tendency in human history as a whole. He is himself submitting to an instinct when he falls into step "with the general movement of the race."[39] The western movement he regards as a rebirth into paradise, which is the state of the soul before it is cut off from the spiritual All in which it had its first home.

> We go eastward to realize history and study the works of art and literature, retracing the steps of the race; we go westward as into the future, with a spirit of enterprise and adventure. The Atlantic is a Lethean stream, in our passage over which we have had an opportunity to forget the Old World and its institutions. If we do not succeed this time, there is perhaps one more chance for the race left before it arrives on the banks of the Styx; and that is the Lethe of the Pacific. . . .[40]

This is assuredly the ultimate in the romantic, in the primitivistic, and at the same time it shares in the spirit of scientific naturalism in its assumption of a "general movement of the race," determined by forces outside the conscious will. It is, for example, suggestive of the scientific determinism that pervades the work of John Steinbeck, himself as ardent a biologist and botanist as Thoreau. The Okies, like the symbolic turtle that precedes them in *Grapes of Wrath*, must move westward; no obstacle they meet is sufficient to stop them. And just as Steinbeck compares this human migration to the deliberate trek of the turtle, Thoreau compares man's westering instinct to that of squirrels that in their migrations are sometimes incomprehensibly and irresistibly prompted by instinct to cross the broadest rivers. For Thoreau was addicted to comparisons of man to animals—a habit that was to become an earmark of naturalistic writers. Furthermore, just as Thoreau feels most nearly at one with nature when he follows his instinct to turn west, so does the old man in Steinbeck's famous story "A Leader of the People." The important thing is that the old man has led a wagon train safely across the desert to the shores of that second Lethe, the Pacific. But, as he says, it was the westering, the feeling that he was part of one great group organism that was somehow fulfilling its destiny, it knew not how or why, by driving on to the western limits of the continent.

With Steinbeck the significance of these movements of "group-man,"[41] to use his phrase, barely stops short of the transcendental. With Thoreau, of course, it crosses deeply into the transcendental. The movements are ultimately symbolic of profound spiritual truths. The saunter in nature, with its inevitable westward drift to the newer Garden of Eden, is actually a drift spiritward. "My desire for knowledge is intermittent; but my desire to bathe my head in atmospheres unknown to my feet is perennial and constant. The highest that we can attain to is not Knowledge, but Sympathy with Intelligence."[42]

The step, then, from the romantic naturalism of Wordsworth, Emerson, and Thoreau to scientific naturalism and its accompanying determinism is not a wide one. In fact, this transition was being made by the Darwinians and others during the lifetimes of most of the transcendentalists. Yet, grappling with the Calvinistic determinism of the past and pretty well routing it, the transcendentalists thought of themselves as indeterminists and did much to reestablish man's concept of himself as a self-determining being.

John Burroughs

The determinism resulting from a fusion of science and transcendentalism is nowhere better exemplified than in certain essays of John Burroughs, a writer at one time of immense popularity whose work appeared in almost every magazine of distinction in the United States from 1860 to 1921—the *Atlantic Monthly, Scribner's, Century, Outlook,* and many others. So widely read were his essays, many of which dealt with problems of science, philosophy, and religion, that a good case could be made for him as a leader and formulator of opinion among educated Americans of his time. In his youth on a Catskill farm, Burroughs was nurtured on the primitive Calvinism of the Old School Baptists. Leaving home to become a teacher and later an author, he fell under the spell of Emerson and Whitman, whose philosophies he adopted and retained, with minor modifications, until his death. But Burroughs was also an avid student of science and an admirer of Huxley, Tyndall, Haeckel, and, especially, Darwin. The effecting of a synthesis of the scientific and transcendentalist visions of the universe became a lifelong goal with him— and he came close to achieving it, at least to his own satisfaction.

The synthesis, of course, had already been partly made by Emerson and Whitman, for both were intellectually hospitable to science and the accomplishments of engineering and industry. Burroughs received further aid from his reading of Henri Bergson, whose *Creative Evolution* he thought did much to undermine the positions of both the predestinarians and the scientific determinists. At any rate, Burroughs was interested all his life in the question of the freedom of the will, and there are more references to it in his writing than to any other theological or philosophical problem. At first he followed closely the thought of Emerson's "Self-Reliance": the promptings of our desires and our volitions are actually the dictates of the divinity within us; our will is an expression of the Oversoul, and it is free because the Oversoul is free. This view he found supported by David Wasson, a lesser transcendentalist, who in an article in the *Atlantic* of January, 1863, attacked Buckley's scientifically oriented determinism.

Burroughs' final and most extended statement on the will was in the essay "Fated to Be Free," published in 1916 in *Under the Apple-Trees* when Burroughs was seventy-eight years old. The title is Emersonian, but by this time Burroughs had abandoned the strictly transcendentalist point of view of his earlier years. Emerson and Wasson argued that the will is free, not as an individual agency but as an organ of indwelling divinity. Burroughs argued in "Fated to Be Free" that the will feels itself to be free because most of our choices and volitions are in harmony with our basic human nature and needs. We have the *illusion* of freedom. Like Bergson, he admits that, logically considered, the question as to whether or not the will is free must be answered negatively. In reality, we will as our fundamental human nature directs us. In other words, we are at liberty to act as we please but not to determine what pleases us—which is the state of affairs described by Edwards. Burroughs, however, remained sufficiently Emersonian to believe that nature is directed by what he called cosmic mind (the equivalent of the Oversoul), which he in turn roughly equated with Bergson's *élan vital*. Since to Burroughs human beings are entirely a part of nature, our wills are thus instruments of the creative energy of the universe as it activates the evolutionary development of man. Emerson, Bergson, Darwin, and science in general contributed to Burroughs' thesis, which is less than libertarian, perhaps, but far from rigidly deterministic. In merging the will with the evolutionary cosmic purpose, he assigns to it a more dignified status than it could occupy either in the block universe of the more inflexible of the naturalists or in the predestinated dispensation of the Calvinists. Though the transcendentalists did not grant the will complete freedom, they endowed it with an unprecedented importance and value. A next and inevitable step would be its full emancipation.

Philosophic Idealism

Another group closely akin to the transcendentalists philosophically—the idealists—require mention here. In the words of Josiah Royce, the best-known spokesman of this school, "the idealist maintains that there is in the universe but one perfectly real being, namely, the Absolute, that the Absolute is self-conscious and that this world is essentially in its wholeness the fulfillment *in actu* of an all-perfect ideal."[43] As to the will, Royce is less equivocal than Emerson: "There is, I doubt not, moral free will in the universe."[44] In his approach to the problem of evil, too, Royce is less cautious than Emerson, who regarded evil as "merely privative, not absolute: it is like cold, which is the privation of heat. All evil . . . is non-entity."[45]

If evil then—as Emerson would have it—is unreal, it is difficult to see how there can be any true choice between good and evil in which a free will might operate. Royce, on the other hand, escapes this dilemma: "The existence of evil . . . is not only consistent with the perfection of the universe, but is necessary for the very existence of that perfection."[46] The conflict between good and evil impulses and the triumph of the good over the evil, Royce believes, are essential to the spiritual life of man and of God, whose spirit man shares.

> It is not those innocent of evil who are fullest of the life of God, but those who in their own case have experienced the triumph over evil. It is not those naturally ignorant of fear . . . who possess the genuine experience of courage; but the brave are those who have fears, but control their fears.[47]

Outside of the deists, Royce is the most thoroughgoing indeterminist thus far encountered in this survey of American attitudes toward the will. Writing, as he did, during the latter part of the nineteenth century, he was bucking a strong tide of naturalistic determinism; and though he may not have made much headway against the current, he was at least not swept backward by it. Idealism, whether Emersonian or Roycean, remained an influence on American thought. One of its chief exponents among belletrists was E. A. Robinson, America's greatest philosophical poet, who too frequently is numbered among the naturalists. There has been much controversy as to just how much of a libertarian Robinson is. There is, to be sure, a strong leaven of fatalism or predestinarianism in his writing, as is not surprising in an author of Puritan cultural heritage. But to suggest, as one recent critic has done, that Robinson is more of a determinist than Edwards can be a result only of the misreading of Edwards.

Robinson, of course, does write of the evils of life: insanity, spiritual bankruptcy, social decay, frustration, and the destructiveness of blind chance; and he is fully aware of the odds against man when confronted by such forces. But never does he reduce man to a soul-less mechanism devoid of will, even in his earliest poetry, which is the most deterministic. In the poem titled "The Night Before," a murderer on the eve of his hanging tells a prison chaplain:

> Perilous
> Things are these demons we call our passions:
> Slaves are we of their roving fancies,
> Fools of their devilish glee.[48]

Yet this condemned man does not totally despair; the universe to him is neither entirely malevolent nor even indifferent to his sufferings. At the end of the poem he puts three questions:

> What are we,—
> Slaves of an awful ignorance? puppets
> Pulled by a fiend? or gods, without knowing it?[49]

This unfortunate obviously leans toward the third suggestion, since he has already said:

> I trust in something—
> I know not what. . . .[50]

Robinson's veering away from the notion of mankind as "puppets" or "slaves of an awful ignorance" becomes plain in another early poem, "The Children of the Night," which places the deterministic and idealistic viewpoints in diametric contrast, with patent preference for the latter. In the following stanzas the resemblances to Royce and Emerson are obvious. Robinson himself in his letters speaks of his interest in Emerson, and it is highly probable that he knew the thought of Royce, who was at Harvard while Robinson was a student there.

> For those that never know the light,
>   The darkness is a sullen thing;
> And they, the Children of the Night,
>   Seem lost in Fortune's winnowing.
> . . . .
> It is the faith within the fear
>   That holds us to the life we curse;—
> So let us in ourselves revere
>   The Self which is the Universe!
>
> Let us, the Children of the Night,
>   Put off the cloak that hides the scar!
> Let us be Children of the Light,
>   And tell the ages what we are![51]

The plight of the determinists (the Children of the Night, for whom "the darkness is a sullen thing") is exactly that of Hemingways' characters—for example, those in "A Clean, Well-Lighted Place" and in *A Farewell to Arms* —who so fear the night and who are so conscious of a meaningless fate that governs their lives and that, for some inscrutable reason, always kills first the good, the gentle, and the kind. The idealistic passages in Robinson's early poems, which also contain much of his gloomy pondering on evil and misfortune, are numerous. Their acceptance of evil is definitely in the spirit of Royce, however. That Robinson was consciously an idealist we know from his letters to his friend Harry De-Forest Smith, in which he reveals his philosophical development. While he was writing "The Night Before" he had not yet fully adopted idealism, though he was clearly tending in that direction. This incipient idealism is reflected mainly in the poem's purpose, which (as Robinson explains in a letter of 1894) was "to show that men and women are individuals,"[52] that is, not machines, who can sustain themselves by faith even when aware of a seemingly blind fate at work in their lives. Such an act of faith, incidentally, is an act of free will incompatible not only with Calvinism, which teaches that faith is a gratuitous gift of God and not attainable by the individual's own efforts alone, but also with naturalism, which would regard faith in this case as a meaningless self-delusion, a product of a sick mind.

By 1896 Robinson is saying that it is his intention in his poems "that there shall always be at least a suggestion of something wiser than hatred and something better than despair."[53] He wonders whether idealism may not be the last resort of those driven to desperation, but decides it is not necessarily so. At any rate his idealism is strong. Of Carlyle's *Sartor Resartus* he writes, also in 1896:

> If the book is anything it is a denial of the existence of matter as anything but a manifestation of thought. Christianity is the same thing, and so is illuminated common sense. . . . Epictetus and Socrates, Emerson and Carlyle, Paul and Christ . . . tell pretty much the same story from a more general point of view. This line of thought took hold of me when I was a Harvard, but my meeting with Jones was the first thing that set it fairly going.[54]

Jones was a friend of Robinson's in Gardiner, Maine, who attempted to convert him to Christian Science. Though highly respectful of the Scientist point of view, which he astutely recognized as a form of idealism and "a stepping stone to the truth," he finally rejected it as being "too dependent on unsubstantiated inferences."[55] What these inferences are he does not state; it is reasonable to guess that one might have been the sect's Emersonian denial of the existence

of evil. However, he did share, temporarily at least, the
Christian Scientists' conviction "that every man has it in his
power to overcome whatever obstacles may be in his way—
even that seeming obstacle we call by the name of Death."[56]
Such a statement is, of course, the extreme opposite of determinism; in all truth, it represents a pinnacle of optimism
that Robinson only rarely reached. Yet it indicates that he,
like Royce, believed that the evils of this world and its temptations are challenges to man's will, not insurmountable evidence of the will's impotence.

Captain Craig in Robinson's poem of that name is a
notable example of man's power to overcome obstacles, in
this case in the form of poverty, illness, and unemployment.
An "apparent failure" in the true Browningesque sense of the
phrase, the captain is a success by right of his achievement of
an idealistic philosophy to which eventually he converts a
number of his friends among the young men of Tilbury Town.
The captain is a listener to what he calls God's music, which
is all the intimations of truth that come to mankind in this
life and which,

> When we have earned our spiritual ears. . . ,
> Then shall at last come ringing through the sun.
> Through time, through flesh a music that is true.
> For wisdom is that music, and all joy
>   That wisdom.[57]

Basic to this wisdom is the knowledge that there are

> Two kinds of gratitude: the sudden kind
> We feel for what we take, the larger kind
> We feel for what we give. Once we have learned
> As much as this, we know the truth has been
> Told over to the world a thousand times;—
> But we have had no ears to listen yet
> For more than fragments of it. . . .[58]

On the strength of man's spiritual affiliations with the All,

Captain Craig has great faith in humanity's power to live joyously and affirmatively, and he cites the passage from Sophocles already quoted in connection with Emerson's similar humanistic view. On the subject of free will the captain's statement is whimsical but unequivocal:

> ". . . There is no luck,
> No fate, no fortune for us, but the old
> Unswerving and inviolable price
> Gets paid: God sells himself eternally,
> But never gives a crust. . . ."[59]

The captain is tolerantly scornful of those determinists who

> would have this life no fairer thing
> Than a certain time for numerous marionettes
> To do the Dance of Death.[60]

Robinson's best-known statement of idealism is "The Man Against the Sky," written in 1919. This poem, Robinson said, "comes as near as anything to representing my poetic vision. . . ."[61] Its purpose, he wrote to Amy Lowell, was "to carry materialism to its logical end and to indicate its futility as an explanation or a justification of existence."[62] He insisted that it is a poem of hope rather than of despair. Its central image is of a man walking over a barren mountain top and disappearing into the sunset beyond. This is a symbol of humanity, and Robinson speculates lengthily on the man's destiny and his thoughts as he vanishes into the fiery west. The man may have been possessed of some sturdy traditional faith that takes full cognizance of good and evil. He may have been one of the tender-minded idealists, an Emersonian or a Christian Scientist, who had never fully faced up to the existence of evil. He may have been a scientific determinist who

> Discovered an odd reason too for pride
> In being what he must have been by laws
> Infrangible and for no kind of cause.[63]

He may have been a potential suicide, a stoic, a pessimist—
any one.

> Where was he going, this man against the sky?
> You know not, nor do I.[64]

Robinson cites some of the sociological and other scientific
explanations of life: laisser-faire, Marxism, Darwinsim. But
none of these supplies a motive

> why one man in five
> Should have a care to stay alive.
> . . . .
> No planetary trap where souls are wrought
> For nothing but the sake of being caught
> And sent again to nothing will attune
> Itself to any key of any reason
> Why man should hunger through another season. . . .[65]

We are forced back to

> an orient Word that will not be erased,
> Or, save in incommunicable gleams
> Too permanent for dreams
> Be found or known.[66]

The "orient Word" is of course the God made flesh of the
Christians, or the idealism which Robinson found to underlie the Gospels.

Pragmatism

A philosophy quite different from idealism appeared that
also was in opposition to the deterministic drift of naturalism.
This was pragmatism, the pluralism of which was intended
as a corrective to idealistic monism. William James, the chief
voice of pragmatism, has dealt with the will in a number
of books and essays, in his capacity both as a psychologist and

as a philosopher. As a psychologist—that is, as a scientist—he finds himself forced to sidestep the question of freedom of the will as an insoluble one. The psychologist, being a scientist in search of immutable laws, naturally has a bias in favor of determinism. Most psychologists, he concludes, deny freedom to the will. But like Tolstoy, James is impressed by man's consciousness of freedom, though James calls it "the sense of the amount of effort that we can put forth."[67] This effort, which is willpower, emanates from within ourselves; it is not an outside influence, some factor in our environment. Effort, then, is the psychologists' equivalent of will; how far it is conditioned—that is, not free—is difficult to gauge, but James assumes that to most of them it is totally so. James personally relegates the question of the will to metaphysics. In the "Epilogue" to his *Psychology*—following directly after the chapter on will—he discusses metaphysics and there goes firmly on record as considering the will to be free. The contrary assumption of psychology he brands as "merely provisional and methodological."[68]

James's thinking on the subject is obviously that of pragmatism—the philosophy that assesses the validity or truth of an idea by its consequences. In his essay "The Dilemma of Determinism" he tests the consequences of determinism and of indeterminism as beliefs by which to live. Determinism he defines as follows:

> It professes that those parts of the universe already laid down absolutely appoint and decree what the other parts shall be. The future has no ambiguous possibilities hidden in its womb. . . . The whole is in each and every part, and welds it with the rest into an absolute unity, an iron block, in which there can be no equivocation or shadow of turning.[69]

As the chief characteristics of the determinist's universe, James underlines its monism and its "antipathy to the idea of chance."[70] Indeterminism, on the other hand, he describes as postulating "that the parts have a certain amount of loose play on one another, so that the laying down of one of them does not necessarily determine what the others shall be."[71] It admits the existence of many possibilities—of chance, that is—and it is thus pluralistic. The consequences of determinism are threefold: (1) One may frankly accept the world as it is and refuse to recognize any such distinction as that between good and evil. This is "hard"[72] determinism, uncompromisingly mechanical. (2) One may develop a profound pessimism resulting from regret that the universe and its inexorable determinism include such events as wars, murders, and similar calamities, coupled with a realization that these miseries are unavoidable. This is the way things are. We do not like them, but what can we do? (3) One may regard the mixture of good and evil as essential "for the production of consciousness, scientific and ethical, in us."[73] According to this third viewpoint, which James calls gnosticism, or subjectivism, "life is one long eating of the fruit of the tree of *knowledge.*"[74] What happens in the universe is "subsidary to what we think or feel about it. . . . The wretch languishing in the felon's cell may be drinking draughts of the wine of truth that will never pass the lips of the so-called favorite of fortune."[75]

James frankly prefers subjectivism to either mechanism or pessimism. Yet he considers it merely a form of romanticism, of which it shares the weakness as well as the attraction. With its emphasis on experience and sensibility for their own sakes, it has won the respect of such great men as Renan and Zola, to mention only two. James's most telling point, perhaps, is that the determinists of any sort are not the realists that they like to think themselves to be, but they are essentially romanticists. Although he can see many reasons in favor of subjectivism, James finds strong practical objections to it.

Once dismiss the notion that certain duties are good in themselves, and that we are here to do them, no matter how we feel about them; once consecrate the opposite notion that our performance and our violations of duty are for a common purpose, the attainment of subjective knowledge and feeling, and that the deepening of these is the chief end to our lives—and at what point on the downward slope are we to stop? In theology, subjectivism develops as its "left wing" antinomianism. In literature, its left wing is romanticism. And in practical life it is either a nerveless sentimentality or a sensualism without bounds.[76]

Examples of this sort of subjectivism are rife in twentieth-century fiction. Outstanding are Hans Castorp in Mann's *The Magic Mountain* and Thomas Wolfe's autobiographic heroes.

Quoting from Thomas Carlyle, however, William James voices strong objections to subjectivism. "Hang your sensibilities! Stop your snivelling complaints, and your equally snivelling raptures! Leave off your general emotional tomfoolery, and get to work like men!"[77] In other words, subjectivism accomplishes no work; it is too passive to make an imprint on the outside world. For subjectivism James proposes to substitute a philosophy of objective conduct and standards—pragmatism—which sets certain limits to our understanding—limits that one need not feel one has to pass beyond. The indeterminism of this philosophy lies in the fact that there are wrong ways and right ways, and one has freedom of choice as to which to follow. That this leaves an element of chance in the universe, James readily admits, though he refuses to regard "chance" as a dirty word. It simply means that things may or may not happen in certain ways; the whole order of events from the beginning to the end of time has not been prearranged according to an unchangeable plan. The great advantage of the attitude of indeterminism, with its concepts of chance and free will, is that it assumes

the chance that in moral respects the future may be other and better than the past has been. This is the only chance we have any motive for supposing to exist. Shame, rather, on its repudiation and its denial! For its presence is the vital air that lets the world live, the salt that keeps it sweet.[78]

John Dewey, a name in pragmatism second only to that of James, holds similar views. Along with James and C. S. Peirce, he has taken a firm stand against determinism. Dewey refuses to admit that freedom of will and empirical facts are inconsistent. To begin with, "uncertainty, doubt, hesitation, contingency and novelty, genuine change which is not mere disguised repetition, are [empirical] facts."[79] In other words, like James, Dewey admits chance into the scheme of things. Man's freedom of choice naturally follows.

> To foresee future objective alternatives and to be able by deliberation to choose one of them and thereby weight its chances in the struggle for future existence, measures our freedom. It is assumed sometimes that if it can be shown that deliberation determines choice and deliberation is determined by character and conditions, there is no freedom. This is like saying that because a flower comes from root and stem it cannot bear fruit. The question is not what are the antecedents of deliberation and choice, but what are their consequences. What do they do that is distinctive? The answer is that they give us all the control of future possibilities which is open to us. And this control is the crux of our freedom.[80]

Dewey does not deny the existence of necessity, of course. One must perceive it and live with it, but not submit helplessly to it. Dewey has no truck with a block universe. Despite an area of necessity, he sees a wide latitude for free and creative human action.

> . . . intelligence treats events as moving, as fraught with possibilities, not as ended, final. In forecasting their possibilities, the distinction between better and worse arises. Human desire and ability co-operate with this or that natural force according as this or that eventuality is judged better. We do not use the present to control the future. We

use the foresight of the future to refine and expand present activity. In this use of desire, deliberation, and choice, freedom is actualized.[81]

This is a far cry from the naturalistic philosophies of such men as Sumner who believe that all human efforts to direct the course of history are silly and futile. It is almost equally opposed to the contemporary Marxist view that one must work with the inevitable laws of history and perhaps aid them, while in no way modifying the final results. According to the views of James and Dewey, there is not one fixed groove that human events must follow. There are many alternatives, and man's will—a *cause* rather than an effect—plays its part in determining the future. This is an eminently practical view; it makes for action rather than passivity. But it does not make for fanatical action, as does the Calvinist belief that one is prompted by God's will or the Marxist belief that one is cooperating with the one sole law and tendency. Making no such grandiose claims, pragmatism directs its appeal to common sense. Most men in their everyday lives are conscious of a certain degree of freedom and act accordingly.

There is small wonder that pragmatism, with its appeal to man's fundamental sense of his own freedom of choice and action, should have attracted many followers. Among these, apparently, are the so-called philosophic naturalists, who are like the scientific naturalists in that they believe that "nature, the world of reality, has a character, a structure, of its own and our opinions are true only insofar as they conform to this actual condition."[82] But these naturalists differ from scientific naturalists in that they believe in two kinds of laws: physical laws, which are permanent; and social laws, which are not permanent but are "largely man-made" and may be imposed on history. Man thus contributes importantly "to the formation of his environment."[83] Such ideas as democracy, freedom, and tolerance, which are potent forces in determining a culture,

. . . have been shaped not in accordance with the eternal laws of the universe, but in accordance with the rational will of man aspiring to become master of his earthly home and of his historical destiny. And it is possible, no doubt, increasingly to realize this long-range ambition, provided man takes steadily into consideration the unalterable character of the ways of physical nature.[84]

Here is a philosophy reminiscent of deism, which also recognized the mechanical nature of the physical universe but left a wide area of free activity for the reason and will of man in his own private and societal affairs.

Humanism

Many pragmatists, or those influenced by pragmatism, have called themselves humanists. This is not a misnomer. The viewpoints of Dewey and James and the philosophical naturalists do not separate man from nature to the extent that the classical humanists do, but they do concede to man a very considerable control over his destiny. His reason and will are factors not found elsewhere in nature, and thus they set him apart; nor is man's potential underrated as it is by the strict naturalists. This brand of humanism is sometimes called scientific humanism. One of its major spokesmen is Corliss Lamont, whose book *Freedom of Choice Affirmed* (1967) is an eloquent plea for indeterminism.

There is another more traditional and more literary type of humanism which came prominently to the fore in the 1920s under the sponsorship of Irving Babbitt, Paul Elmer More, and Stuart Sherman. This group rejected the monisms of both transcendentalism and of naturalism. It stressed a dualism of man and nature, deploring the mystical merging of them by the romantics and the mechanical merging of them by the naturalists. They believed in what Irving Babbitt called "a higher will"[85]—that is, a will which is more than appetite or instinct and which serves to keep appetite and instinct under control; and they believed in a set of standards or values based on "the law of measure,"[86] which the higher will could use as a guide. Whether the higher will originates in God's grace or elsewhere is not of paramount importance to these thinkers. Babbitt writes:

> The person who declines to turn the higher will to account until he has grasped its ultimate nature is very much on a level with the man who should refuse to make practical use of electrical energy until he is certain he has an impeccable theory of electricity. Negatively one may say of the higher will . . . that it is not the absolute, nor again the categorical imperative; not the organic and still less the mechanical. . . . Positively one may define it as the higher immediacy that is known in its relation to the lower immediacy—the merely temperamental man with his impressions and emotions and expansive desires—as a power of vital control (*frein vital*). Failure to exercise this control is the spiritual indolence that is for both Christian and Buddhist a chief source, if not the chief source, of evil.[87]

Though Babbitt aligned himself with religion and considered the existence of the higher will to be one of the mysteries of faith, the humanists did not insist on a belief in God as essential to their philosophy. What they did insist on was the dualism of a "law for man" and a "law for thing"[88] (they were fond of quoting these phrases from Emerson) and the uniqueness and dignity of man's position in the universe. They were constantly and militantly on guard against any threats to this unique position of man, whether the threats came in the form of a Rousseauean mysticism or scientific mechanism. Naturalistic authors like Dreiser were the target of their fiercest attacks. Their battle cry is most forcefully worded by Stuart Sherman:

The great revolutionary task of nineteenth-century thinkers . . . was to put man into nature. The great task of twentieth-century thinkers is to get him out again—somehow to break the spell of those magically seductive cries, "Follow Nature," "Trust your instincts," "Back to Nature."[89]

To the humanists, man's potential is vast; his place is distinct; he has his own set of laws, which he can obey or disobey at will. This was the standpoint which the humanists, many of them clever writers, set out to maintain.

American Libertarian Novelists

Influence of Russian Humanistic Novelists

All the libertarian tendencies discussed in the previous chapter were reflected in various American novels—always the literary form most sensitive to current schools of thought. But just as the stimulus for the naturalistic novelists came from abroad, so were there strong indeterministic influences at work on American fiction. Among these was the nineteenth-century Russian novel, the impact of which on this country, though not yet carefully assessed, was demonstrably great. "To conceive of a man as having no freedom is impossible except as a man deprived of life,"[1] wrote Leo Tolstoy in *War and Peace*. Turgenev and Dostoevski would agree.

From 1870 onward Tolstoy and Turgenev were exerting a strong influence on American letters through Henry James and Wiliam Dean Howells. The most cogent statement, however, of the Russian novelists' dissatisfaction with naturalism is in Dostoevski's *The Brothers Karamazov*, although the superlative literary and spiritual qualities of this novel were not appreciated in this country until well into the twentieth century, after Constance Garnett's translation appeared. Dostoevski's attack on naturalism is frontal—against ideas and at times against personalities,as, for example, his singling out of Zola's mentor, Claude Bernard, for special dismemberment.

Though some will argue the point, Dostoevski was essentially a humanist, one of the greatest of modern times, standing staunchly for freedom of the will and the transcendence of man's spirit over matter. The entire confrontation of naturalism and humanism in *The Brothers Karamazov*—so tragically dramatized—cannot be outlined here, but a few episodes may give some indication of its scope and power.

To begin with, the most famous chapter in the novel, that of "The Grand Inquisitor" (which Freud called the high point in world literature), was written, according to Dostoevski's own statement to his editor, against the socialists of the day. The Inquisitor himself is a poetic creation of Ivan Karamazov's. Ivan is a student of natural science, a reformer or revolutionist, who would eradicate suffering from the world and who, if not an atheist, is a rebel against God's ordering of the universe. Furthermore, in rejecting God and immortality, he has been more consistent than Zola in that he has rejected all distinction between right and wrong.

"Do you despise or respect mankind, you, its coming saviours?"[2] was the question Dostoevski was asking in the Grand Inquisitor chapter. The Inquisitor himself, the embodiment of Ivan's ideas, obviously does not respect mankind. He upbraids Christ for withstanding the temptations of the devil during the forty days in the wilderness, because, by succumbing to them, Christ would have been able to bribe and bedazzle man into following him. He could have offered men bread, miracle, and mystery in return for the surrender of their freedom of will: and they would have jumped at the bargain. Thus in control, Jesus could have led mankind to perpetual peace, plenty, and happiness. The world would have become a vast kindergarten inhabited by millions of happy babes, spiritually dead, to be sure, and destined to eternal death, but free from earthly suffering and guilt.

By standing on the worth of each individual soul and demanding *free* acceptance of himself, or none at all, Christ has plunged all but a handful of the spiritual and intellectual elite into misery and uncertainty here and probable damnation in the hereafter. The vast majority of men, according to Ivan and the Grand Inquisitor, are incapable of the exertions of the will necessary freely to choose to follow Christ. Thus the Inquisitor must revise Christ's work. His impulse, like that of so many reformers, is humanitarian, even self-sacrificial, since in bringing the happiness and security of the nursery to his fellow beings he knows he is damning himself.

Human beings, to the Inquisitor, as to Ivan, are virtually will-less, soulless—thus resembling machines. You can feel sorry for man and wish to help him, but to do so you must manipulate him and his society as you would a mechanism. Zola's program—"to be the master of good and evil, to regulate life, to regulate society, to solve in time all the problems of socialism"[3]—this would meet the approval of the Inquisitor and of Ivan. But more honest than Zola, or more logical, they made no claims that this is "being the most useful and most moral workers in the human workshop."[4] In these three— Ivan, the Inquisitor, and Zola—we have archetypes of the social experimentalists (Dostoevski's would-be saviours of mankind) who pursue their way, as Zola says, "without troubling [themselves] . . . with the origin of the mechanism,"[5] certainly without bothering themselves about God or God in man.

But it is precisely God and God in man with which Dostoevski and most humanists are concerned. A favorite chant of Dmitri in *The Brothers Karamazov* is:

> Glory to God in the world,
> Glory to God in me![6]

Dmitri is sensual, impulsive, and not particularly brilliant. But his moral sense is strong, as is his sense of God's dwelling within him. He inflicts and endures much suffering; he loves and hates violently; he oscillates between humility and pride;

but always he reveals in his own humanity, his vast, limitless potential. Although brainwashed by the police and seemingly totally stripped of his individuality, he finds within himself resources of redemptive love for mankind unknown by the Grand Inquisitor or Ivan in their own lives. Joyous in his discovery of new springs of being, Dmitri faces a probable sentence to the mines, to him a way of atonement not only for his own criminal past but for the sufferings and crimes of all humanity. At this point his former fiancée and Ivan hire a physician from Moscow to declare him insane and thus not responsible for the murder everyone is convinced he committed. Dmitri is incensed. Not only is he not insane; he has been responsible for his actions, though he did not actually commit murder. To be adjudged *non compos mentis* is to be adjudged a machine: he is not a machine, but a human being, with a human being's potential for suffering and happiness, crime, and sacrificial service.

But the influence of Claude Bernard reaches even to the cell where Dmitri is awaiting trial. It reaches there through Rakitin, a liberal and opportunist journalist, who is making a name for himself in the Russian newspapers by reporting the Karamazov murder case and commenting on its social significance. Dmitri asks his brother, Alyosha, who is visiting him in prison:

> "Who was Karl Bernard? . . . No, not Karl. . . . Claude Bernard. What was he? Chemist or what?"
>
> "He must be a savant," answered Alyosha; "but I confess I can't tell you much about him, either. . . ."
>
> "Well, damn him then! I don't know either," swore Mitya [Dmitri]. "A scoundrel of some sort, most likely. They are all scoundrels. And Rakitin will make his way. Rakitin will get on anywhere; he is another Bernard. Ugh, these Bernards! They are all over the place."
>
> "But what is the matter?" Alyosha asked insistently.
>
> "He wants to write an article about me, about my case, and so begin his literary career. That's what he comes for; he said so himself. He wants to prove some theory. He wants

to say 'he couldn't help murdering his father, he was corrupted by his environment,' and so on. He explained it all
to me. He is going to put in a tinge of Socialism, he says."[7]

Of his lawyer, who along with the alienist was brought from
Moscow by his fiancée and his brother, Dmitri speaks just
as disparagingly. "He's a soft, city-bred rogue—a Bernard!
But he doesn't believe me—not a bit of it! Only imagine, he
believes I did it. 'In that case,' I asked him, 'why have you
come to defend me?' Hang them all! They've got a doctor
down, too, want to prove I'm mad. I won't have that!"[8]

We have already seen that Tolstoy referred to the scientific
determinists of his day as "a mob of ignoramuses" and avowed
that their reasonings did "not advance one hair's-breadth
the solution of the question [of free will], which has another
opposite side, founded on the consciousness of freedom."[9]
A good example of the "ignoramuses" who have swallowed
whole, and added to, the pretensions of science is Bazarov in
Turgenev's *Fathers and Sons*. Turgenev does not despise Bazarov, although at times he presents him as an oaf, as in the
love-making episode in which he rushes at Madame Odintsov
with an "almost animal face."[10] Ultimately Bazarov, who is
in fact intellectually brilliant, emerges as a tragic figure. But in
spite of his intelligence and sensitivity, he insists on forcing
himself into a mold which leads him to make love like a
beast, threaten his best friend with strangulation, and finally
allow himself to die in a manner strongly suggestive of suicide.

What are the ideas that so dehumanize this otherwise
superior person? As to his views on the individual, he has this
to say:

"I assure you, studying separate individuals is not worth
the trouble. All people are like one another, in soul as in
body; each of us has brain, spleen, heart, and lungs made
alike; and the so-called moral qualities are the same in all;
the slight variations are of no importance. A single human
specimen is sufficient to judge us all by. People are like

trees in a forest: no botanist would think of studying each individual birth-tree."[11]

Like Zola, Bazarov deprecates the "follies of the poets and the philosophers."[12] He asserts: "A good chemist is twenty times as useful as any poet."[13] Instead of Pushkin, he recommends Büchner's *Stoff und Kraft*. Büchner was a German materialist whose book on matter and force was a bible to Bazarov as was Bernard's *Introduction à la Médicine Expérimentale* to Zola.

Regarding man's place in the universe, Bazarov's view is the standard naturalistic one:

> "The tiny space I occupy is so infinitely small in comparison with the rest of space, in which I am not, and which has nothing to do with me; and the period of time in which it is my lot to live is so petty beside the eternity in which I have not been, and shall not be. . . . And in this atom, this mathematical point, the blood is circulating, the brain is working and wanting something. . . . Isn't it loathsome? Isn't it petty?[14]

Thus the fruits of Bazarov's philosophy—which he chooses to call nihilism—are hatred of himself and of the rest of humanity. Having reduced man to the status of a birch tree, he now hates man, exactly as Ivan in *The Brothers Karamazov* hates individual humans. "One reptile will devour the other,"[15] Ivan says in regard to his quarreling father and brother. Men are little different from snakes. And elsewhere Ivan avers, "I could never understand how one can love one's neighbors."[16] Yet we have seen that, like the Grand Inquisitor, Ivan would go to any limit to reform humanity as a whole. Ivan can love his neighbors only in the abstract. And Bazarov—who says, "I felt such a hatred for this poorest peasant, this Philip or Sidor, for whom I'm to be ready to jump out of my skin, and who won't even thank me for it"[17]—is similar.

The three great Russian novelists made the earliest and perhaps the strongest attack on literary naturalism. All three were humanists essentially; all three rejected a predominantly mechanistic concept of man; none was a thoroughgoing determinist; all three were moralists—which naturalists can never consistently be. The influence of these novelists, we must repeat, has been strong upon the American novel—as strong, at least, as the influence of the French naturalists and stronger than that of any British novelists of the period, for since the Civil War American literature in general has had closer connections with the Continent than with England.

Moreover, American literature, as D. H. Lawrence has pointed out, is deeply preoccupied with morals, and the same may be said of Continental literature—especially its novelists, and especially the Russian novelists. Hence arose Howells's lifelong admiration for the European novel and his idolizing of Tolstoy. This also is the reason for the affinity between Henry James and Ivan Turgenev—both of them living in self-imposed exile from their native lands. Morally speaking, Turgenev also had much in common with Hawthorne, the American author to whom James acknowledged a great debt and whose all-inclusive theme was the dehumanized heart. Dehumanization in Hawthorne's fiction can come about from fanatical devotion to some idea—scientific, religious, or social—or through isolation from the rest of humanity, either through personal guilt as with Arthur Dimmesdale, or through hereditary guilt as with the Pyncheons in *The House of the Seven Gables.* In Turgenev the dehumanization is the result of fanaticism, as with Bazarov and to some extent with Insarov in *On the Eve,* or of isolation—segregation, Dostoevski called it—of the intelligentsia and the gentry from the masses, as with Rudin and with most of the characters in *Virgin Soil.* But most important here is that to each—the Russians and the Americans under discussion—naturalism would be distasteful. For naturalism has some of the characteristics of fanaticism; and both are oversimplified approaches to human problems based on oversimplified and hence somewhat degrading concepts of mankind. The consciousness of freedom, to use Tolstoy's apt phrase, cannot be divorced from the recognition of man's complexity—the myriad opposing forces and impulses at work within him, the bewildering variety of his moods, and the mazes through which his choices of action lead him. On the other hand, the simplified man, the naturalistic man, can be conceived of not as a free man but as a machine, something less than human.

William Dean Howells

Among the many American novelists who rejected determinism insofar as is justifiable by common sense are William Dean Howells, Henry James, Edith Wharton, and Willa Cather. To all of these the consciousness of freedom of action and of choice was stronger than their sense of humanity's bondage to uncontrollable forces. Thus in their insistence on the individual's ability to shape his own destiny they can be classed as humanists rather than as naturalists.

Howells's "realism," which is an ethical as well as aesthetic philosophy, is based on the assumption that human beings are capable of exerting significant control over their own emotions and over their environment as it affects their lives. It is difficult to generalize about an author who produced over eighty volumes during a lifetime of over eighty years. The best we can do is to examine one of his most competent and most popular novels, *The Rise of Silas Lapham,* and, assuming it to be reasonably representative, to assess its affirmation of freedom of the will. To begin with, though not actively religious, the Laphams as rural Vermonters in origin have been conditioned by orthodox Calvinist doctrine. For example, we are told that Mrs. Lapham experiences that "helpless longing, inbred in all Puritan souls, to have some one specifically suffer for the evil in the world, even if it must be herself."[18] And her daughter Penelope says of her lover, "Mr. Corey seems fated to come in, somewhere. I guess it's Providence, mother."[19]

But more important than these ingrained vestiges is the wide scope of choice that confronts Lapham in his business dealings. The *rise* in the title of the novel refers ironically to Lapham's social rise, which is followed by a fall in status that turns out to be a real moral rise. Bound by conventional goals common to his class and times, Lapham has striven to make money—which he has done successfully and reasonably honestly—and to gain recognition in the fashionable circles of proper Bostonians. To the extent that such goals shape his life beyond the limits of common sense, he is not a free agent. But when the real test comes, he *rises* above such conventionalities. Presented almost providentially (a Puritan might so regard it and take advantage of it) with the chance to shore up his collapsing fortune, he chooses failure and bankruptcy rather than save himself by means which would victimize a number of unsuspecting investors, even though these latter are in England and personally unknown to him.

Obviously the climax of a novel should be the point at which the protagonist's freedom of action, or lack of it, becomes most evident. A revealing comparison can be made between the climactic moments of Lapham's life and those of the businessmen in Dreiser's *Sister Carrie* and *The Financier.* In *Sister Carrie* Hurstwood's theft of his employers' money results from a series of causes over which he has little control. Hurstwood is a weak man dominated by instinct, chance, and blood chemistry. Cowperwood in *The Financier,* though a strong man, is strong only in the strength of his potent, ruthless intellect combined with an irresistible drive for power. There is no question of Cowperwood's controlling his impulses; to be able to do so would be a violation of his character as presented by Dreiser through a thousand pages. He is simply carried along by his drives, never wishing to do differently. He is as much a natural force as the tides, serving nature's inscrutable ends as inevitably and as undeviatingly. But Lapham is given a true choice—survival at the expense of many innocent people or bankruptcy with personal honor.

After an agonizing night he chooses the latter, much to his wife's approval, though it means the loss of wealth and social position.

Howells emphasizes the element of freedom in Lapham's decision: "It was for him alone to commit this rascality—if it was a rascality—or not."[20] Appropriately in describing this moral struggle of a son of the Puritans, Howells quotes from Scripture: "And there wrestled a man with him until the breaking of the day. . . . And he said, Let me go, for the day breaketh. And he said, I will not let thee go, except thou bless me."[21]

In their personal lives also the Laphams are able to effect modifications that a strict naturalist would never concede to be possible. In addition to social pretensions and desire for wealth, there is another powerful force, again conventional, in the lives of the Laphams. This is sentimentality, a quality that blinds those who possess it and that therefore is alien to Howells's ethical realism, which demands the application of reason and common sense to life's troublesome involvements. The fact is that Lapham's business failure was the result in part of his and his wife's sentimentality in trying to rehabilitate Rogers, Lapham's former partner, whom he had "driven" out of business. It so happens that Rogers had been treated as justly as he had deserved, for he was not only a weakling but a scoundrel. Lapham's renewed association with Rogers was neither morally nor financially sound; because of it Lapham is brought to the point where he has to make his momentous and financially ruinous choice.

However, it is in the love affairs of Lapham's daughters, Irene and Penelope, that sentimentality, in the form of an irrational yearning for self-sacrifice, is most apparent. Sentimentality decrees that Tom Corey, a desirable young scion of a Brahmin family of Boston, must be in love with Irene, for she is the prettier. When it turns out that he is actually in love with the homely but witty Penelope, the sisters vie in sacrificing their feelings for one another. A minister is consulted, and he states Howells's well-known theory of economy of pain, with the result that the family is returned to its senses. If neither marries Tom, he and both girls will be miserable. If Tom marries Irene, whom he does not love, all three will alike suffer. If he marries Penelope, only Irene will be hurt. Better one wretched person than three. Common sense triumphs; freedom of choice and action have been exercised.

Henry James

As might be expected, Henry James's attitude toward the will and its freedom is more complicated than Howells's; yet he definitely belongs among the libertarian novelists. From the many characters inhabiting the numerous novels and stories of James, examples can be found of every degree of free will and of determinism. Again, as with Howells, consideration will be limited to two or three works, several characters of which are reasonably typical in respect to their control over their own destinies. Daisy Miller, Christopher Newman, and Isabel Archer will serve as well as any. In a sense the actions of all three are determined by their personalities—a statement which pretty well sums up James's theory of fiction. Two questions remain: Are these persons responsible for their characters as we find them at the beginning of the stories? And are they able to modify their characters during the course of the stories?

Daisy Miller, like the other two, is strong on what James considered to be the dominant American traits of self-confidence and innocence, traits which in combination can lead their possessors to disaster. With Daisy, one of the least complicated of James' characters, self-reliance becomes recklessness, and innocence becomes folly. A young girl brought up by an indulgent mother of small intelligence and less common sense, more or less ignored by her father, and spoiled by money, she can hardly be held entirely to blame for her headstrong behavior. Neither can she be held responsible for the accident of birth that made her an American, nor for the environment that instilled into her the standard national strengths and weaknesses.

Whether James intentionally meant to level a criticism against the Emersonian doctrine of self-reliance is not known. In any event, the book does constitute such a criticism. Emerson's essay on the subject was a classic read in all the schools. Its thesis is that every human being, possessing as he does a spark of the Oversoul, can by being true to himself or herself be certain of his or her own rightness, innocence, and invincibility. Daisy is sure of these things and dies as a result. Because of her early death, her character has little opportunity to change. She certainly does what she wishes, with the exception of contracting the fatal Roman fever; but it is doubtful if she has had much to do with choosing what she wishes. Her chief freedom is that of being at liberty to permit her unconsciously acquired character traits to destroy her. She is one of the more deterministically treated of James's Americans, and hers is a good example of a freedom that is actually a bondage.

Christopher Newman in the novel *The American* is less deterministically conceived. As the book opens, he has already made a momentous decision—to give up his life of moneymaking and broaden his experience and sensitivities by foreign travel. The decision is made in a moment in a hackney coach and is so strong and comprehensive as to resemble a religious conversion. As an American he, too, is amply endowed with self-assurance as well as with a good nature that stems from his sense of innocence. So this New American Man reverses the direction followed by his namesake Christopher Columbus and sails from America to discover Europe. One need not rehearse his adventures. Among his projects for self-improvement is the acquisition of a French wife. With his usual confidence he sets about the fulfillment of this desire, and he almost suceeds in marrying a beautiful countess

of charming personality and spotless character. Only the
shameless perfidy of the lady's family—a perfidy that the
good-natured innocence of Newman was incapable of enter-
taining as a possibility—shatters his dream.

Later, provided with knowledge of a crime that could send
his former fiancée's mother and brother to jail or worse, Newman allows his good nature to reassert itself, and he burns
the incriminating document. The French aristocrats, knowing
Newman better than he knew himself, gauged his good nature
so accurately as to foresee that he would never exact his revenge, and they continued to treat him with the normal
arrogance of their class. But Newman has his choice as to
whether to use or destroy the damning evidence. His moral
nature certainly does not suffer from his decision, which is
in accord with his character but has not been fully determined
by it. Revenge, as he would have got it, would have been a
shabby business. There is an element of impulse in his tossing
the paper into the fire, just as an instant later he has the impulse—too late—to extricate it. But at least there are two impulses to choose between, and Newman's choice of the first
one seems freely made. Furthermore, unlike Daisy Miller,
Newman grows in understanding and thus achieves a change
in his personality. He learns, specifically, that innocence is
not an invulnerable armor; that to be right and good is not
enough to assure the attainment of one's goals.

Even more complex than Newman's is the motivation of
Isabel Archer in *The Portrait of a Lady*. Equipped with the same
self-confidence, love of independence, and innocence as are
Daisy Miller and Christopher Newman, eager to experience
life to the full, as they are, and sure of her powers to make
her own way, she is nevertheless oppressed by the sense of
being under a fate. As a chief reason for not marrying her
wealthy English suitor, Lord Warburton, she says simply,
"It's that I can't escape my fate."[22] And later in explanation
she adds, "I can't escape unhappiness. In marrying you [Lord
Warburton] I shall be trying to."[23] Yet, later still, when she

contemplates marrying Osmond, she asserts to those who offer objections: "I've only one ambition—to be free to follow out a good feeling."[24] Above all she values liberty. "The idea of a diminished liberty," James writes, "was particularly disagreeable to her. . . ,"[25] and she repeatedly announces, "I like my liberty. . . ."[26] Only occasionally, as when she inherits Mr. Touchett's fortune, does she express any misgivings about liberty: "A large fortune means freedom, and I'm afraid of that."[27] And once, in her interior monologue, she questions her whole attitude, her prudence itself: "Who was she, what was she, that she should hold herself superior? What view of life, what design upon fate, what conception of happiness, had she pretended to be larger than these large, these fabulous occasions?"[28] Truly, as James points out, she is, in one sense, "affronting her destiny."[29] To affront one's destiny requires a considerable measure of freedom of will.

Isabel is not hampered by any sporadic misgivings she may feel. She turns down two highly acceptable suitors, Lord Warburton and Caspar Goodwood, and marries the rotter Osmond. Why does she behave so perversely? To begin with, it is *not* the result of Madame Merle's machinations. "Madame Merle might have made Gilbert Osmond's marriage, but she certainly had not made Isabel Archer's. That was the work of—Isabel scarcely knew what: of nature, providence, fortune, of the eternal mystery of things."[30] But Isabel—and James— quickly back away from this assignment of causes, as if fortune, providence, and the rest were mere figures of speech rather than actual influences in human lives. Soon realizing that she has made a mistake in her marriage, Isabel insists on taking responsibility squarely on herself. "It was impossible to pretend that she had not acted with her eyes open; if ever a girl was a free agent she had been. A girl in love was doubtless not a free agent; but the sole source of her mistake had been in herself."[31] The spell of Europe had been upon her; the manner, appearance, and superficially brilliant conversation of Osmond had impressed her. To the extent that these influences aroused her love, and to the extent that she was in love, she may have been under what the naturalists would call a biological determinism. But this is not enough to enable Isabel to excuse herself before her own conscience. "She had looked and considered and chosen";[32] on this she insists, and now that she has made her choice she will "accept it."[33] Her final conclusion is: "I married him before all the world; I was perfectly free; it was impossible to do anything more deliberate."[34]

One may object that elements in Isabel's character—her zest for experience, her insistence on liberty, her innocence, and her self-confidence—made some such mistake as hers inevitable. Perhaps—but they do not make inevitable the manner in which she confronts that mistake. "Whatever happens to me let me not be unjust . . . ; let me bear the burdens myself and not shift them upon other!"[35] Isabel takes full responsibility, not only as regards her errors but also as regards Pansy, whose life she begins to influence when she marries Osmond, the child's father. She has a duty toward Pansy, a duty that she does not overlook. Self-confident, innocent, inexperienced persons may be prone to making foolish marriages, but they are not compelled to face up to their mistakes as does Isabel. Daisy Miller has all these qualities and still is incapable of admitting that she can be wrong. Isabel's distinction (and the beginning of growth and change in her character) is that she does admit her error, assuming full blame for it herself, and then goes on to live under it in a manner that is fair for all those involved. Her initial weakness is that of too much Americanness, cocksureness in the face of life. To this extent some determinism is involved, doubtless, despite her assertions to the contrary. But her reassessment of herself, in the great chapter in which she ponders all night her past life and her calamitous marriage, marks the beginning of a radical change in her outlook and character. Such change in character and motive, such growth in understanding—surely these are tokens of a freedom at the farthest remove from determinism.

Edith Wharton

In the novels of Edith Wharton an anthropological determinism—social taboos, class customs, and deeply ingrained mores—appreciably delimits freedom of choice and action. These forces can be seen most strongly at work in *Ethan Frome,* in which, reinforced by economic stresses, they seem to amount to an almost total determinism. Yet *Ethan Frome* exemplifies a pattern common to most of Mrs. Wharton's novels: the protagonists are given a choice between two courses of action—one suggested by more or less selfish human desires, the other by social custom. The choice is a real one, marked by intense struggle, though social pressures usually carry the day. In *Ethan Frome* the two neutralize each other. Ethan must decide whether to run away with a newfound lover, thus escaping his wretched marriage, or to abide by the moral standards of society by remaining with his wife. His sense of duty seemingly prevails, and he prepares to take his sweetheart to the railroad station to leave him forever. On the way to the station, the two become overwhelmed by a suicidal impulse. But as the sled races down a hill toward a collision with the tree that is to dash out their brains, a vision of his wife causes Ethan to swerve ever so slightly, though enough to render the "accident" less than lethal. The two drag out their lives as hopeless cripples under the care of Ethan's wife, who suddenly recovers from her hypochondriacal ailments.

Against this sense of duty inherited from generations of Puritan ancestry and against the socially sanctioned bonds of marriage, Ethan is relatively helpless; yet in at least his decision to run off with his lover, one feels he has exercised some freedom of choice. The element of freedom is stronger in other novels by Edith Wharton, notably in *The Age of Innocence.* Again, the choice to be made by the hero and heroine—Newland Archer and Madame Olenska—is beset by strong considerations of social convention. Should the love of these two for one another take precedence over Newland's obligations to another girl, May Welland, to the extent, first, of breaking his engagement to her, and, later, after he has married her, of terminating their union? Social pressures are indeed powerful, but in these cases they are not so overwhelming as in *Ethan Frome.* Newland is intellectually sophisticated enough to realize that the mores of the New York high society into which he has been born and in accordance with the rituals of which he has become engaged and married are not essentially different from the mores and rituals of the primitive tribes with which his own interest in anthropology has acquainted him. Such knowlege is often liberating. But Newland realizes there are rational and moral reasons other than mere taboos for the breaking of a relationship that promises much unhappiness for innocent people. In his decision and Madame Olenska's, social mores are not the sole or dominant factor. Rather it is a sense of decency that swerves them away from gratification of personal desire; it is a consideration of the pain involved for May and her family. True, May's pregnancy is a last-minute pressure in Newland's resolve to stick by his marriage, but the decision is still very much his own.

Furthermore, the apparent sacrifice made by Newland and Ellen Olenska does not doom either to lifelong misery. Having made their choice, they both proceed to live satisfying and useful lives, in which regret for what might have been is little more than a spice that adds zest to their days. Mrs. Wharton is very clearly saying that human beings in a predicament, faced with momentous choices, are able to choose on a basis of reason and human feelings, without placing the remainder of their lives under some immutable curse. Men and women are free agents. In *The Age of Innocence* something like Howells's theory of economy of pain has been put in practice as a result of the good sense and sensitivity of the main characters. Mrs. Wharton sums up her attitude in the words: "He [the novelist] must, above all, bear in mind at each step that his business is not to ask what the situation would be likely to make of his characters, but what his characters, being what they are, would make of the situation"[36]— a thought with which Henry James would surely concur.

Willa Cather

In a preface to the 1932 edition of her novel *The Song of the Lark*, Willa Cather wrote of her heroine, Thea Kronberg: "She seemed wholly at the mercy of accident; but to persons of her vitality and honesty, fortunate accidents will always happen."[37] The statement suggests the one just quoted from Edith Wharton. It could be argued, of course, that vitality is inborn, that it is not a matter over which the individual has control. Perhaps this is so, but honesty is not innate, and though it can be inculcated by early training, it is a quality that one can develop in oneself. What Willa Cather seems to be saying is that certain persons can wrest good fortune from circumstances that would spell disaster to many others.

In direct contrast to Thea is her first music teacher, the alcoholic old Wunsch, who has become fatalistic in his conviction "that whatever he hoped for was destined not to be; that his affection brought ill fortune, especially to the young; that if he held anything in his thoughts, he harmed it."[38] Yet Wunsch tells Thea: "There is one big thing—desire. And before it, when it is big, all is little."[39] This remark fires her ambition, later realized, to become a great musician; for, in addition to honesty and vitality, Thea has a stubborn will combined with a vivid imagination of what she would like to be in her life. Moreover, she has the power—which is a part of her vitality—to imbue other people with enthusiasm for her own potential for greatness, persons like Wunsch and like the railroad conductor who senses in her as a little girl that she is "bound for the big terminals of the world"[40] and who, on his death in an accident is found to have bequeathed her the money that will provide her education as an artist.

As she gradually grows to a mastery of her art, that of singing, Thea learns that all art is but "fragments of [humanity's] desire."[41] Art is the will incarnating itself. This she first divines at a pueblo that she visits in a lonely canyon by one of those blind chances that to others would be insignificant but that to her serve as an awakening to a full meaning of her proposed life as an artist. The pueblo evokes many thoughts. One is a painful awareness of the hardness of man's lot against a background of an indifferent and sometimes hostile nature. But whereas this recognition would plunge many into a naturalistic resignation before the insuperable forces of the universe, to Thea it has other consequences. The fact that puny man was able to survive against such odds in such distant ages is in itself an inspiration for further effort. But more compelling is the realization that the bits of Indian pottery she finds scattered about are representative of all art in all times, for what is art except a

> mould in which to imprison for a moment the shining, elusive element which is life itself—life hurrying past us and running away, too strong to stop, too sweet to lose[?] . . . The Indian women had held it in their jars. . . . In singing, one made a vessel of one's throat and nostrils and held it in one's breath, caught the stream in a scale of natural intervals.[42]

To this extent, art is a supreme exertion of the will—the will to perpetuate life in a universe where natural law permits permanence to no material thing. To the degree to which an artist is successful, he has liberated his will from circumstance.

Artistic achievement, then, represents a victory for the will. To be sure, there is an element of chance in such achievement. "All the intelligence and talent in the world can't make a singer. The voice is a wild thing. It can't be bred in captivity. It is a sport like the silver fox. It happens."[43] The germ that will grow and blossom into an artist is therefore innate. But the birth of the artist from this germ is a function of effort. Thea's later teacher tells her: "Every artist makes himself born. It is very much harder than the other time, and longer. Your mother did not bring anything into the world to play a piano. That you must bring into the world yourself."[44] Artistic achievement is not a matter of inspiration operating more or less independently of the will. Final fruition comes only as the end result of a long process of "refining and perfecting."[45] With Thea, at least, it is the entering into an "inheritance that she herself had laid up, into the fullness of the faith she had kept before she knew its name or meaning."[46]

A determinist would find in the unpromising circumstances of Thea's early life a near certainty that she would never rise above mediocrity. Willa Cather believed otherwise—not only as regards Thea but as regards others among her fictional protagonists. For example, Ántonia Shimerda in *My Ántonia* from early childhood seems slated for a life of frustration and pain. Years of living in an immigrant's sod hut, her daily round of toil in the fields of her brother's farm, her father's suicide, and her lack of all formal education constitute a deterministic formula for failure—a formula frequently used by naturalists like Stephen Crane, Dreiser and James Farrell. And for a time, as Ántonia runs off with the railroad man and has an illegitimate child by him, the formula gives the appearance of validity in her case. But Ántonia is a woman of vitality, honesty, and intelligence. From a wrecked life she manages to shape a significant future for her husband, herself, and her numerous children, and above all for her sophisticated childhood friend, Jim Burden, who finds in her a symbol of whatever makes life worth living—not the least of which is the conviction that character can rise above circumstances.

Ernest Hemingway

The tendency in American literature since the middle 1920s has been away from strict determinism, whether theological, philosophical, or scientific. Writers in the humanistic tradition, like Willa Cather or Robert Frost, quite regularly endowed their imaginary characters with freedom of will, although even Cather in her early career was sufficiently under the spell of naturalism to write the completely deterministic short story "Paul's Case." The vitality of humanism, indeed, must never be underrated. In an age that produced the biochemical determinism of Dreiser, the physicomathematical determinism of Henry Adams with his fanciful interpretation of history by the law of phase and by the second law of thermodynamics, the Freudian determinism of Eugene O'Neill's greatest plays, the Marxist determinism of the early John Dos Passos, and the sheer fatalism of the early Hemingway—in this same age not only Willa Cather and Robert Frost but other such distinguished authors as Ellen Glasgow and William Faulkner (despite their vestigial Calvinism) were insisting that mankind, either individually or collectively, could exert a very real control over its destiny. At no time was determinism an all-engrossing philosophy.

The decline of determinism (which is still, of course, very much with us) from its high point in the first quarter of the century can be illustrated in the works of several authors whose lives and productivity spanned the period. It is noticeable, we have seen, in the career of Theodore Dreiser, whose posthumous *The Bulwark* recorded a marked drift towards humanism and idealism. It appears with the suddenness of a religious conversion in T. S. Eliot's transition from the period of "The Hollow Men" and "The Waste Land" to that of "Ash Wednesday" and the verse dramas. Less spectacular but perhaps more typical is the modification of mood and outlook discernible during the four decades of Ernest Hemingway's creative life. Hemingway's work, which enjoyed a more or less uniformly high esteem among the intelligent reading public from the beginning to the end of his career, may serve as a barometer of the changing temper of the times.

Hemingway's first two important novels, *The Sun Also Rises* and *A Farewell to Arms,* are restrictively and gloomily deterministic. In the first, the hero's life is blighted by his physical maiming in World War I, and the heroine's life is wracked by uncontrollable lust. That the two should be in love is a mean trick charactistic of whatever "brute and blackguard" rules the universe. These persons, along with an entourage of acquaintances who reel alcoholically through the novel, are denied any decisive control over their own destinies and only a minimum of choice and freedom in their day-to-day activities. They can choose, apparently, only among drinking, making love (if physically equipped to do so), trout fishing, attending bullfights, and occasionally saying a prayer that they suspect is futile.

In *A Farewell to Arms* the restrictions are even more rigid, since the action takes place in the midst of war. The hero does commit one act of free will when he severs his connection with the Italian army, and he successfully rises above his environment to the extent that he avoids court-martial by fleeing to Switzerland with his sweetheart. Yet, to use Hemingway's simile, their predicament is comparable to that of ants futilely trying to escape from a burning log. Frederic Henry and Catherine Barkley escape from Italy only to be stamped under the heel of fate in Switzerland, where Catherine dies in childbirth—because, according to Hemingway, the good and the gentle always die young—and where Frederic, after a groveling prayer to a deity in whom he seems scarcely to believe, disappears in bitter despair into a rainy night. Catherine dies bravely at least, but Frederic is reduced to a whimpering cynicism.

Catherine's brave death is the first libertarian glimmer through the thick wall of Hemingway's determinism. At least, within the very narrow restrictions imposed by life and fate, one can exert some sway over one's conduct and mood. One can adopt or invent a code and then live by it and in that way achieve some stature as a free agent. Thus we have from Hemingway a story ("The Undefeated") in which an aging bullfighter dies stoically in pursuit of his calling; a story ("The Short Happy Life of Francis Macomber") in which a big-game hunter fulfills his destiny by standing up to and killing a charging buffalo and at the same instant is shot through the head by his wife, who apparently could not face the prospect of living henceforth with a man who has so signally proved himself; and even a story ("The Killers") in which a gangster, doomed by his fellows according to the gang code, resignedly walks out onto the street where he knows he will be mowed down by bullets.

In his last two novels of importance—*For Whom the Bell Tolls* and *The Old Man and the Sea*—the shackles of determinism are much looser. In the former, Robert Jordan, an American intellectual, chooses to fight fascism in Spain rather than remain at home in uncommitment. In Spain he accomplishes by dint of bravery, ingenuity, and idealism what amounts to a considerable contribution to the cause he has joined, though he loses his life in the process. With the help of his friend Anselmo, who also believes that fulfillment lies in doing a necessary job as well as possible, he blows up a strategic bridge; and, when wounded, he holds off the pursuing fascists long enough to ensure the escape of his comrades. In addition, he engages in a love affair of more than merely carnal significance. His life is short but good and happy—much more so at least than that of the ill-starred Francis Macomber.

In *The Old Man and the Sea*, the old man, Santiago, battles the Gulf Stream and a huge fish to the limit of his aging strength and wins to the extent of capturing the fish. Sheer willpower and courage, rather than physical strength, are triumphant over the forces of nature. According to Carlos Baker, Hemingway hoped that in this little book Santiago "had shown what a human being could do, and something about the dignity of the human soul."[47] That the reward of Santiago's efforts, the fish, is consumed by sharks in no way detracts from his victory of self-assertion and fulfillment. He has done all a man can do, and it has been much.

The drift away from determinism discernible in Hemingway gives promise of continuing. At any rate, strong philosophical and theological stimuli are at hand to give it impetus. Since the Second World War, existentialism—an import from Germany and France—has been exerting more and more influence on the American intellectual scene in the direction of indeterminism, although, with the possible exception of several of Norman Mailer's later books, there has yet to appear in America a major literary work that is self-consciously existialist. For our existential novels and plays we still depend upon such European writers as Sartre and Camus. Yet certain existentialist themes—for example, those of alienation, engagement, and anxiety—are beginning to find literary expression here on a widespread scale.

The basic concept of existentialism is that of freedom: the freedom of the individual to choose for himself, even "to make himself" by the nature of his choosing; for without such choice there can be no existence at all. Indeed, as Sartre expresses it, "no limits to [our] freedom can be found except freedom itself or, if you prefer, . . . we are not free to cease being free."[48] This overwhelmingly significant tenet of existentialism has recently made a strong impact on theologians of the "neo-reformed" camp and on the more radical ones of the "Godless" persuasion. Man, on his own now in the universe, undirected by either a stern or kindly deity, must fend for himself within the limits of natural laws which impose on him death and other limitations. What a man is is the result of his own free choices and efforts, though not of his successes, which must always be provisinal and restricted. Such is the drift of theology, philosophy, and pyschology today.

Can it be that after millennia of reliance on predestination or submission to a block universe man is now assigning himself more freedom than he can sustain? The answer will be given by the writers and artists of the remainder of this century.

Notes

Definitions and Introduction

1. William James, "The Dilemma of Determinism," in *Essays in Pragmatism*, ed. Alburey Castell (New York, 1954), pp. 40–41.
2. Ibid., p. 41.
3. For example, see John Hospers's "Free Will and Psychoanalysis," in *Freedom and Responsibility,* ed. Herbert Morris (Stanford, Calif., 1961), pp. 463–73.

Chapter 1: The Predestinated Will

1. St. Augustine, *The City of God,* trans. G. G. Walsh et al. (Garden City, N.Y., 1958), pp. 279, 306.
2. Ibid., p. 103.
3. Ibid., pp. 104–5.
4. Ibid., pp. 106–7.
5. John Calvin, *Institutes of the Christian Religion,* ed. J. T. MacNeill, trans. Fred Lewis Battles (Philadelphia, 1960), 2:926.
6. Ibid., 1:261.
7. Ibid.
8. Ibid., p. 268.
9. Ibid., p. 278.
10. Ibid., p. 296.
11. Ibid., p. 298.
12. Ibid., p. 299.
13. Ibid., pp. 297, 307–8.
14. Ibid., p. 307.
15. Ibid., p. 309.
16. Ibid., p. 316.
17. Ibid., p. 318.
18. Ibid. Also see Aristotle, *The Nicomachean Ethics,* trans. D. P. Chase (London, 1911), pp. 55–56.
19. Calvin, *Institutes,* 1:322.
20. Quotations from the Thirty-nine Articles, or Articles of Religion, are from *The Book of Common Prayer* of the Protestant Episcopal Church of the United States of America as certified in 1945. The articles may be found in any other prayerbook of the Anglican Communion.

21, Quotations are from George S. Hendry, *The Westminster Confession for Today: A Contemporary Interpretation* (Richmond, 1965). The sections referred to can be easily located in Hendry's or other editions without the aid of page numbers.

22. Michael Wigglesworth, "The Day of Doom," in *Colonial American Writing*, ed. Harvey Pearce (New York, 1950), p. 274.

23. Ibid., pp. 275, 276.

24. Edward Taylor, *The Poems of Edward Taylor*, ed. D. E. Stanford (New Haven, Conn., 1960), p. 467.

25. Ibid., p. 467.

26. Ibid., p. 162.

27. Ibid., p. 438.

28. Ibid., p. 442.

29. Henry Ward Beecher, *Norwood: or, Village Life in New England* (New York, 1868), p. 38.

30. Walter G. Muelder et al., *The Development of American Philosophy* (Boston, 1960), p. 3.

31. Jonathan Edwards, *Freedom of the Will*, ed. Paul Ramsey (New Haven, Conn., 1957), p. 367.

32. Thomas Hooker, "A True Sight of Sin," in *The American Puritans*, ed. Perry Miller (Garden City, N.Y., 1956), p. 155.

33. Edwards, *Freedom of the Will*, p. 370.

34. Ibid., p. 258.

35. John Milton, *The Poetical Works of John Milton*, vol. 1 (Boston, 1841), Book 3, ll. 98–99. Henceforth, book and line numbers will be given after each quotation.

36. William James, "The Will to Believe," in *Essays in Pragmatism*, ed. Alburey Castell (New York, 1954), p. 89.

37. Edwards, *Freedom of the Will*, p. 370.

Chapter 2: The Predestinated Will in American Fiction of the Nineteenth Century

1. Nathaniel Hawthorne, *The Scarlet Letter* and *The Blithedale Romance* (Boston, 1883), p. 210.

2. Ibid., p. 241.

3. Ibid., p. 253.

4. See John Calvin, *Institutes of the Christian Religion*, ed. J. T. MacNeill, trans. F﹐ Lewis Battles (Philadelphia, 1960), 1:634, 663 ff., 704; 2:1229 ff. 40. Also see George S. Hendry, *The Westminster Confession for Today: A Contemporary Interpretation* (Richmond, Va., 1965), chapter 17.

5. Hawthorne, *The Scarlet Letter* and *The Blithedale Romance*, p. 259.

6. Ibid., p. 260.

7. Ibid., p. 299.

8. Ibid., pp. 299–300.

9. Ibid., p. 301.

10. Ibid., p. 304.

11. Ibid., p. 512.

12. Ibid., p. 515.

13. Nathaniel Hawthorne, *The Marble Faun or the Romance of Monte Beni* (Boston, 1888), p. 141.

14. Hawthorne, *The Scarlet Letter* and *The Blithedale Romance,* p. 545.

15. Nathaniel Hawthorne, *The House of the Seven Gables* and *The Snow Image* (Boston, 1883). p. 14.

16. Ibid., p. 110.

17. Ibid., p. 182.

18. Herman Melville, *Billy Budd and Other Prose Pieces,* ed. Raymond Weaver (New York, 1963), p. 321.

19. Herman Melville, *Pierre, or the Ambiguities* (New York, 1957), p. 69.

20. Melville, *Billy Budd and Other Prose Pieces,* p. 45.

21. Melville, *Pierre,* p. 402.

22. Ibid., p. 200.

23. Ibid., p. 268.

24. Ibid., p. 90.

25. Ibid., p. 223.

26. Ibid., p. 96.

27. Ibid., p. 254.

28. Ibid., p. 400.

29. Ibid., p. 85.

30. Ibid., p. 192.

31. Ibid., p. 396.

32. Fyodor Dostoevsky, *The Brothers Karamazov,* trans. Constance Garnett (New York, 1929), p. 110.

33. Herman Melville, *Selected Poems of Herman Melville,* ed. Hennig Cohen (Garden City, N.Y., 1964), p. 89.

34. Ibid., p. 24.

35. Hawthorne, *The Scarlet Letter* and *The Blithedale Romance.* p. 155.

36. Title of a chapter in Fred Pattee, *Sidelights on American Literature* (New York, 1922).

37. Mary E. Wilkins [Freeman], *Pembroke* (New York, 1894), p. 19.

38. Ibid., p. 297.

39. Ibid., p. 328.

40. Ibid., p. 239.

41. Ibid., p. 240.

42. Thomas Le Duc, *Piety and Intellect at Amherst College, 1865–1912* (New York, 1946), p. 25.

43. Ibid., p. 31.

44. George L. Walker, *Some Aspects of the Religious Life of New England* (Boston, 1896), pp. 132–33.

45. Joseph Haroutunian, *Piety vs. Moralism: The Passing of the New England Theology* (New York, 1932), p. 165.

46. Heman Humphrey, "Revival Conversation," in *Revival Sketches and Manual* (New York, 1859), p. 438.

47. Ibid., p. 457.

48. Ibid., p. 459.

49. Arthur C. Cole, *A Hundred Years of Mt. Holyoke College* (New Haven, Conn., 1940), p. 107.

50. Sarah D. Stow, *History of Mt. Holyoke Seminary, 1837–88* (South Hadley, Mass., 1887), p. 178.

51. Emily Dickinson, *The Letters of Emily Dickinson*, ed. Thomas H. Johnson and Theodora Ward (Cambridge, Mass., 1958), 1:306.

52. George Whicher, *This Was a Poet* (Ann Arbor, Mich., 1957), p. 9.

53. Ibid.

54. Charles Wadsworth, *Sermons* (New York, 1869), pp. 153–54.

55. Ibid., pp. 154–57.

56. Emily Dickinson, *Poems of Emily Dickinson*, ed. Thomas Johnson (Cambridge, Mass., 1958), 2:455.

57. Ibid., p. 405.

58. Ibid., 1:182.

59. Ibid., p. 299.

60. Ibid., 2:385.

61. Ibid., 1:227–8.

62. Ibid., p. 238.

63. Ibid., p. 341.

64. Ibid., p. 225.

Chapter 3: Nineteenth-Century Authors Actively Hostile to Calvinist Predestination

1. Charles B. Brown, *Wieland, or The Transformation* (New York, 1960), pp. 204–5.

2. Ibid., p. 251.

3. Oliver Wendell Holmes, *Elsie Venner: A Romance of Destiny* (New York, 1892), pp. ix–xi.

4. Ibid., p. 247.

5. Ibid.

6. Ibid., p. 248.

7. Ibid., p. 74.

8. Ibid., p. 94.

9. Ibid., pp. 111–12.

10. Ibid., p. 228.

11. Ibid., p. 317.

12. Ibid., p. 435.

13. Ibid., p. 145.

14. Ibid., p. 208.

15. Oliver Wendell Holmes, *The Professor at the Breakfast Table* (Boston, 1890), p. 42.

16. Ibid., p. 43.

17. Leo Tolstoy, *War and Peace,* trans. Constance Garnett (New York, The Modern Library, n.d.), pp. 1134–35.

18. Oliver Wendell Holmes, *Pages from an Old Volume of Life* (Boston, 1892), p. 261.

19. Ibid., p. 285.

20. Ibid., p. 293.

21. Ibid., p. 301.

22. Ibid., p. 302.

23. Ibid., p. 303.

24. Ibid.

25. Ibid., pp. 304–5.

26. Ibid., p. 303.

27. Ibid., p. 305.

28. Ibid., p. 308.

29. Ibid.

30. "Crime and Automatism," ibid., p. 353.

31. Charles H. Foster, *The Rungless Ladder* (Durham, N.C., 1954), p. 134.

32. Holmes, *Elsie Venner,* p. 228.

33. Harriet Beecher Stowe, *The Minister's Wooing* (New York, 1859), pp. 343–45.

34. Harriet Beecher Stowe, *Oldtown Folks* (Boston, 1869), p. 463.

35. Ibid., p. 464.

36. Ibid., p. 463.

37. Mark Twain, *Pudd'nhead Wilson* (New York, 1899), p. 22.

38. Ibid., p. 113. Mark Twain, "The Mysterious Stranger," in *The Portable Mark Twain,* ed. Bernard DeVoto (New York, 1946), p. 695.

40. For evidence that in the last years of his life Mark Twain had modified, though by no means abandoned, his mechanistic views, or at least was becoming less doctrinaire concerning them, see John S. Tuckey, "Mark Twain's Dialogue: The 'Me' and the Machine," *American Literature* 51 (January 1970): 532–42.

41. Twain, "The Mysterious Stranger," p. 669.

Chapter 4: The Law for Things: Naturalism

1. Ralph Waldo Emerson, *Poems* (Boston, 1884), p. 73.

2. As quoted by Émile Zola in *The Experimental Novel and Other Essays* (New York, 1964), pp. 14–16. The passage may also be found in different translation in Claude Bernard, *An Introduction to the Study of Experimental Medicine,* trans. Henry Copley Greene (New York, 1957). p. 60. For quick reference, many of the passages quoted in this chapter may be found in *What Was Naturalism?*, ed. Edward Stone (New York, 1959).

3. Zola, *Experimental Novel,* p. 17.

4. Ibid., p. 8.

5. Ibid., p. 9.

6. Willard O. Eddy, "The Scientific Bases of Naturalism," *The Western Humanities Review* 8 (Summer 1954):219-20.

7. Eddy, "The Scientific Bases of Naturalism," p. 224, note 23.

8. Zola, *Experimental Novel,* pp. 38-39.

9. Ibid., p. 17.

10. Ibid., p. 29. For Bernard's statement see *An Introduction to the Study of Experimental Medicine,* p. 219.

11. Ibid., p. 39.

12. See Eddy, "The Scientific Bases of Naturalism," for discussion of the weaknesses of Zola's position.

13. Zola, *Experimental Novel,* p. 31.

14. Ibid., p. 29.

15. Ibid., p. 25. Cited in Eddy, "The Scientific Bases of Naturalism," p. 226.

16. Zola, *Experimental Novel,* p. 26.

17. Thomas R. Malthus, *An Essay on Population* (London, 1958), 1:8-11.

18. Ibid., 2:151.

19. Thomas B. Malthus, *First Essay on Population, 1798* (New York, 1965), p. 353.

20. Ibid., p. 395.

21. Ibid., p. 396.

22. Karl Marx, *Capital: A Critical Analysis of Capitalist Production,* trans. Samuel Moore and Edward Averling, ed. Frederick Engels (Chicago, 1906), 1:13.

23. Ibid., p. 15.

24. Ibid., p. 23.

25. John Somerville, "Dialectical Materialism," in *Twentieth Century Philosophy,* ed. Dagobert D. Runes (New York, 1947), p. 488.

26. Charles Darwin, *The Origin of Species* (London, 1920), p. 45.

27. Charles Darwin, *The Variation of Animals and Plants under Domestication* (London, 1868), 2:432.

28. Ibid.

29. Charles Darwin, *The Descent of Man and Selection in Relation to Sex* (New York, 1872), 2:378.

30. Ibid., p. 387.

31. Ibid.

32. Ibid.

33. Ibid., p. 369.

34. Ibid., p. 375.

35. Ibid., p. 386.

36. Herbert Spencer, *First Principles of a New System of Philosophy,* Second Edition (New York, 1872), p. 555.

37. Ibid., p. 558.

38. Ibid., p. 559.

39. Herbert Spencer, *The Principles of Biology* (New York, 1871), 1:355.

40. Herbert Spencer, *The Principles of Sociology* (New York, 1890), 2:240.

41. Ibid., p. 241.
42. Ibid.
43. Herbert Spencer, *The Principles of Psychology* (New York, 1888), 1:500–501.
44. Ibid., I:503.
45. Ibid.
46. Richard Hofstadter, *Social Darwinism in American Thought* (Boston, 1955), p. 45.
47. Andrew Carnegie, "Wealth," *North American Review* 148 (June 1889): 663.
48. Ibid.
49. William Graham Sumner, "The Absurd Effort to Make the World Over," *Forum* 17 (March 1892): 94.
50. Ibid., pp. 95–96.
51. Ibid., p. 96.
52. Ibid., p. 99.
53. Ibid., p. 102.
54. Ibid.
55. Henry George, *Social Problems* (New York, 1900), p. 9.
56. Ibid., p. 16.
57. Ibid., p. 18.
58. Quoted by Lester Ward in *The Psychic Factors of Civilization* (Boston, 1897), p. 320.
59. Ibid., p. 327.
60. H. A. Taine, *History of English Literature*, trans. H. Van Laun (New York, 1879), 1:5–6.
61. Ibid., p. 11.
62. Ibid., p. 13.
63. Ibid., p. 14.
64. Ibid., p. 20.
65. Ibid., p. 19.
66. Sigmund Freud, *A General Introduction to Psychoanalysis*, trans. Joan Riviere (Garden City, N.Y., 1943), p. 27.
67. Ibid., pp. 95–96.

Chapter 5: Election and Natural Selection

1. Andrew Carnegie, "Wealth," *North American Review* 148 (June 1889): 655–56. See Richard Hofstadter, *Social Darwinism in American Thought,* and R. H. Tawney, *Religion and the Rise of Capitalism* (New York, 1926), for further light on the point of view represented by Carnegie.
2. See any Anglican or Episcopal *Book of Common Prayer.* This article has already been quoted in Chapter 1.
3. *The American Puritans,* ed. Perry Miller (Garden City, N.Y., 1956), p. 192.
4. Ibid.

5. Ibid., p. 195.

6. Ibid., p. 196.

7. Ibid., pp. 206–207.

8. See chapter 13, "The Covenant of Grace," in Perry Miller, *The New England Mind,* (Boston, 1961), pp. 355–97.

9. William Graham Sumner, "Sociology," in *American Thought: Civil War to World War I,* ed. Perry Miller (New York, 1954), p. 80.

10. Edwards, *Freedom of the Will*, p. 436.

11. Cotton Mather, *Bonifacius: An Essay upon the Good,* ed. David Levin (Cambridge, Mass., 1966), p. 107.

12. Quoted in *Benjamin Franklin and the American Character,* ed. Charles L. Sanford (Boston, 1955), p. 43.

13. *American Puritans,* p. 173.

14. Ibid., p. 175.

15. Ibid.

16. Carnegie, "Wealth," p. 653.

17. Ibid., p. 657.

18. *American Puritans,* p. 174.

19. *Benjamin Franklin and the American Character,* p. 42.

20. The Right Reverend William Lawrence, "The Relation of Wealth to Morals," *World's Work* 1 (January 1901):287.

21. Ibid.

22. Ibid., p. 288.

23. Ibid., p. 287.

24. Ibid.

25. Ibid., p. 289.

26. Carnegie, "Wealth," p. 264.

27. *American Puritans,* pp. 118–19.

28. Quoted in *Democracy and the Gospel of Wealth,* ed. Gail Kennedy (Boston, 1949), p. xii.

29. Andrew Carnegie, *Autobiography* (Boston, 1920), p. 327.

30. Jonathan Edwards, "Personal Narrative," in R. H. Pearce, *Colonial American Writing,* p. 348.

31. Walt Whitman, "Democratic Vistas," in *Specimen Days, Democratic Vistas, and Other Prose,* ed. Louise Pound (Garden City, N.Y., 1935), p. 261.

32. Walt Whitman, "With Antecedents," *Complete Poetry and Selected Prose,* ed. James Miller (Boston, 1959), p. 176.

33. Whitman, "Passage to India," *Complete Poetry and Selected Prose,* p. 288.

34. Whitman, "As I Ebb'd with the Ocean of Life," *Complete Poetry and Selected Prose,* p. 186.

35. Whitman, "Song of the Redwood Tree," *Complete Poetry and Selected Prose,* p. 152.

36. *American Puritans,* pp. 113–14.

37. Whitman, "Democratic Vistas," p. 261.

Chapter 6: Four Deterministic Novelists

1. Stephen Crane, "Maggie—A Girl of the Streets," *Selected Prose and Poetry,* ed. William M. Gibson (New York, 1950), p. 1.
2. Ibid., p. ix.
3. Stephen Crane, *The Red Badge of Courage* (New York, Modern Library, n.d.), p. 41.
4. Ibid., p. 13.
5. Frank Norris, *The Pit* (New York, Grove Press, n.d.), pp. 283–84.
6. Ibid., p. 388.
7. Jack London. *The Sea-Wolf* (New York, 1917). p. 102.
8. Ibid., p. 50.
9. Ibid., p. 98.
10. Jack London, *Martin Eden* (New York, 1917), p. 197.
11. Ibid.
12. Ibid., 318.
13. Ibid., pp. 321–22.
14. Ibid., p. 410.
15. Theodore Dreiser, *Sister Carrie* (New York, Modern Library, n.d.), p. 83.
16. Ibid., pp. 286–88.
17. Ibid., pp. 288–89. In possession of the money, Hurstwood does act decisively on several occasions, as when he virtually abducts Carrie; but later he sinks back into passivity. Carrie is even more consistently passive than Hurstwood, breaking away from him only after he has become totally helpless.
18. Theodore Dreiser, *An American Tragedy* (New York, 1925), 2:76–77.
19. Ibid., p. 77.
20. Ibid., p. 78.
21. Ibid., p. 79.
22. Ibid.
23. Ibid., p. 389.
24. Theodore Dreiser, *The Financier* (Cleveland, 1946), pp. 271–72.
25. Theodore Dreiser, *The Titan* (New York, 1972), p. 32.
26. Ibid., p. 189.
27. Theodore Dreiser, *Hey Rub-A-Dub-Dub* (New York, 1920), p. 80.
28. *American Puritans,* p. 195.
29. Dreiser, *Hey Rub-A-Dub-Dub,* pp. 84–87.
30. Ibid., p. 90.
31. Ibid., p. 209.
32. Ibid., p. 208.
33. Ibid., p. 121.
34. Ibid., p. 163.
35. Ibid., p. 125.
36. Ibid.

37. Theodore, Dreiser, *The Bulwark* (Garden City, N.Y., 1946), p. 330.
38. Ibid., p. 318–19.
39. Ibid., p. 331.
40. Quoted in Robert Elias, *Theodore Dreiser: Apostle of Nature* (New York, 1949), pp. 282–83.
41. Ibid., p. 286.
42. Ibid., p. 285.
43. Theodore Dreiser, "What I Believe," *Forum* 82 (November 1929):313.

Chapter 7: Ellen Glasgow and William Faulkner: Vestigial Calvinism and Naturalism Combined

1. *I Believe,* ed. Clifton Fadiman (New York, 1943), p. 94.
2. Ellen Glasgow, *A Certain Measure* (New York, 1938), p. 58.
3. Ellen Glasgow, *The Woman Within* (New York, 1954), p. 102.
4. *I Believe,* p. 94.
5. Frederick P. W. McDowell, *Ellen Glasgow and the Ironic Art of Fiction* (Madison, Wis., 1960), p. 13.
6. Glasgow, *A Certain Measure,* pp. 168–69.
7. Ellen Glasgow, *Barren Ground* (New York, 1957), p. 328.
8. Glasgow, *The Woman Within,* p. 270.
9. Glasgow, *Barren Ground,* pp. 81, 133, 141, 194, and 367.
10. Ibid., p. vi.
11. Glasgow, *A Certain Measure,* p. 169.
12. See the doctrine of the assurance of grace and salvation in *The Westminster Confession For Today,* ed. George S. Hendry, 20. References are to chapters and paragraphs.
13. Glasgow, *A Certain Measure,* p. 169.
14. Glasgow, *Barren Ground,* p. 133.
15. *The Westminster Confession for Today,* 19:1–2.
16. Ibid., 20:1.
17. Glasgow, *Barren Ground,* p. 7.
18. Glasgow, *The Woman Within,* p. 168.
19. Glasgow, *Barren Ground,* p. 271.
20. *Westminster Confession,* 18:2.
21. Glasgow, *Barren Ground,* pp. 268–71.
22. *Westminster Confession,* 15:2.
23. Glasgow, *Barren Ground,* pp. 285–86.
34. Ibid., p. 239.
25. Ibid., p. 322.
26. *Westminster Confession,* 3:1.
27. Glasgow, *Barren Ground,* p. 405.
28. Ibid., p. 265.
29. Ibid., p. vi.
30. *Westminster Confession,* 20:4.

31. Dreiser, *The Financier*, pp. 468–69.
32. Norris, *The Pit*, p. 417.
33. Glasgow, *Barren Ground*, p. 48.
34. Ibid., p. 80.
35. Ibid., p. 185.
36. Ibid., p. 188.
37. *Westminster Confession*, 12:1.
38. Glasgow, *Barren Ground*, p. 408.
39. Ibid., p. 228.
40. Glasgow, *A Certain Measure*, p. 161.
41. Glasgow, *Barren Ground*, p. 258.
42. Ibid., pp. 323–24.
43. Ibid., p. 398.
44. Ralph Waldo Emerson, *The Selected Writings*, ed. Brooks Atkinson (New York, 1964), p. 6.
45. Ibid.
46. Ibid.
47. Glasgow, *The Woman Within*, p. 166.
48. *I Believe*, p. 101.
49. Glasgow, *A Certain Measure*, p. 248.
50. Ellen Glasgow, *Vein of Iron* (New York, 1935), p. 217.
51. Ibid., p. 373.
52. Ibid., p. 278.
53. Ibid., p. 135.
54. Ibid., p. 260.
55. Ibid., p. 427.
56. William Faulkner, *Light in August* (New York, 1950), p. 337.
57. Ibid., p. 338.
58. Ibid., p. 335.
59. Ibid., p. 87.
60. Ibid., p. 322.
61. Ibid., p. 341.
62. Ibid., p. 115.
63. Ibid., p. 107.
64. Ibid., p. 121.
65. Ibid., p. 180.
66. Ibid., p. 225.
67. Ibid., p. 232.
68. Ibid., p. 236.
69. Ibid., p. 103.
70. Ibid., pp. 244–45.
71. Ibid., p. 223.
72. Ibid., p. 221.
73. Ibid.
74. Ibid., p. 222.

Chapter 8: Libertarian Philosophies Opposed to Predestination and Naturalistic Determinism

1. Wiliam James, *Psychology* (New York, 1905), p. 460.

2. *The Journal of John Wooman,* ed. T. S. Kepler (Cleveland, 1954), pp. 100–101.

3. Samuel Johnson, "Ethics: or Moral Philosophy," in *The Development of American Philosophy,* ed. Walter G. Muelder et al. (Boston, 1960), p. 50.

4. William Ellery Channing, *Unitarian Christianity and Other Essays,* ed. Irving Bartlett (New York, 1957), p. 30.

5. Thomas Jefferson, Letter to John Adams, April 11, 1823, *The Writings of Thomas Jefferson* (Washington, D.C., 1904), 15:425.

6. Elihu Palmer, "Principles of the Deistical Society of the State of New York," in *The Development of American Philosophy,* p. 82.

7. Ethan Allen, *Reason the Only Oracle of Man* (New York, 1940), pp. 97–98.

8. Thomas Paine, "Common Sense," in *Political Works,* part of *Complete Works* (Chicago, 1879), pp. 24–26.

9. Quoted by Conrad Wright, in *The Beginnings of Unitarianism in America* (Boston, 1966), p. 162.

10. Channing, *Unitarian Christianity and Other Essays,* p. 24.

11. Oliver Wendell Holmes, *The Autocrat of the Breakfast Table* (Boston, 1889), p. 312.

12. Theodore Parker, "Transcendentalism," in *The Development of American Philosophy,* p. 128.

13. Ibid., p. 131.

14. Ibid., p. 132.

15. Ralph Waldo Emerson, *The Selected Writings,* ed. Brooks Atkinson (New York, 1964), p. 153.

16. Ibid., p. 169.

17. Ralph Waldo Emerson, *The Conduct of Life* (Boston, 1904), p. 6.

18. Ibid., p. 19.

19. Ibid., p. 15.

20. Ibid., pp. 22–23.

21. Ibid., pp. 27–28.

22. Ibid., p. 40.

23. Ibid., p. 42.

24. Ibid., p. 41.

25. Ibid., p. 42.

26. Emerson, *The Selected Writings,* p. 156.

27. Ibid., p. 161.

28. Ibid., p. 190.

29. Vivian Hopkins, *Spires of Form* (Cambridge, Mass., 1951), pp. 19–20.

30. See *The Literature of the United States,* ed. Walter Blair et al. (Chicago, 1953), 1:73.

31. Emerson, *Poems,* p. 73.

32. Sophocles, *Antigone,* trans. R. C. Jeb, in *The Complete Greek Drama,* ed. W. J. Oates and Eugene O'Neill, Jr. (New York, 1938), 1:432.

33. Emerson, *Conduct of Life,* p. 33.

34. Ibid., p. 23.

35. Ibid., p. 35.

36. Henry David Thoreau, *Walden and Other Writings,* ed. Brooks Atkinson (New York, 1937), pp. 117–25.

37. Ibid., p. 597.

38. Ibid., p. 598. Thoreau's derivation of saunterer is erroneous. It is derived from the Middle English *santren,* meaning *to muse.*

39. Ibid., p. 608.

40. Ibid.

41. John Steinbeck, *In Dubious Battle* (New York, 1936), pp. 143ff.

42. Thoreau, *Walden and Other Writings,* p. 626.

43. Josiah Royce, "The Problem of Job," *Studies of Good and Evil* (New York, 1898), p. 15.

44. Ibid., p. 10.

45. Ralph Waldo Emerson, "Divinity School Address," *The Selected Writings,* p. 69.

46. Royce, "The Problem of Job," p. 25.

47. Ibid., p. 23.

48. E. A. Robinson, *Selected Early Poems and Letters,* ed. Charles T. Davis (New York, 1961), p. 45.

49. Ibid., p. 48.

50. Ibid., p. 46.

51. Ibid., pp. 28–30. This poem and "The Night Before" were omitted from the collected editions of E. A. Robinson's verse, probably because of their inferiority as poetry. But they are useful statements of Robinson's views.

52. E. A. Robinson, *Untriangulated Stars,* ed. D. Sutcliffe (Cambridge, Mass., 1947), p. 182.

53. Ibid., p. 247.

54. Ibid., p. 263.

55. Ibid., p. 280.

56. Ibid., p. 279.

57. E. A. Robinson, "Captain Craig," *Collected Poems* (New York, 1937), p. 118.

58. Ibid., pp. 115–16.

59. Ibid., pp. 121–22.

60. Ibid., p. 129.

61. E. A. Robinson, *Tilbury Town,* ed. Lawrance Thompson (New York, 1953), p. 143.

62. Ibid.

63. Robinson, *Collected Poems,* p. 64.

64. Ibid., p. 66.

65. Ibid., p. 67.

66. Ibid., p. 66.

67. James, *Psychology,* p. 458.

68. Ibid., p. 461.

69. William James, *Essays in Pragmatism,* ed. Alburey Castell (New York, 1954), pp. 40–41.
70. Ibid., p. 42.
71. Ibid., p. 41.
72. Ibid., p. 52.
73. Ibid.
74. Ibid., p. 51.
75. Ibid., pp. 51–55.
76. Ibid., pp. 55–56.
77. Ibid., p. 57.
78. Ibid., p. 61.
79. John Dewey, *Human Nature and Conduct* (New York, 1930), p. 310.
80. Ibid., p. 311.
81. Ibid., p. 313.
82. Ralph B. Winn, "Philosophic Naturalism," in *Twentieth Century Philosophy,* p. 516.
83. Ibid., p. 528.
84. Ibid., p. 536.
85. Irving Babbitt, "Humanism: An Essay at Definition," in *Humanism and America,* ed. Norman Foerster (New York, 1930), p. 39.
86. Ibid., p. 32.
87. Ibid., pp. 40–41.
88. Irving Babbitt, *The New Laokoön* (Boston, 1910), p. 200.
89. Stuart Sherman, *On Contemporary Literature,* (New York, 1917), p. 10.

Chapter 9: American Libertarian Novelists

1. Leo Tolstoy, *War and Peace,* p. 1134.
2. See Ernest Simmons, *Dostoevsky: the Making of a Novelist* (London, 1950), p. 284.
3. *Experimental Novel,* p. 26.
4. Ibid.
5. Ibid., p. 39.
6. Fyodor Dostoyevsky, *The Brothers Karamazov,* trans. Constance Garnett (New York, 1929), p. 104.
7. Ibid., p. 634.
8. Ibid., p. 640.
9. Tolstoy, *War and Peace,* pp. 1134–35.
10. Ivan Turgenev, *Fathers and Sons,* trans. Constance Garnett (New York, 1950), p. 121.
11. Ibid., p. 96.

12. *The Experimental Novel,* p. 39.

13. Turgenev, *Fathers and Sons,* p. 28.

14. Ibid., pp. 148–49.

15. Dostoyevsky, *The Brothers Karamazov,* pp. 146 and 660.

16. Ibid., p. 248.

17. Turgenev, *Fathers and Sons,* p. 152.

18. William Dean Howells, *The Rise of Silas Lapham* (New York, 1950), p. 296.

19. Ibid., p. 368.

20. Ibid., p. 351.

21. Ibid., p. 356.

22. Henry James, *The Portrait of a Lady* (New York, 1966), p. 130.

23. Ibid., p. 131.

24. Ibid., p. 346.

25. Ibid., p. 114.

26. Ibid., p. 160.

27. Ibid., p. 221.

28. Ibid., pp. 109–10.

29. Henry James, *The Art of the Novel,* ed. R. P. Blackmur (New York, 1937), p. 48.

30. James, *The Portrait of a Lady,* p. 402.

31. Ibid., p. 404.

32. Ibid.

33. Ibid.

34. Ibid., p. 488.

35. Ibid., p. 403.

36. Edith Wharton, *The Writing of Fiction* (New York, 1966; rpt. 1924), p. 140.

37. Willa Cather, *The Song of the Lark* (Boston, 1943), p. vi.

38. Ibid., p. 37.

39. Ibid., p. 95.

40. Ibid., p. 187.

41. Ibid., p. 399.

42. Ibid., p. 378.

43. Ibid., p. 258.

44. Ibid., p. 221.

45. Ibid., p. 571.

46. Ibid.

47. Carlos Baker, *Ernest Hemingway: A Life Story* (New York, 1969), p. 500.

48. Jean-Paul Sartre, *Being and Nothingness,* trans. Hazel E. Barnes (New York, 1956), p. 439.

Bibliography

For the most part this bibliography is limited to a listing of the writings cited in the footnotes. Works not cited or receiving only passing mention in the text have been omitted. However, a small number of books of general critical or philosophical interest—which, although not referred to elsewhere, have provided useful ideas and background—have been included for the benefit of readers who may wish to explore further the knotty problems of free will and determinism.

Ahnebrink, Lars. *The Beginnings of Naturalism in American Fiction.* Cambridge, Mass.: Harvard University Press, 1950.

Allen, Ethan. *Reason the Only Oracle of Man.* New York: Scholars' Facsimiles and Reprints, 1940.

Aristotle. *The Nicomachean Ethics.* Translated by D. P. Chase. London: J. M. Dent and Sons, 1911.

Assaglio, Roberto, M. D. *The Act of Will.* Baltimore: Penguin Books, 1974.

Augustine, St. *The City of God.* Translated by G. G. Walsh et al. Garden City, N.Y.: Image Books, Doubleday and Company, 1958.

Babbitt, Irving. "Humanism: An Essay at Definition." In *Humanism and America.* Edited by Norman Foerster. New York: Farrar and Rinehart, 1930, pp. 25–51.

——————. *The New Laokoön.* Boston: Houghton Mifflin Company, 1910.

Beecher, Henry Ward. *Norwood; or, Village Life in New England.* New York: Charles Scribner and Company, 1868.

Bergson, Henri. *Time and Free Will.* New York: Harper and Brothers, 1960.

Bernard, Claude. *An Introduction to the Study of Experimental Medicine.* Translated by H. Copley Greene. New York: Dover Publications, 1957.

Berofsky, Bernard. *Determinism.* Princeton: Princeton University Press, 1971.

The Book of Common Prayer of the Protestant Episcopal Church of America, as certified in 1945. The Church Pension Fund.

Brown, Charles Brockden. *Wieland, or The Transformation.* New York: Hafner Publishing Company, 1960.

Burroughs, John. *Under the Apple-Trees.* Boston: Houghton Mifflin Company, 1916.

Calvin, John. *Institutes of the Christian Religion.* 2 Vols. Translated by Fred Lewis Battles. Edited by J. T. MacNeill. Philadelphia: Westminster Press, 1960.

Cargill, Oscar. *Intellectual America.* New York: The Macmillan Company, 1941.

Carnegie, Andrew. "Wealth." *North American Review* 148 (June 1889): 653–64.

Cather, Willa. *The Song of the Lark.* Boston: Houghton Mifflin Co., 1943.

Channing, William Ellery. *Unitarian Christianity and Other Essays.* New York: Liberal Arts Press, [1957].

Cole, Arthur C. *A Hundred Years of Mt. Holyoke College.* New Haven: Yale University Press, 1940.

Crane, Stephen. "Maggie—A Girl of the Streets." In *Selected Prose and Poetry.* Edited by William Gibson. New York: Rinehart and Company, 1950, pp. 1–69.

Crane, Stephen. *The Red Badge of Courage.* New York: Modern Library, 1930.

Darwin, Charles. *The Descent of Man and Selection in Relation to Sex.* Vol. II. New York: D. Appleton and Company, 1872.

——————. *The Origin of Species.* London: John Murray, 1920.

——————. *The Variation of Animals and Plants Under Domestication.* Vol. II. London: John Murray, 1868.

Dewey, John. *Human Nature and Conduct.* New York: Modern Library, n.d.

Dickinson, Emily. *The Letters of Emily Dickinson.* Vol. I. Edited by Thomas H. Johnson and Theodora Ward. Cambridge, Mass.: The Belknap Press of Harvard University Press, 1958.

——————. *The Poems of Emily Dickinson.* Vols. I and II. Edited by Thomas H. Johnson. Cambridge, Mass.: The Belknap Press of Harvard University Press, 1955.

Dostoevsky, Fyodor. *The Brothers Karamasov.* Translated by Constance Garnett. New York: The Macmillan Company, 1929.

Dreiser, Theodore. *An American Tragedy.* 2 vols. New York: Boni and Liveright, 1925.

——————. *The Bulwark.* Garden City, N.Y.: Doubleday and Company, 1946.

——————. *The Financier.* Cleveland: The World Publishing Company, 1946.

_____ . *Hey Rub-A-Dub-Dub.* New York: Boni and Liveright, 1920.

_____ . *Sister Carrie.* New York: Modern Library, n.d.

_____ . *The Titan.* In *Trilogy of Desire.* New York: World Publishing Company, 1972.

Eddy, Willard O. "The Scientific Bases of Naturalism in Literature." *Western Humanities Review* 8 (Summer 1954): 219–30.

Edwards, Jonathan. "A Divine and Supernatural Light." In *The Literature of the United States.* Vol. I. Edited by Walter Blair et al. Chicago: Scott, Foresman and Company. 1953, pp. 140–50.

_____ . *Freedom of the Will.* Edited by Paul Ramsey. New Haven: Yale University Press, 1957.

_____ . "Personal Narrative." In *Colonial American Writing.* Edited by Roy Harvey Pearce. New York: Rinehart and Company, 1950, pp. 346–61.

Elias Robert. *Theodore Dreiser: Apostle of Nature.* New York: Alfred A. Knopf, 1949.

Emerson, Ralph Waldo. *The Conduct of Life.* Boston: Houghton Mifflin Company, 1904.

_____ . *Poems.* Boston: Houghton Mifflin Company, 1884.

_____ . *The Selected Writings.* Edited by Brooks Atkinson. New York: Modern Library, 1964.

Fadiman, Clifton. *I Believe.* New York: Simon and Schuster, 1939.

Farrelly, Dom M. John, O.S.B. *Predestination, Grace, and Free Will.* London: Burns and Oates, 1964.

Faulkner, William. *Light in August.* New York: Modern Library, 1950.

Foster, Charles H. *The Rungless Ladder: Harriet Beecher Stowe and New England Puritanism.* Durham, N.C.: Duke University Press, 1954.

[Freeman], Mary E. Wilkins. *Pembroke.* New York: Harper and Brothers, 1894.

Freud, Sigmund. *A General Introduction to Psychoanalysis.* Translated by Joan Riviere. Garden City, N.Y.: Garden City Publishing Company, 1943.

George, Henry. *Social Problems.* New York: Doubleday and McClure Company, 1900.

Glasgow, Ellen. *Barren Ground.* New York: Hill and Wang, 1957.

_____ . *A Certain Measure: An Interpretation of Prose Fiction.* New York: Harcourt, Brace and Company, 1943.

_____ . *Vein of Iron.* New York: Harcourt, Brace and Company, 1935.

_____. *The Woman Within.* New York: Harcourt, Brace and Company, 1954.

Haroutunian, Joseph. *Piety vs. Moralism: The Passing of the New England Theology.* New York: H. Holt and Company, 1932.

Hartwick, Harry. *The Foreground of American Fiction.* New York: American Book Company, 1934.

Hawthorne, Nathaniel, *The House of the Seven Gables* and *The Snow Image* [in one volume]. Boston: Houghton, Mifflin and Company, 1883.

_____. *The Marble Faun or the Romance of Monte Beni.* Boston: Houghton, Mifflin and Company, 1888.

_____. *The Scarlet Letter* and *The Blithedale Romance* [in one volume]. Boston: Houghton, Mifflin and Company, 1883.

Hendry, George S. *The Westminster Confession for Today: A Contemporary Interpretation.* Richmond, Va.: John Knox Press, 1960.

Hofstadter, Richard. *Social Darwinism in American Thought.* Boston: Beacon Press, 1955.

Holmes, Oliver Wendell. *The Autocrat of the Breakfast Table.* Boston: Houghton, Mifflin and Company, 1889.

_____. *Elsie Venner: A Romance of Destiny.* Boston: Houghton, Mifflin and Company, 1892.

_____. *Pages from an Old Volume of Life.* Boston: Houghton, Mifflin and Company, 1892.

_____. *The Professor at the Breakfast Table.* Boston: Houghton, Mifflin and Company, 1890.

Hook, Sidney, ed. *Determinism and Freedom in the Age of Modern Science.* New York: Collier Books, 1961.

Hopkins, Vivian. *Spires of Form: A Study of Emerson's Aesthetic Theory.* Cambridge, Mass.: Harvard University Press, 1951.

Hospers, John. "Free Will and Psychoanalysis." In *Freedom and Responsibility.* Edited by Herbert Morris. Stanford, Calif.: Stanford University Press, 1961.

Howells, William Dean. *The Rise of Silas Lapham.* New York: Modern Library, 1951.

Humphrey, Heman. *Revival Sketches and Manual.* New York: American Tract Society, 1859.

James, Henry. *The Art of the Novel.* Edited by R. P. Blackmur. New York: Charles Scribner's Sons, 1937.

_____. *The Portrait of a Lady.* Edited by Fred Millett. New York: Modern Library, 1966.

James, William, "The Dilemma of Determinism." In *Essays in Pragmatism*. Edited by Alburey Castell. New York: Hafner Publishing Company, 1954, pp. 37–64.

_____ . *Psychology* (Briefer Course). New York: Henry Holt and Company, 1905.

_____ . "The Will to Believe." In *Essays in Pragmatism*. Edited by Alburey Castell. New York: Hafner Publishing Company, 1954, pp. 88–109.

Jefferson, Thomas. "Letter to John Adams, April 11, 1823." In *The Writings of Thomas Jefferson*. Vol. XV. Washington, D.C.: The Thomas Jefferson Memorial Association, 1904, pp. 425–30.

Johnson, Samuel. "Ethics: or Moral Philosophy." In *The Development of American Philosophy*. Edited by Walter G. Muelder et al. Boston: Houghton Mifflin Company, 1960, pp. 45–50.

Kennedy, Gail, ed. *Democracy and the Gospel of Wealth*. Boston: D. C. Heath and Company, 1949.

Krause, Sydney J. ed. *Essays on Determinism in American Literature*. Kent, Ohio: Kent State University Press, 1964.

Lawrence, The Right Reverend William. "The Relation of Wealth to Morals." *World's Work* 1(January 1901):286–92.

Le Duc, Thomas. *Piety and Intellect at Amherst College, 1865–1912*. New York: Columbia University Press, 1946.

London, Jack. *Martin Eden*. New York: The Review of Reviews Company, 1917.

_____ . *The Sea-Wolf*. New York: The Review of Reviews Company, 1917.

McDowell, Frederick P. W. *Ellen Glasgow and the Ironic Art of Fiction*. Madison, Wis.: University of Wisconsin Press, 1963.

Malthus, Thomas R. *An Essay on Population*, Vols. I and II. New York: E. P. Dutton and Sons, 1958.

_____ . *First Essay on Population, 1798*. New York: Augustus M. Kelley, 1965.

Marx, Karl. *Capital: A Critique of Political Economy*. Vol. I. Translated by Samuel Moore and Edward Averling. Edited by Frederick Engels. Chicago: C. H. Kerr and Company, 1906.

Mather, Cotton, *Bonifacius: An Essay upon the Good*. Edited by David Levin. Cambridge, Mass.: The Belknap Press of Harvard University Press, 1966.

Melville, Herman. *Billy Budd and Other Prose Pieces*. Edited by Raymond Weaver. New York: Russell and Russell, 1963.

_____ . *Pierre, or, The Ambiguities*. New York: The Grove Press, 1957.

_____ . *Selected Poems.* Edited by Hennig Cohen. Garden City, N.Y.: Doubleday and Company, 1964.

Miller, Perry, ed. *The American Puritans: Their Prose and Poetry.* Garden City, N.Y.: Doubleday and Company, 1956.

_____ . *The New England Mind: The Seventeenth Century.* Boston: Beacon Press, 1961.

Milton, John *The Poetical Works.* Vol. I. Boston: Hilliard, Gray, and Company, 1841.

Norris, Frank. *The Pit.* New York: The Grove Press, n.d.

Paine, Thomas. "Common Sense." In *The Political Works of Thomas Paine* (part of *Complete Works of Thomas Paine*). Chicago: Belford, Clarke and Company, 1879.

Palmer, Elihu. "Principles of the Deistical Society of the State of New York." In *The Development of American Philosophy.* Edited by Walter G. Muelder et al. Boston: Houghton Mifflin Company, 1960, pp. 81–82.

Parker, Theodore. "Transcendentalism." In *The Development of American Philosophy.* Edited by Walter G. Muelder et al. Boston: Houghton Mifflin Company, 1960, pp. 127–35.

Pattee, Fred L. *Sidelights on American Literature.* New York: The Century Company, 1922.

Robinson, Edwin Arlington. *Collected Poems.* New York: The Macmillan Company, 1937.

_____ . *Selected Early Poems and Letters.* Edited by Charles T. Davis. New York: Holt, Rinehart and Winston, 1960.

_____ . *Tilbury Town: Selected Poems of Edwin Arlington Robinson.* Edited by Lawrance Thompson. New York: The Macmillan Company, 1953.

_____ . *Untriangulated Stars: Letters of Edwin Arlington Robinson to Harry de Forest Smith.* Edited by Denham Sutcliffe. Cambridge Mass.: Harvard University Press, 1947.

Royce, Josiah. *Studies of Good and Evil.* New York: D. Appleton and Company, 1898.

Sanford, Charles L., ed. *Benjamin Franklin and the American Character.* Boston: D. C. Heath and Company, 1955.

Sartre, Jean-Paul. *Being and Nothingness: An Essay in Phenomenological Ontology.* Translated by Hazel E. Barnes. New York: Philosophical Library, 1956.

Sherman, Stuart P. *On Contemporary Literature.* New York: Henry Holt and Company, 1917.

Simmons, Ernest J. *Dostoevsky: The Making of a Novelist.* London: John Lehmann, 1950.

Simon, Yves R. *Freedom of Choice*. Edited by Peter Wolff. New York: Fordham University Press, 1969.

Somerville, John. "Dialectical Materialism." In *Twentieth Century Philosophy*. Edited Dagobert D. Runes. New York: Philosophical Library, 1947, pp. 469–509.

Sophocles. *Antigone*. Translated R. C. Jobb. In *The Complete Greek Drama*. Vol. I. Edited by W. J. Oates and Eugene O'Neill, Jr. New York: Random House, 1938, pp. 421–60.

Spencer, Herbert. *First Principles of a New System of Philosophy*. New York: D. Appleton and Company, 1872.

———. *The Principles of Biology*. Vol. I. New York: D. Appleton and Company, 1871.

———. *The Principles of Psychology*. Vol I. New York: D Appleton and Company, 1888.

———. *The Principles of Sociology*. Vol II. New York: D. Appleton and Company, 1890.

Steinbeck, John. *In Dubious Battle*. New York: Modern Library, 1936.

Stone, Edward, ed. *What Was Naturalism? Materials for an Answer*. New York: Appleton-Century-Crofts, 1959.

Stow, Sarah D. *History of Mt. Holyoke Seminary During Its First Half Century, 1837–1887*. [Springfield]: Springfield Printing Company, 1887.

Stowe, Harriet Beecher. *The Minister's Wooing*. New York: Derry and Jackson, 1859.

———. *Oldtown Folks*. Boston: Fields, Osgood, and Company, 1869.

Sumner, William G. "The Absurd Effort to Make the World Over." *Forum* 17 (March 1892):92–102.

———. "Sociology." In *American Thought: Civil War to World War I*. Edited by Perry Miller. New York: Rinehart and Company, 1954, pp. 71–92.

Taine, Hippolyte A. *History of Englilsh Literature*. Two volumes in one. Translated by H. Van Laun. New York: Henry Holt and Company, 1879.

Tawney, R. H. *Religion and the Rise of Capitalism*. New York: Harcourt, Brace and Company, 1926.

Taylor, Edward. *The Poems of Edward Taylor*. Edited by D. E. Stanford. New Haven: Yale University Press, 1960.

Thoreau, Henry David. *Walden and Other Writings*. Edited by Brooks Atkinson. New York: Modern Library, 1950.

Tolstoy, Leo. *War and Peace*. Translated by Constance Garnett. New York: Modern Library, n.d.

Tuckey, John S. "Mark Twain's Later Dialogue: The 'Me' and the Machine." *American Literature* 41 (January 1970):532–42.

Turgenev, Ivan. *Fathers and Sons.* Translated by Constance Garnett. New York: Modern Library, 1950.

Wadsworth, Charles. *Sermons.* New York: A. Roman and Company, 1869.

Walcutt, Charles C. *American Literary Naturalism: A Divided Stream.* Minneapolis: University of Minnesota Press, 1956.

Walker, George L. *Some Aspects of the Religious Life of New England.* Boston: Silver Burdett and Company, 1896.

Ward, Lester. *The Psychic Factors of Civilization.* Boston: Ginn and Company, 1893.

Wasson, David Atwood. "Mr. Buckle as a Thinker." In *Beyond Concord: Selected Writings of David Atwood Wasson.* Edited by Charles H. Foster. Bloomington: University of Indiana Press, 1965.

Wharton, Edith. *The Writing of Fiction.* New York: Octagon Books, 1966.

Whicher, George F. *This Was a Poet: A Critical Biography of Emily Dickinson.* Ann Arbor, Mich.: The University of Michigan Press, 1957.

Whitman, Walt. *Complete Poetry and Selected Prose.* Edited by James Miller. Boston: Houghton Mifflin Company, 1959.

_____ . *Specimen Days, Democratic Vistas, and Other Prose.* Edited by Louise Pound. Garden City, N.Y.: Doubleday Doran and Company, 1935.

Wigglesworth, Michael. "The Day of Doom." In *Colonial American Writing.* Edited by Roy Harvey Pearce. New York: Rinehart and Company, 1950, pp. 233–97.

Winn, Ralph B. "Philosophic Naturalism." In *Twentieth Century Philosophy.* Edited by Dagobert D. Runes. New York: Philosophical Library, 1947, pp. 511–37.

Woolman, John. *The Journal of John Woolman.* Edited by T. S. Kepler. Cleveland: The World Publishing Company, 1954.

Wright, Conrad. *The Beginnings of Unitarianism in America.* Boston: Beacon Press, 1966.

Wright, George Henrik von. *Causality and Determinism.* New York: Columbia University Press, 1974.

Zola, Émile. *The Experimental Novel and Other Essays.* Translated by Belle M. Sherman. New York: Haskell House, 1964.

Index